D0899102

WITHDRAWN
UTSA Libraries

Nigerian federal finance: its development, problems and prospects

By the same author

NIGERIAN ADMINISTRATION AND ITS POLITICAL SETTING

Nigerian federal finance

Its development, problems and prospects

Adebayo Adedeji

AFRICANA PUBLISHING CORPORATION · NEW YORK
An affiliate of International University Booksellers, Inc.

Published in the United States of America 1969 by
Africana Publishing Corporation
101 Fifth Avenue
New York, N.Y. 10003

© Adebayo Adedeji 1969

All rights reserved

Library of Congress Catalog Card No. 77-80848

Printed in Great Britain

This book is dedicated to the memory of my late father, L. S. Adedeji

Contents

    First moves: quasi-federalism, 1952–4   72
    Fiscal system under the 1951 Constitution   82
    Central-regional finances, 1952–4   85
    Conclusions   91

5   Operation of federal finance in Nigeria: first phase   96

    Emergence of federal finance   96
    Fiscal implications of regionalising the marketing boards   108
    Federal and regional finances, 1955–9   112
    An appraisal   118

6   Operation of federal finance in Nigeria: second phase   125

    A review of the fiscal system   125
    Federal and regional finances, 1959–66   133
    Federal finance and public expenditure   144
    Over-all appraisal and conclusions   152

7   Federal finance and taxation: indirect taxes   157

    The development of the Nigerian tax structure   157
    Export taxation   161
    Import and excise taxes   169
    Taxation of extractive industry   179

8   Federal finance and taxation: direct taxes   186

    Personal income taxation   186
    Company income taxation   202
    Conclusion   206

9   Federal finance, loans and public debt policy in Nigeria   208

    Monetary role of the marketing boards   210
    Internal borrowing   214
    External borrowing   216

Tables

Figures and maps

Foreword

The finances of the older countries with federal constitutions, such as the USA, Canada and Australia, have evoked a good deal of discussion over the years. Inevitably, there is much less literature available on the finances of more recent federations. In this book, Dr A. Adedeji, Director of the Institute of Administration, University of Ife, Nigeria, sets out in detail the experience of Nigeria, one of the most important of the post-war federations. From his account, which will surely prove to be definitive, we can see the ways in which the general principles of federal finance have had to be tailored to the particular needs and interests of the several regions in a large underdeveloped country.

The detailed listing of the various changes in the system over the years contains many lessons of great interest and importance to other federations, both old and new. The lessons of fiscal adjustment in India and Australia, as seen from an African standpoint, and the prospects for the future in Nigeria, with twelve states instead of four regions, will also be studied closely by all who are interested in this field.

It requires expertise in the field of government and in the field of economics to write on these matters. Dr Adedeji has used his knowledge in both areas to produce a most valuable addition to the literature of federal finance.

A. R. PREST

Preface

This book is the outcome of a study which began five years ago for the PhD degree of the University of London. It is a shortened and revised version of the thesis subsequently submitted. During these five years, Nigeria has witnessed a series of political upheavals which have culminated in two military coups and a civil war. Although it is not yet clear what kind of a Nigeria will emerge after the cessation of hostilities, there is a genuine desire on the part of the leadership and the majority of Nigerians to maintain a sense of national unity and consciousness which the tragic events of the past two years, 1966 to 1968, have engendered There is growing belief in Nigeria and abroad that a new nationhood forged in the discipline and sacrifice of these tragedies is being created. The country's future federal financial arrangements will play a decisive role for better or worse in the achievement of this objective. Thus, if for no other reason than this, a comprehensive study of the development and problems of federal finance in Nigeria during the two decades after World War II will have been valuable.

This is, I believe, the first attempt to provide such a study. Apart from Arthur Hazlewood's pioneering work, *The Finances of Nigerian Federation* (Oxford University Press, 1956), the only published work on public finance in Nigeria is P. N. C. Okigbo's *Nigerian Public Finance* (Longman, London, 1965). The former, which is a series of articles first published in the weekly magazine, *West Africa*, was written during the formative stage of federal finance in Nigeria. The latter, concentrating mainly on the period

1958–62, is more concerned with the broad issues of public finance than with the specific problems of federal finance. And, as this book shows, the problems of federal finance in Nigeria date back to the year of the amalgamation of the Protectorate of Northern Nigeria and the Colony and Protectorate of Southern Nigeria in 1914, even though they came to a head only in the fifties. There are of course the works of the various fiscal commissions of enquiry as well as a number of specialised studies on specific aspects of federal finance. All these have been cited in the book.

In addition to tracing the evolution and analysing the problems of federal finance, the book also undertakes an evaluation of the country's tax system, its revenue structure and its pattern of expenditure during the past decade or so. It ends with a discussion of the future prospects for federal finance in Nigeria against the background of the new states structure. After the civil war, a new fiscal system which will be conducive to a rational and equitable allocation of fiscal resources, minimise inter-state conflict and thus promote national unity will have to be devised. If this book contributes in any small way to achieving this goal, it will have served its purpose.

I therefore hope that politicians, administrators and other leaders of thought will find the book useful. I also hope that it will be of some value to scholars, University students and students of Nigerian and African affairs to whom the lack of a comprehensive textbook on the Nigerian federal finance system must have constituted a main and constant source of frustration. In order that the book may be readable to the non-economist, I have tried to reduce to the minimum the use of technical language. I hope my colleagues will bear with me in this respect.

In undertaking the study on which this book is based and in preparing it for publication, I have inevitably become indebted to more people than I can remember or name here. My first and deepest gratitude is to Professor A. R. Prest who has maintained interest in the work right from its inception. I have benefited immensely from his authoritative knowledge of fiscal problems in developing countries in general and of Nigerian public finances in

particular. I am also grateful to Professor A. C. Callaway of the
Nigerian Institute of Social and Economic Research, Dr O Teriba
of the Department of Economics, University of Ibadan, and
Professor M. C. Taylor of Michigan State University who read
the manuscripts and made very helpful comments. The officials of
the Federal Ministries of Finance and Mines and Power, the Central
Bank of Nigeria and of the States Ministries of Finance and
Economic Planning/Development have been very helpful and co-
operative. In particular, I am grateful to my good friend, Mr A. O.
Ogunniyi, Assistant Chief Statistician to the Government of
Western Nigeria, for his invaluable assistance in providing some
essential data not readily available.

My gratitude also goes to Mr Dickson Agidee, A.L.A., F.L.A.,
who, in addition to his most invaluable services in obtaining for
me from other libraries publications which were not available in
the Institute's and University's libraries, helped in preparing the
index.

I am greatly indebted to the authorities of the University of Ife
in general and those of the Institute of Administration in particular
for their financial and moral support. Through their generosity I
was able to spend the 1965 long vacation in the United Kingdom.
During this period, I made an extensive use of the libraries of the
Commonwealth Office, the Royal Institute of Public Administration, and of the Australian, Canadian and Indian High Commissions in London. The officials of these libraries were very helpful.
So also were the officials of the former Western Nigeria Agent-
General's Office, particularly its last Official Secretary, Mr M. S.
Adigun, who in spite of heavy official engagements continued for
quite a while after my return to Nigeria to assist me in obtaining
from the United Kingdom publications which were not available
in Nigeria.

All the secretarial and typing staff (past and present) of my
Institute have assisted in the typing of this work, which has
inevitably gone through many drafts. Most of the burden has
fallen on Mrs Ruth Kolade who has bravely and skilfully borne
the brunt of it. I also acknowledge the help of Mrs Charline

Baldwin, a Peace Corps Volunteer, for editorial assistance and of Miss Susan Phillpott for getting the book published on time. Let me hasten to add, however, that all errors and inadequacies which may be found in the book remain my responsibility.

Finally, I must express my profound thanks to my family for their love and understanding. The extent to which I have taxed their forbearance during the past five years was recently brought home to me forcibly one afternoon, when after lunch I prepared to return to the office to put finishing touches to the final manuscript in order to meet the publisher's deadline. 'Where are you going again, Daddy?' asked my seven-year-old son, Kunle. 'Back to work, of course,' I answered. 'Why can't you stay at home with us like the other daddies always do with their children? If you go, I'll call the police,' he threatened. I dismissed this threat and left home only to be informed later that he did try to dial 999 but his nine-year-old brother, Doyin, and their mother dissuaded him from doing so!

ADEBAYO ADEDEJI

Institute of Administration
University of Ife
Nigeria

1 Introduction

Purpose and scope

The purpose of this study is fivefold: (1) to trace the evolution of federal finance in Nigeria; (2) to analyse the socio-political, economic, and fiscal problems encountered by the governments of the federation in the course of this development; (3) to examine the main features of the fiscal system which eventually emerged; (4) to analyse some of the main problems of federal finance in Nigeria; and (5) to consider the future development and prospects for federal finance in the country.

The study covers the period 1946–66, although full cognisance has been taken of new developments which have taken place in 1967 and 1968. This twenty-year period, unique in Nigerian history, has been one of exceptionally rapid political and economic change. At the beginning of the period, a new fiscal system was introduced along with a new constitution. Fourteen years later the country became an independent, sovereign nation. The year 1966 marked a new phase in the political development of Nigeria; it saw the end, at least for a season, of parliamentary democracy in Nigeria and the assumption of political power by the country's armed forces—consequent upon a *coup d'état* on 15 January. Politically and constitutionally, the year 1967 is perhaps the most historic; in that year, a decree of the military rulers divided Nigeria's four regions and the federal territory of Lagos into twelve states. Also, in 1967, a civil war began, aimed at preserving the political and territorial integrity of the country. These two developments have far-reaching implications. The division of the powerful regions into smaller units has removed, once and for all, one of the major causes of disunity which has threatened the survival of Nigeria as a nation. The nation-wide support for the military efforts to 'keep Nigeria one' also marks a considerable change of attitude. Nigeria has ceased to be a mere geographical expression created by the British colonial power. Rather it has become, at least to the majority of Nigerians, a country which should be preserved at all costs—even at the cost of a terrible civil war.

Changes in the fiscal system did not lag behind the political and constitutional development which took place during the period of our study. Between 1946 and 1958, four commissions inquired into Nigeria's fiscal system specifically to make recommendations about the distribution of tax jurisdiction and revenue allocation amongst the federal and regional governments. In 1964, a fiscal review commission was set up to make recommendations about fiscal adjustments. Another commission to review the fiscal system under the new twelve-states structure will no doubt convene immediately after the cessation of hostilities and the establishment of a new constitution.

This study provides a comprehensive and systematic analysis of the evolution of federal finance in Nigeria and of the major problems which the country's federal fiscal system has posed to economic, monetary, social, and political issues. It reveals that federal finance in Nigeria has developed and operated virtually in complete disregard of the main objectives of public finance— allocation, efficiency, and equity. In the sharing of revenues, particularly among the regions, such principles of federal finance as need, equity, stability, and national interest have played secondary roles. Emphasis has been placed on the derivation principle as the basis of revenue allocation. This, together with the lack of a built-in process of adjustment in the fiscal system, has hampered the development of national unity and inhibited the growth of an effective, development-oriented national fiscal policy.

One hopes that the lessons of the past twenty-one years will not be forgotten when Nigeria's fiscal system is reviewed against the background of the new states structure and in the light of the allocation of functions between the federal and the state governments. This study contains proposals which are designed to facilitate a rational and equitable allocation of relatively scarce fiscal resources, to minimise inter-state conflict, and to promote the emergence of a sense of national unity.

Political and administrative structure

Nigeria is the largest country on the west coast of Africa, both in

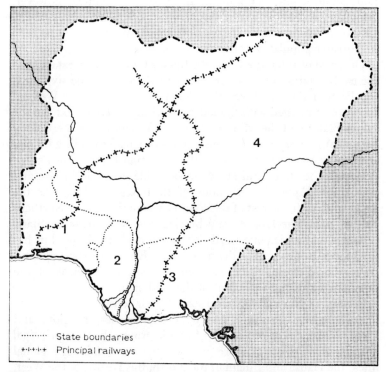

KEY   1   Western Region   2   Mid-Western Region
            3   Eastern Region   4   Northern Region

MAP I *The regions of Nigeria*

its land size and in its population of over fifty-six million. Having gained independence on 1 October 1960, until May 1967 the country was organised politically into a federation of four regions and a relatively small federal territory of Lagos (see map 1). Northern Nigeria was dominant among the regions in land area (seventy-nine per cent) and population (53·5 per cent). Eastern Nigeria and Western Nigeria each had somewhat less than ten per cent of the land area, and populations of 12·4 million and 10·3 million respectively, while the Mid-West Region, formed three years after independence, was the smallest region in size with a population of only 2·5 million. In an African context, however, even the Mid-West had a population greater than that of the Gambia, Mauritania, or Togo; Eastern and Western Nigeria each had greater populations than Kenya or Uganda.

On 27 May 1967, the Federal Military Government established the twelve states. The former Northern Region became six states; the Eastern Region three; the Colony Province in the Western Region was merged with the federal territory of Lagos to form the Lagos State; and the Mid-Western and Western (less the Colony Province) Regions were renamed states (see map 2). The administrations of the new states started to function from 1 April 1968. Although the states still show considerable variation in size and population (Appendix A), none of them has anything like the dominance over the rest of the country which the former Northern Region had. The largest state by size, the North-Eastern State, occupies just under one third of the country's total area but has only fourteen per cent of the population. Even the most populous state, the Western State, has only seventeen per cent of the population and eight per cent of the land area.

Because of Nigeria's physical size, there is considerable diversity in geography, climate, economic characteristics, religion, and ethnic traits. There are scores of ethnic groups, but the principal ones have followed (or more precisely have determined) regional lines: the Hausa and Fulani of the North, the Yoruba of the West, the Ibo of the East. Mid-West Nigeria is more diversified, with several tribal groups. At the present time, tribalism—the struggle of each ethnic group for power to promote its self-interest—

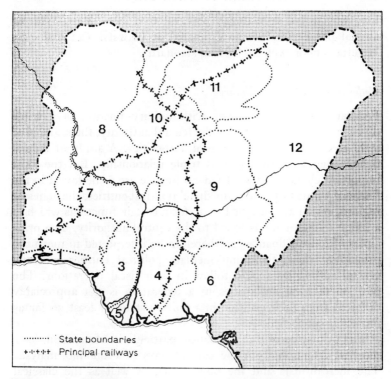

KEY	1	Lagos State	7	Kwara State
	2	Western State	8	North-Western State
	3	Mid-Western State	9	Benue-Plateau State
	4	Central-Eastern State	10	North-Central State
	5	Rivers State	11	Kano State
	6	South-Eastern State	12	North-Eastern State

MAP 2 *The new states of Nigeria*

is a more powerful social force in Nigeria than nationalism.

Not only is Nigeria physically large, but natural resources are plentiful and relatively untapped. If it were possible to divide the countries of Africa into two groups—those that have a clear potential for growth and those where economic development will be more difficult to achieve—the Federal Republic of Nigeria would undoubtedly be included in the former. But Nigeria has a long way to go, even though it is off to a flying start. With an annual per capita income estimated at between £22 and £29, Nigeria is poor even by African standards.

Federalism and public finance

Federal finance, in contrast with unitary finance, is a triple division of resources between the federal authority, the regional or state governments, and the local authorities. A study of federal finance therefore involves this triple relationship. But the most important characteristics of federal finance are to be found in the financial status of the 'intermediate' political entities, the states or regions, which are designed to perform certain functions which in a unitary system are assigned to the central authority. The principles of federal finance can therefore be interpreted to mean the principles which these intermediate political entities and the central authorities should follow in their fiscal operations. The position of local authorities in a federation is not appreciably different from their position in a unitary state, at least so far as finance is concerned.

The principles of public finance, particularly of taxation, have received attention from the earliest days of economic analysis. The mercantilists and the physiocrats, as well as the classical economists, advanced propositions concerning tax principles. David Ricardo and John Stuart Mill recognised the division of the subject-matter of public finance into three aspects—revenue, expenditure, and public debt. Each devoted a great deal of attention to the principles which should govern the different aspects of public finance. For example, Adam Smith is famous for his canons of taxation. In the 1920s, Hugh Dalton and A. C. Pigou developed principles of taxation based essentially on the application of the theory of economic welfare.[1]

The sacrifice-benefit approach to the theories of taxation and of

[1] Hugh Dalton, *Principles of Public Finance* (London: Routledge and Kegan Paul, fourth edition, 1954), chapters II and IX, pp. 5–11 and 59–67; and A. C. Pigou, *A Study in Public Finance* (London: Macmillan, third edition, 1956), pp. 40–5.

expenditure assumes that the central government in a unitary state will tend to equate over-all marginal sacrifices of taxation with over-all marginal benefits of public expenditure. That is to say, the optimum of public finance is reached, according to these approaches, when taxation and expenditure are carried to the point where the benefit derived from the marginal unit of expenditure is equal to the sacrifice imposed in raising that unit of revenue. By equating marginal social costs, the government would achieve 'maximum social advantage'[1] or 'maximum aggregate welfare',[2] or 'maximum net aggregate welfare'.[3]

This theory of public finance has two corollaries—the principle of taxation, and the principle of public expenditure. The principle of taxation rests on the least aggregate sacrifice theory; and individual sacrifice is 'the difference between the net satisfaction he would have enjoyed had there been no tax system and the net satisfaction which, under the aegis of this tax system, he does enjoy'.[4] The theory of public expenditure holds that each line of governmental activity should be extended to the level at which the marginal social benefit from the activity is equal to the marginal social cost. This equality of marginal social benefit with marginal social cost for each activity would bring about equi-marginal social benefit per unit of money spent to produce the services.

In recent years, increasing doubts have been raised about the usefulness of this sacrifice-benefit doctrine of public finance. Instead, emphasis has shifted to resource mobilisation and allocation, the distribution of income, and the stabilisation aspects of public finance.[5] But since federal finance is concerned not only with issues of inter-regional but also with inter-personal equity, it

[1] Hugh Dalton, op. cit., p. 7.
[2] A. C. Pigou, op. cit., p. 43.
[3] R. N. Bhargava, The Theory and Working of Union Finance in India (London: Allen and Unwin, 1956), p. 17.
[4] A. C. Pigou, op. cit., p. 42.
[5] Two recent standard books which have followed this approach are R. A. Musgrave, The Theory of Public Finance—A Study in Public Economy (New York: McGraw-Hill Book Company, Inc., 1959), and A. R. Prest, Public Finance in Theory and Practice (London: Weidenfeld and Nicholson, 1963).

is appropriate to examine the relevance of the sacrifice-benefit theory of public finance to the particular problems of federal finance.

While the federal authority as well as each of the state or regional governments might be expected to equate marginal sacrifice with marginal benefit, there is no guarantee that the principle will operate for the country as a whole, since the federating states are invariably at different levels of economic prosperity. In a comparatively high-income state, the sacrifice imposed by the marginal unit of taxation is, other things being equal, less than that in a low-income state. On the other hand, the benefit derived from an expenditure out of this marginal unit is comparatively less in a high-income state. Thus, over-all marginal equilibrium cannot be taken for granted in a country with a federal constitution, even if each government in the federation succeeds in equating the marginal sacrifice imposed by its taxation with the marginal social benefit derived from its expenditures.

The failure to achieve this equilibrium has been called the 'opportunity cost of federalism'[1] and if equilibrium is ever to be brought about, the federal government cannot be content with only following the basic principle of public finance in its own sphere of activity. It should also act as a coordinator to effect such transfers as may be necessary to achieve the over-all marginal equilibrium. Unless the federal government assumes this coordinating function, a federal form of government will suffer from a serious defect in the field of public finance. It is thus an essential function of the federal government to follow the basic principle of public finance for the country as a whole, taking into account the fiscal activities of the states.

Yet the 'federal principle' requires that the federal and state governments be coordinate but independent of each other within their spheres of competence.[2] In the field of public finance, this means independent and coordinate tax jurisdictions. And with

---

[1] A. Scott, 'The Economic Goals of Federal Finance', in *Public Finance*, vol. XIX, No. 3, 1964, pp. 241–88.
[2] K. C. Wheare, *Federal Government* (Oxford University Press, fourth edition, 1963), p. 10.

independent financial resources and distinct functions goes independent public expenditure policy. The 'federal principle', carried to its logical conclusion, limits the federal government's ability to act as a coordinator to induce over-all equilibrium. For example, where independent sources of revenue are assigned to the federal and state governments, each might tax its own sphere according to the principle of least aggregate sacrifice. Because of differences in the level of economic development of the different states, the marginal sacrifice of the taxpayers of each state is unlikely to be the same as the marginal sacrifice of the taxpayers of the other states.

Yet if the basic principle of taxation is to be achieved, the marginal sacrifice of the sum total of federal and state taxation must be equal for each person, or as nearly equal as possible, thus giving similarly placed persons in different states similar burdens of federal plus state taxation. Since inter-state and inter-personal equality of marginal sacrifice will not occur automatically in a federation, it has been suggested that federalism must suffer from a theoretical defect: this defect can only be removed, in theory at least, if the federal government is given the constitutional power to tax all the people of the federation, and to levy direct taxes which can be closely related to the ability to pay. In addition, the federal government should have the power to levy some indirect taxes, principally customs and excise duties. These powers will make its scheme of taxation both progressive and comprehensive. Finally, the federal government should be given the constitutional power to provide grants-in-aid so as to be able to bring about equimarginal social benefit.

The application of a theory of federal finance, however, has been circumscribed by a variety of historical, political, cultural, and economic factors in most federations. A federal system of government is the answer to an immediate problem—a compromise between centrifugal and centripetal forces. It rests on a particular attitude on the part of the population of the federating units who desire union but not unity. Its architecture, therefore, invariably takes on local colouring in different countries. A study of federal constitutions shows clearly how complex are the motives and factors involved in the formation of federal systems. But in spite of the variations, it is possible to discern what might be termed the essential features of federal finance.

There is, first, the allocation of functions between the centre and the regions. Whatever may be the basis for dividing the spheres of government between these two levels, each should be given adequate fiscal powers if it is to be able to discharge its duties and responsibilities and still preserve its autonomy. Fiscal independence is a concomitant of local self-government, which the federating units desire to preserve. It is, however, a rarity for the fiscal powers granted to federal and state governments to prove adequate for all time. As W. A. Mackintosh has observed: 'Nothing is more certain in a federal constitution than that division of functions made reasonably decades ago will prove impracticable under the changed circumstances of a later age and that a disparity between functions and revenue sources will emerge.'[1]

The Australian Commonwealth Grants Commission, in its first report published in 1934, also observed that 'it is impossible in a federation nicely to adjust the functions entrusted to the members to their financial resources; some member may have more financial power than actually needed, and another less. Consequently, some adjustment may have to be made in the form of a redistribution of the revenue from the more favoured to the less fortunate member or members of the union. This must be accounted as one of the weaknesses of a federation. It renders it difficult to apply the principle of financial responsibility necessary to sound politics. However, some redistribution must be accepted as almost inevitable in any federation and especially at certain stages of development'.[2]

This disparity between fiscal needs and revenue sources has operated at both the federal and state levels. In the older federa-

[1] W. A. Mackintosh, 'Federal Finance' in Geoffrey Sawyer (Ed.), *Federalism: An Australian Jubilee Study* (Melbourne: Cheshire, for Australian National University, 1952), p. 94.
[2] Australian Grants Commission, *Report on the Application Made by the States of South Australia, Western Australia and Tasmania for Financial Assistance from the Commonwealth Under Section 96 of the Constitution* (First Report, 1934), p. 15.

tions, it has been one of the principal causes of the assumption by the federal governments of powers which originally did not belong to them and/or of the assumption of exclusive control of tax jurisdiction which they originally exercised concurrently with the state governments.

The second feature of federal finance is the freedom that both the central and unit governments exercise in the disbursement of revenue. In other words, '. . . full freedom of financial operations must be extended to both federal as well as to state governments in order that they may not suffer from a feeling of cramp in the discharge of their normal activities and in the achievement of their legitimate aspirations'.[1]

Thirdly, resources available to the various levels of government must be adequate, as far as possible, to meet the needs and responsibilities of each government. Such resources must also be elastic in response to expanding needs. Adequacy and elasticity of resources are two requirements which must go hand in hand. It is desirable to allocate sources of revenue to the unit government in order to achieve stability. It is more important for local revenue to be stable than for state revenue, and more important for state revenue to be stable than federal. In an emergency, the federal government, with its greater recourse to internal and external borrowing, is better able to bear financial shocks and strains than the state governments. For example, whereas revenues from property taxes or personal (capitation) taxes fluctuate little with changes in the level of income, revenues from export taxes are relatively unstable. Thus, while property and capitation taxes are appropriate as sources of revenue for the unit governments, export taxes, because of the volatility of their revenues, are more appropriate as a federal source of revenue.

The fourth essential feature of federal finance is administrative economy and efficiency. The fiscal system should minimise fraud, evasion, cost of collection, and double taxation. These objectives can only be achieved if tax jurisdiction is allocated between the federal and unit governments in full recognition that certain taxes

[1] B. P. Adarkar, *The Principles and Problems of Federal Finance* (London: King & Son, 1933), p. 219.

are better administered in the interest of efficiency and minimisation of cost at the federal level, while others are better administered at the local level. In modern federations, where attempts have been made to allocate fiscal powers in such a way as to achieve the criterion of minimising cost, a great deal of centralisation of tax administration has taken place, with the unit governments being left with little fiscal autonomy. Thus, the efficiency criterion tends to conflict with the principle of fiscal independence. Yet, given the scarcity of administrative resources, it seems that it is an inevitable feature of federal finance that fiscal power should tend to be concentrated in the central government.

Finally, if economic equilibriun is to be achieved, not only should the federal government have constitutional authority to impose direct and indirect taxes, but it should also be given constitutional powers to transfer resources from the relatively more developed parts of the country to the relatively less developed parts by means of grants-in-aid. Indeed, poverty anywhere in a federation is a limitation to prosperity everywhere.

These then are the basic requirements of federal finance. A study of federations all over the world will no doubt reveal considerable variation in the extent to which these features are present in various federations. In discussing the development, problems, and prospects of federal finance in Nigeria in the succeeding chapters, we shall endeavour to show *inter alia* the extent to which these requirements are met in the country's fiscal system.

Principles of fiscal adjustment in a federation

If fiscal adjustment is a necessary concomitant of federal finance, particularly to bring about over-all marginal equilibrium, on what principles should such adjustments be made? The orthodox treatment of the principle of fiscal adjustment has tended to concentrate attention on equity considerations while ignoring the consequences of such adjustment on several other worthwhile federal goals, such as the achievement of a nation-wide minimum standard of public services; the restriction of local irresponsibility due to excessive dependence on grants from the federal government; the maintenance of the federal parliament's responsibility for the funds it has raised; the encouragement of local efficiency and initiative; the reduction of administrative costs from multiple tax collection authorities; and the prevention of tax evasion by geographical migration.

J. M. Buchanan emphasises the equity goals more than any of the other objectives. In his articles on the subject, 'The Pure Theory of Government Finance: A Suggested Approach'[1] and 'Federalism and Fiscal Equity',[2] he argues against a system of fiscal adjustment which would enable all regional governments in a federation to provide a national average level of public services at average tax rates. He favours, instead, an inter-governmental system of fiscal adjustment that facilitates 'equal treatment of equals'. Arguing that in a federation the individual has 'a plurality of political units with which to deal fiscally',[3] he rejects what he calls 'organismic theory' as being of little use in practical problems because it regards the regional unit as an organic unit.[4] He questions limiting the application of the equity principle to single fiscal systems within a federation. If this were done, he argues, 'individuals similarly situated would be subjected to equal fiscal treatment only if they were citizens of the same subordinate unit of government. There would be no guarantee that equals living in different subordinate units would be equally treated at all'.[5] Therefore, he concludes, 'the principle of equity must be of use in solving the fiscal problem of federalism'.

Buchanan accordingly introduces the concept of the 'fiscal residuum', which he defines as being equal to an individual's tax burden minus his benefits from public services. 'Only by a comparison of the residuums of individuals,' he writes, 'can the total effects of a fiscal system be analysed and evaluated.'[6] Thus the

---

[1] *Journal of Political Economy*, vol. LVII, December 1949, pp. 496–505.
[2] *American Economic Review*, vol. XL, September 1950, pp. 583–99.
[3] J. M. Buchanan, 'Federalism and Fiscal Equity', p. 588.
[4] J. M. Buchanan, 'The Pure Theory of Government Finance: A Suggested Approach', pp. 496–8.
[5] J. M. Buchanan, 'Federalism and Fiscal Equity', p. 588.
[6] J. M. Buchanan, 'The Pure Theory of Government Finance: A Suggested Approach', p. 501. If 't' represents the tax burden of an individual and

B

satisfaction of the equity criterion will require that the fiscal
residua of similarly-placed individuals should be the same regardless of where they live in the federation, and the policy objective
for inter-governmental transfers will become one of providing or
ensuring 'equal fiscal treatment for equals'.

The acceptance of this principle would yield at least three
important results. First, it would establish a firm basis for the
claim that citizens of the low-income states within a national
economy possess the 'right' that their states receive transfers sufficient to enable these citizens to be placed in positions of fiscal
equality with their equals in other states. Thus, inter-governmental fiscal adjustment would no longer be regarded as an outright
subsidisation of the poorer areas, nor as charitable contributions
from the rich to the poor. Secondly, the principle would
provide justification for inter-area transfers, independent of any
particular public service or group of services. Federal grants to
regional governments for the purpose of furthering certain national
interests would thus be divorced from basic equalisation grants.
And thirdly, Buchanan's principle would necessitate the elimina-
tion of matching grants which, he claims, have served to prevent
the accomplishment of equalisation between the richer and the
poorer areas.

Buchanan's analysis has been described as 'a most ingenious
proposal for obtaining the best of both worlds. Its implementation
would leave the provinces or regions fairly autonomous, yet would
oblige the central government to take account of the net tax-benefit
residuum.'[1] But his proposal has a number of practical and
operational objections, as well as some theoretical difficulties.

There is first the question of provincial or regional autonomy.
In a federation with a strong tradition of regional fiscal autonomy,
would the regions tolerate a federal tax-benefit structure that varies

'b' has benefits from public services, his fiscal residuum is (t—b). It will
be negative where b<t and positive where t<b. John F. Graham in his
*Fiscal Adjustment and Economic Development: A Case Study of Nova
Scotia* (University of Toronto Press, 1963), has defined the residuum the
other way as being equal to b—t. Thus defined, an individual with a
positive residuum would have an excess of benefits over burdens.

[1] A. Scott, op. cit., p. 253.

from one region to another? And would such a varying federal tax-benefit structure be constitutional? The answer to both questions is in the negative. In addition there would be severe administrative difficulties in the operation of such a system of fiscal adjustment. If, for constitutional reasons, the federal government cannot impose a tax-benefit structure that varies from region to region, the only way of achieving horizontal fiscal equity as defined by Buchanan is through unconditional grants which would vary among regions. Once such grants are received, each region would be free to use them as it pleases, with the result that horizontal equity may not in fact be achieved.

On theoretical grounds, it is doubtful if the equalising of fiscal residua of similarly situated taxpayers would necessarily make their over-all fiscal treatment the same. Apart from the net fiscal pressure on a person, the level of public services available to him has a bearing on his welfare. But it is the legislators rather than the individual citizens who determine through the legislative processes of appropriations the level of public services for all the residents of the region or federation. It is therefore likely that some taxpayers will feel that their welfare would be enhanced by more public services and less private goods while others may feel the reverse. Thus, the equalising of fiscal residue is, in itself, insufficient to equalise the over-all fiscal treatment of similarly situated individuals. It is only when the levels of public services are the same in all the regions that equalising fiscal residua could achieve the over-all fiscal treatment of similarly situated individuals.[1]

If the residua could be equalised, Buchanan argues that the whole fiscal structure would be as neutral as is geographically possible. A fiscal residuum will fit many combinations of taxes and benefits.[2] However, a person with a given income and tastes may be indifferent among many tax-benefit combinations even though

---

[1] J. F. Graham, op. cit., p. 178.
[2] For example, tax-payer X in region Y, whose b=£600 and t=£400, has a fiscal residuum of £200. On the other hand, tax-payer N in region M, whose b=£2,000 and whose t=£1,800, also has a fiscal residuum of £200.

the fiscal residuum of each combination differs. Thus 'to guarantee to a person of given income that he will receive the same fiscal residuum wherever he lives is not to guarantee that he will remain on the same indifference curve. On the contrary (except by accident), it is almost certain to guarantee that, by moving to an area with the same fiscal residuum but a different tax-benefit combination, he will be made better or worse off, i.e., moved to a higher or lower indifference curve.'[1] Thus, the Buchanan proposal for achieving equity would not necessarily bring about neutrality in a geographic sense between different tax-benefit combinations whose residua are the same.

But in spite of these limitations on the Buchanan fiscal equity approach, it does take into account both taxes and benefits in the discussion of the principles of fiscal adjustment in a federation. It also removes from equalising federal grants the stigma which is often attached to them as being subsidies that are little different from handouts.

Richard A. Musgrave, in his paper 'Approaches to a Fiscal Theory of Political Federalism,'[2] presents a series of approaches which combine the various principles of fiscal adjustment and take into account not only efficiency considerations but also other objectives which a federal government may wish to pursue. These objectives may relate the central government fiscal adjustment to the groups of individuals comprising the various regions of the federation: the federal government respects the right of the regional or state governments to determine fiscal policies at the regional or state level. In other words, the federal government may choose to equalise the fiscal operations of the various regions in the federation. Alternatively, the objective might be to ensure a minimum level of regional services or to provide incentives to the regions to raise the levels of their services.

The fiscal adjustment process aimed at placing all the regions in a federation in a more or less equal fiscal position might be used to

---

[1] A. Scott, op. cit., p. 254.
[2] Published in *Public Finances: Needs, Sources and Utilization*, A Report of the National Bureau of Economic Research (Princeton University Press, 1961), pp. 97–122; Comments pp. 122–33.

bring about various forms of equalisation, namely, actual fiscal performance, fiscal capacity, or fiscal potential. Musgrave analyses in turn the effects of each form of equalisation on regional taxation.

First, he shows that a fiscal adjustment aimed at equalising the per capita expenditure on regional services in all regions, while resulting in the transfer of resources from high-income to low-income regions, results in a disincentive effect on regional taxation. Second, a fiscal adjustment aimed at equalising regional performance also has a disincentive effect on regional taxation, but the disincentive is smaller for the more needy regions and greater for the less needy. Third, in the case where adjustment is aimed at equalising the differentials in fiscal need and capacity rather than in actual outlays for performance, there are no disincentive effects in regional taxation. Fourth, when the objective is to equalise fiscal potentials, due account should be taken of the potential tax effort of each region by assessing the tax base before any adjustment is made. Under this plan, resources would be distributed from regions with larger tax bases to regions with smaller ones. This approach would permit each region to determine its own level of taxation, while leaving the federal government to equalise the fiscal opportunities of the various regions. It would make it possible for a region to receive support only to the extent that it qualified for support by its own tax effort.

In most of the literature dealing with the subject of federal grants-in-aid, the substitution of federal for regional and local revenues is often ignored. It is often contended that federal grants stimulate state expenditures on the subsidised services. Musgrave in his analysis has shown the reverse to be the case in regard to equalisation grants. Using micro-economic analysis, it is also possible to demonstrate the theoretical possibility of federal revenue being substituted for state revenue.

Other things being equal, a reduction in the price of a service will lead to an increase in the quantity demanded. Assuming that a regional government will behave like an individual consumer,[1]

---

[1] The regional legislature is assumed to be representative of the preferences of the community between public and private goods and between one governmental service and another.

and assuming, also, elastic demand for a particular government service, there will be some, however small, increase in the quantity of a service if its supply price is reduced to the region as the result of federal assumption of part of the total price. But an increase in the quantity consumed does not, of course, result in an increase in total outlay on the part of the region. Whether or not total outlay increases depends on the elasticity of demand for the service: if it is elastic, the region's outlay will increase, but if it is inelastic, then outlay will decrease.

The region's demand for the subsidised service will be influenced by a number of factors. First, if the service absorbs a large proportion of income, the demand for it is more likely to be elastic than if the service absorbs only a small proportion of its income. Second, unless the subsidised service is an 'inferior' good, the demand for it will increase as the tax base of the region increases. Finally, a region with a limited conception of the role of government would have a system of indifference curves different from that of a region which is more welfare-oriented, and where, therefore, a high marginal rate of substitution of private for governmental services exists.

Figure 1 shows the foregoing analysis diagrammatically. The figure illustrates the effect of federal grants-in-aid on regional finances. The quantity of the subsidised service is measured along the X-axis, while the price of the service is measured along Y-axis. The curve TE shows the demand schedule of region R_1, while the curve MV shows that of region R_2. The total outlay of region R_1 before the federal subsidy is represented by the area OUTL, while the pre-subsidy total outlay of region R_2 is represented by the area ONML. A federal subsidy for the service which reduces its unit price from OL to OC will make region R_2 substitute BQRN for LCBM, causing a reduction in the region's total outlay but an increase in its consumption of the service from OU to OR. On the other hand, region R_1, given the same subsidy, will increase its own expenditure by WUDA even though the federal subsidy only amounts to LTWC (WUDA>LTWC). Its consumption of the service also increases from OU to OD.

Thus in the case of region R_1, federal grants have stimulated a

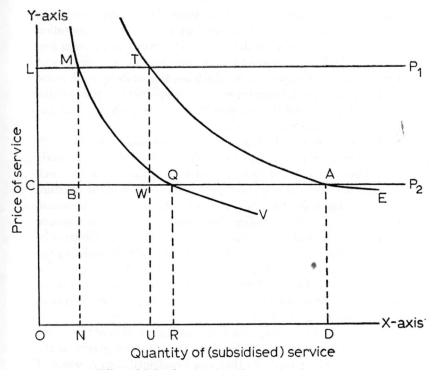

FIGURE I *Effect of federal grants-in-aid on regional finances*

large increase in the quantity of the subsidised service consumed, and also a large increase in its total outlay on the service. The increased outlay might be financed by increased taxation or a reduction in expenditure on other services. In the case of region R_2, federal grants have led to a reduction in its outlay on the service. The resources thus released might be used in providing unsubsidised services, or the region might reduce its taxes.

The above analysis and that of Musgrave both show that fiscal adjustment aimed at equalisation or at stimulation does sometimes lead to the substitution of federal revenues and taxes for regional revenues and taxes. However, its net effect would depend on the type of adjustment used. But whatever system of federal grants-in-aid is used (whether specific or lump-sum, or constant matching or variable matching grants), there would be some substitution effect, and therefore some distortion. The extent of the substitution of federal for regional funds would depend on a number of factors, the most important of which are the elasticity of demand for the service, the relative importance of a particular service in the region's budget, and the community's scale of preferences as between private and public goods.

Of course, in the Buchanan theory emphasising equity, fiscal adjustment is aimed at equalising the fiscal residua of similarly placed persons in a federation, regardless of the region in which he resides, rather than equalising the fiscal position of the different regions in the federation. It is claimed, *inter alia*, that this system of adjustment will neutralise the distorting effects on resource allocation. The validity of this claim has already been shown to be doubtful, but even if it were valid, it would result in restricting the flow of resources from the poorer regions, where they are not being used efficiently, to the relatively richer regions, where they could be employed in optimum use. This would affect the rate of growth of the economy as a whole.

Five conclusions emerge from the foregoing review of the theory of fiscal adjustment in a federation. First, federal grants to the states must adopt methods that will avoid inefficiency, waste of public money, and a distortion of a rational allocation of resources. Second, the criteria for adjustment may vary from time to time, and/or from one country to another, depending on the goals which a federation intends to achieve. Third, adjustments should minimise the substitution of federal grants for state revenues by taking into account such factors as tax-effort, expenditure economy, and fiscal capacity. This will ensure that the states do not relax their effort to resolve their own problems. Fourth, if conditional grants are used, they should be kept at a minimum so that they are marginal to the total adjustments. Finally, in order to achieve an effective adjustment process it is essential to have a satisfactory machinery (like the Australian Grants Commission or the Finance Commission of India) which will be responsible for making recommendations for adjustment. It is highly desirable that such an institution should be both permanent and independent. In chapter 10 we shall examine the experience of two well-known federations—Australia and India—in fiscal adjustment, with a view to identifying the lessons which Nigeria can learn from the experience of these two countries.

2 The background to federal finance in Nigeria

The problem of federal finance is by no means merely a financial problem; its proper study requires a knowledge of the political, social, and economic circumstances which give it its special local character in a particular federation. A study of the evolution of federal finance in Nigeria and of the problems of operating such a federal fiscal system should therefore begin with a brief sketch of the broad cultural background within which federal finance developed and has operated since 1954.

Historical, political, and constitutional

Nigeria as a political entity came into being on 1 January 1914, when the British Colonial Government amalgamated the Protectorate of Northern Nigeria with the Colony and Protectorate of Southern Nigeria. The various steps which led to this amalgamation and the political justification for it is not the concern of this study. It is sufficient to emphasise that Nigeria was an artificial creation, a mere geographical expression (to borrow Metternich's famous description of Italy), and at the time of its birth it was just a country 'inhabited by a medley of formerly warring tribes with no common culture and only united in so far as they were governed by a single power'.[1]

It is also worth emphasising that even the two protectorates that

[1] Sir Alan C. Burns, *In Defence of Colonies* (London: Allen and Unwin, 1957), p. 67.

were amalgamated in 1914 were each an artificial creation. Neither sprang into being as a complete whole. Each came into existence as British jurisdiction, trying to facilitate peaceful trading, spread its influence to the slave-trading and tribal-warring hinterlands. This gradual process occupied the best part of half a century, beginning with the cession of Lagos to the British Crown in 1861 and ending with the creation of both protectorates in 1906. Thus, Nigeria from the very beginning was a composite of states. Federalism in Nigeria is therefore not, as it is sometimes supposed, the 'fragmentation of a long established natural unity but in some measure a reversion, though with great differences, to the past'.[1]

The amalgamation of 1914 did not bring forth appreciable constitutional change, and until 1946 the North and South continued to be governed as they had before 1914. Although a new constitution in 1922 gave the Governor executive and legislative councils for advice, the latter had an overwhelming majority of official and nominated members and its powers did not extend to the North. Legislative powers over Northern Nigeria, except in so far as financial proposals were concerned, were exercised by the Governor-in-Council by means of proclamation.

The fact that the North and South continued to be governed separately between 1914 and 1946 made assimilation between the two difficult. Lord Lugard, the 'creator' of Nigeria and its first Governor-General, resisted all attempts at centralisation and assimilation. He rejected all the advice given to him to break the country into four or more groups of provinces[2] on the grounds that:

'. . . each of the former Administrations was under a separate body of laws. A territory re-division, which transferred portions of one Administration to the other, or included portions of each in a new Administration, would have been productive of chaos and interminable appeals for "Ruling" at a moment when the insatiable pressure on the Central Government was greatest. Moreover, the

[1] *Report of the Commission on Revenue Allocation, 1951* (Government Printer, Lagos), p. 10.
[2] K. D. Morel in his book, *Nigeria, its People and Problems* (second edition, 1912), suggested dividing the country into four great provinces.

multiplicity of Secretariats, and the reduplication of Departmental Heads . . . appeared to be an insuperable objection involving unnecessary correspondence, duplication of work and needless cost.'[1]

The administrative areas of Northern and Southern Nigeria were placed under two Lieutenant-Governors without any territorial change and each with a secretariat and departmental organisation. Those departments which were practically indivisible and whose functions were Nigeria-wide in nature (the Judiciary, Military, Railway, Posts and Telegraphs, and Audit) were centralised under the direct control of the Governor-General assisted by a Central Secretariat. The Colony of Lagos was constituted into a separate administration under an administrator, sharing its departmental staff with Southern Nigeria Provinces.

Prior to amalgamation, Northern Nigeria had been divided into thirteen provinces (two small provinces, Ilorin and Kabba, were later amalgamated into one), under 'Residents'. Southern Nigeria had comprised three 'Divisions'—East, Central and West—under Provincial Commissioners. After amalgamation, Southern Nigeria was divided into nine provinces, each under a Resident. In 1916, the former colony of Cameroons was added to the South.

This administrative structure given to Nigeria by Lord Lugard had existed practically unchanged for fifty-three years. The North had remained a single political entity within Nigeria until the creation of new states on 27 May 1967, in spite of suggestions from time to time that it be divided into three or more regions. The South had been re-divided into three—West, East, and Mid-West —by August 1963. The first step in that direction had come in 1939 when Southern Nigeria was split into Western and Eastern Provinces, and the second step had come in 1963 when the Mid-Western Region was carved out of the Western Region. Now, however, both South and North consist of six states each.[2]

[1] Sir F. D. (later Lord) Lugard, *Report on the Amalgamation of Northern and Southern Nigeria, and Administration, 1912–1919*, Cmd. 468, p. 10.
[2] It should be pointed out here that although the Federal Military Government issued a decree in May 1967, dividing the country into twelve states, this new structure is subject to a nation-wide referendum which is to be held after the current civil war in the country. As the fiscal consequences of the creation of twelve states out of the existing four

A new constitution was introduced in 1946. Its threefold objective was: to promote the unity of Nigeria; to recognise its diversity; and to increase the participation of Nigerians in the management of their own affairs. It sought to promote unity by the establishment of a legislative council for the whole of the country. It acknowledged the diversity of Nigeria by the creation of regional councils for the Northern, Western, and Eastern groups of provinces. And finally, the constitution provided for an African majority on the legislative and regional councils. In the view of its architect, Sir Arthur Richards, who was then the Governor of Nigeria:

'. . . the problem of Nigeria . . . is how to create a political system which is itself a present advance and maintains the living possibility of further orderly advance—a system within which the diverse elements may progress at varying speeds amicably and smoothly, towards a more closely integrated economic, social and political unity, without sacrificing the principles and ideals inherent in their divergent ways of life.'[1]

From 1946 onwards, the constitutional advancement of Nigeria was relatively swift. The regional councils created under the 1946 Constitution were purely advisory in their role: they debated bills and passed resolutions on them, but the legislative council alone had the power to enact the bills. The regional councils served principally as electoral colleges for the election of members of the legislative council and as a training ground for members of that assembly.

In 1951 (even though the 1946 Constitution was intended to operate for nine years), a new constitution was introduced which considerably strengthened the regional councils. They became legislative bodies and could make laws on certain enumerated subjects like education, agriculture and public health. Although the central legislature could veto regional legislation and could also

regions and the federal territory of Lagos belong to the future rather than to the past and the present, we shall defer their consideration until the last chapter, where the future development and prospects of federal finance in Nigeria are considered.

[1] *Despatch to the Secretary of State by the Governor*, 6 December 1944.

legislate on all subjects within the regional list, the 1951 Constitution really marked the first decisive step towards federalism in Nigeria. The regional governments it established behaved from the very beginning as if they had coordinate powers with the central government. The decision of the leaders of the major political parties in the country to participate in the regional governments rather than in the central government enhanced the status of the former at the expense of the latter.

But since the regional governments were constitutionally subordinate to the central government it was inevitable that there were frequent frictions between the two levels of government. This eventually led to the breakdown of the constitution and to the introduction of a more truly federal constitution in 1954. Thus, exactly forty years after amalgamation, the Federation of Nigeria was finally born. Although three constitutional conferences were held between 1954 and the time of independence in 1960,[1] these were concerned with providing necessary federal institutions and with settling outstanding matters in connection with the country's approaching independence.

While the amalgamation of Nigeria in 1914 was imposed on the people by the British, the adoption of a federal constitution was 'the creation from below of a natural and democratic unity by the peoples themselves'.[2] And three years after independence, when the Federation of Nigeria became the Federal Republic of Nigeria, the Republican Constitution formally affirmed that the people of Nigeria are 'firmly resolved to establish the Federal Republic of Nigeria with a view to ensuring the unity of [the] fatherland . . . so as to further the ends of liberty, equality and justice . . .'[3]

---

[1] In 1957, 1958 and 1960. One outcome of the 1957 Constitutional Conference was the granting of internal self-government to Western and Eastern Regions. At the 1958 Conference, Northern Nigeria was granted a similar measure of internal self-government.

[2] Margery Perham, *Lugard, the Years of Authority, 1898–1945* (London: Collins Clear-Type Press, 1960), p. 408.

[3] *Constitution of the Federation.* Act No. 20 of 1963.

Fiscal

Important as were the political and administrative factors which led to the amalgamation of Northern and Southern Nigeria, the fiscal and economic forces were even more compelling. With the creation of the Colony and Protectorate of Southern Nigeria in 1906, the material prosperity of Southern Nigeria increased very rapidly. There developed a prosperous trade in spirits from which Southern Nigeria derived considerable revenue. The demand was so vigorous that the quantities imported increased rapidly in spite of increased duty. As was to be expected, therefore, the government of Southern Nigeria had no financial problems. In fact, its revenue was always in excess of its expenditure, and it was able to build up reserves. These reserves were over one million pounds (sterling) by the time of amalgamation.

On the other hand, the government of the Protectorate of Northern Nigeria was unable to balance its budget and was dependent on annual grants from the British government. Even with these grants, which in the year before amalgamation were at the level of £136,000 and had averaged £314,500 for the eleven years ending March 1912, the Northern government could balance its budget only with the most parsimonious economy. While the country as a whole had an 'aggregate revenue practically equal to its needs',[1] its division by an 'arbitrary line of latitude' was responsible for the dependence of one part on imperial grants. Amalgamation was the only solution to this anomalous situation.

In addition to the fiscal problems of Northern Nigeria, there were trade and economic difficulties. Trade between the two parts of Nigeria was far from free. There were customs stations on inland frontiers where a surtax was levied on salt brought into the North, and all non-Northerners trading in the North had to obtain licences. Although the Southern government was paying £70,000 annually to the Northern government as its share of the revenues from import duties, the latter government, in order to secure direct customs duties, connected Baro, a port on the Niger,

[1] Sir Frederick (later Lord) Lugard, op. cit., p. 7.

with a railway line from Kano. The South then retaliated by extending its railway as far north as Minna.

If the northern trade was to expand, it was seriously in need of this outlet to the sea. Also, the two railway systems developing separately in the two protectorates needed unification and a single controlling authority if unnecessary duplication and competition were to be avoided. This belief in the fiscal and economic viability of an economically integrated Nigeria was justified by subsequent events.[1] By making possible the integration of the economies of both parts of the country, an impetus was given to trade and development. The value of domestic exports rose from £6·78 million in 1913 to £14·50 million in 1919 (an increase of 214 per cent), while the value of imports increased from £6·28 million to £10·80 million (an increase of 172 per cent) during the same period. And in spite of the fear that the amalgamation might prove 'an unfruitful union',[2] the new country established its fiscal viability during the first years of its creation.

Both the governments of Northern Nigeria Protectorate and of the Colony and Protectorate of Southern Nigeria had separate and widely different fiscal systems, which had to be integrated to create true amalgamation. Even their financial years began on different dates—the North from 1 April and the South from 1 January. The systems of accounts kept by the governments were also separate. A uniform fiscal system reflecting the political and administrative changes was needed to replace the two systems which had existed before amalgamation.

Given the political and administrative structure established with effect from 1 January 1914, and the concern of the Governor-General for a large degree of devolution (what in the fifties came to be known as 'regional autonomy'), it is not surprising that separate

[1] It should be pointed out that many people, including the then Secretary of State for the Colonies, were less sanguine as to whether Nigeria would be able to balance its budget for some time to come even with the most careful economy in administration. Hence a grant-in-aid of £100,000 per annum for five years was promised by the British government. See *Amalgamation Report*, p. 45.

[2] Lord Hailey, *An African Survey* (Oxford University Press, 1957), p. 528.

estimates of revenue and expenditure were prepared for each of the three governments—Central, Northern, and Colony and Southern. Certain sources of revenue were taken over by the new central administration, the principal ones being revenues from customs duties, railway receipts, posts and telegraph earnings, and interests accruing from investments and loans. The 'regional' governments' main sources of revenue became licences and internal revenue, fees of court and offices (including reimbursements), rent on government property, direct taxes, and, in the case of the North, imperial grants-in-aid which were received during the first five years after amalgamation. Direct taxation, which had been introduced in the North before amalgamation, was not extended to the South until some years thereafter. Even then, it never really became an important source of 'regional' revenue in the South until the 1920s.

This system of revenue 'allocation' meant that the South would suffer financially, since customs, its most important source of revenue, was now transferred to the central authority. Before amalgamation the level of revenue of the Southern Nigeria government had been about £2·5 million while that of the Northern Nigeria government was only £0·5 million. Due to the new fiscal system, however, the revenue of the Southern Nigeria government fell to just a little over £0·2 million in 1914. Problems of fiscal adequacy did not arise, though, since under the new system all the revenues of the three governments were deposited into a single general revenue fund. Aggregate expenditures were met from this fund without the requirement that each government should balance its own budget. All that was required, instead, was that the aggregate budget of all the governments should be in balance.

This fiscal system remained practically unchanged until 1926/7, when the estimates of revenue and expenditure of the three governments ceased to be shown separately. From that year and until the re-introduction of regional estimates in 1948/9, the Nigerian fiscal system was completely unified. Thus, Lord Lugard's claim that 'the financial unification'[1] of Nigeria was complete on amalgamation never really materialised until 1926. However, this integration

[1] Sir F. D. (later Lord) Lugard, op. cit., p. 45.

of the finances of the three governments later proved an unfortunate development; for as we shall see in subsequent chapters, it made the evolution of federal finance extremely difficult.

The remaining part of this section is devoted to a brief review and analysis of the two distinct phases of public finances in Nigeria during the thirty-two years after amalgamation. As was noted above, separate budgets were published each year in a single document, and all the revenues of the three governments were treated as belonging to one general revenue fund from 1914 to 1925/6. Analysis of revenues and expenditures during this period gives some indication of the revenue-raising efforts of the three governments. In the second phase, 1926/7 to 1947/8,[1] devolution of powers was replaced by a complete centralisation of administrative and fiscal powers. The supremacy of the central government was established when the revenue and expenditure of the provincial governments ceased to be shown separately and were integrated with the central government estimates of revenue and expenditure. It was also during this period that the Protectorate of Southern Nigeria was split into Eastern and Western groups of provinces, each with its own administrative machinery.

The financial needs of the North, as noted above, were one of the compelling reasons for amalgamation. Of the total liquid assets taken over by the new central government on 1 January 1914, 93·5 per cent (about £1·7 million) came from the South. Nevertheless, during the first year of its existence, the country was able to balance its budget. Thus, the solvency of Nigeria during this period was made possible by the favourable revenue position of the Colony and Southern Provinces.

Table 2.1 shows the over-all budgetary position of the governments during the first twelve years after the amalgamation. During this period, Nigeria was unable to balance its budget only on three occasions (1915, 1916 and 1921/2), in spite of the cessation of the imperial grants after 1918. During this period also, revenue increased almost threefold and expenditure more than doubled. It would, however, be misleading to give the impression that the

[1] Although the 1946 constitution became operative from March 1947, changes in the fiscal system were not effected until 1 April 1948.

finances of the Nigerian governments were adequate. For no sooner did the amalgamation take place than World War One began. By disrupting international trade, the war affected not only the growth of Nigeria's revenue, but also its expenditure on essential services, which had to be reduced because orders for goods and services from Britain could not be filled. The country was also

TABLE 2.1 *Revenue and expenditure, 1914–1925/6*

(£'000s)

Year	Revenue	Grants-in-Aid from the British Treasury	Total Revenue	Total Expenditure	Budgetary Surplus (+) or Deficit (—)
1914	2,948	100	3,048	2,968	+ 80
1915	2,603	100	2,703	2,802	— 99
1916	2,731	100	2,831	3,067	— 236
1917	3,375	75	3,450	3,105	+ 345
1918	3,964	50	4,014	3,429	+ 585
1919	4,911	—	4,911	4,353	+ 558
1920	6,738	—	6,738	6,081	+ 657
1921/2	4,869	—	4,869	6,553	— 1,684
1922/3	5,562	—	5,562	5,467	+ 95
1923/4	6,304	—	6,304	5,545	+ 759
1924/5	6,990	—	6,990	5,814	+ 1,176
1925/6	8,269	—	8,269	6,583	+ 1,686

SOURCE: *Nigerian Estimates*, 1914–1925/6

made to contribute to the war effort from its rather meagre resources.[1] But the most severe financial problem to be faced came in 1918, when the importation of spirits was prohibited by the government on moral grounds. As a result, Nigeria suffered a loss of sixty per cent of its pre-war revenue from import duties, imposing considerable budget constraints since the loss of this potentially great source of revenue had been unforeseen at the time of amalgamation. No new sources of revenue were immediately

[1] See *Legislative Council Debates, Official Report*, 1 November 1923.

available. As the Chief Secretary to the government rightly observed during the Legislative Council debate:[1]

'Northern Nigeria was amalgamated to Southern Nigeria because, quite openly stated, Southern Nigeria was rich. And further, Southern Nigeria was rich because it had the spirits duties. . . . If it had been foreseen in 1914 that the spirits duties were going to be withdrawn a few years afterwards, it would have been quite impossible to amalgamate Northern and Southern Nigeria on the financial terms on which they were amalgamated.'

And as if the country's financial predicaments were not enough, the Cameroons were added to Nigeria shortly after the war. They were a financial burden, always running budget deficits which had to be covered by Nigerian subsidy. Rising revenues from export duties, increased quantities of imported manufactured goods—the revenue from which gradually replaced the decreased revenues from spirits—and strict economy measures in public expenditure kept the country financially viable.

As Table 2.2 shows, the government of the Colony and Protectorate of Southern Nigeria consistently had budget deficits between 1914 and 1925/6. Besides the loss of customs jurisdiction, the government of Southern Nigeria continued to be responsible, at least for some years, for the maintenance of two major central departments—the Customs and Marine Departments. Had the

TABLE 2.2 *Revenue and expenditure of the northern and southern governments, selected years, 1914–1925/6*

	|							(£'000s)
	1916 Rev.	Exp.	1918 Rev.	Exp.	1922/3 Rev.	Exp.	1923/4 Rev.	Exp.
Northern Government	545	326	612	326	651	347	757	350
Southern Government	289	856	509	1,052	266	702	296	752

SOURCE: *Estimates of the Nigerian Government*, 1914–1925/6

[1] loc. cit.

two parts of Nigeria been federated rather than amalgamated, the assignment of duties and responsibilities would have been more rationally accomplished, and the allocation of revenue and tax powers more equitably distributed. For example, before amalgamation, only seven per cent of the revenue from customs went to the North, the balance being retained by the South for its use. This point is mentioned now to foreshadow the importance these twelve years of 1914–26 have when moves toward a federal constitution began in the forties and fifties. Separate estimates prepared for the three governments during this period became crucial evidence for the allegations by the northern leaders that the North had been unfairly treated in the past and that revenues from the North had been used to develop the South.

As the Hicks-Phillipson Fiscal Commission showed in its 1951 report,[1] this allegation was unfounded, or to use the Commission's words 'not proven'. Because the colonial administration was more interested in integrating the country's fiscal system than in ensuring a rational distribution of functions and an equitable allocation of revenue, little consideration had been given to the problems of inter-governmental and inter-regional fiscal equity. This issue assumed great importance later on, and it will be discussed in subsequent chapters.

The years between 1926 and 1948 are of little significance for this study on the development and problems of federal finance in Nigeria. In this period, central government control was so complete that no distinction was made between northern and southern revenues and expenditures. The fiscal arrangements after amalgamation were not retained throughout this period. Had this been done, there is no doubt that subsequent discussion on the type of federal fiscal system to be adopted by Nigeria and on the allegation of 'unfair treatment' would have had greater light thrown on them.

It is, however, worth noting the two important events which affected the country's economy and therefore its public finances during this period: the economic crisis of 1931–4 and the World War Two. In spite of the strenuous efforts made by the govern-

[1] J. R. Hicks and S. Phillipson, *Report of the Commission on Revenue Allocation*, 1951 (Lagos: Government Printer), p. 71.

ment to reduce expenditures, there were budget deficits in ten of the twenty-two years.

Economic

The economic setting within which public finance has operated in Nigeria will be considered in this section not as an analysis of general economic inter-relationships but as an identification of the main features of the Nigerian economy relevant to our understanding of the nature and problems of federal finance in Nigeria.

It is sometimes argued that Nigeria has achieved much more rapid economic and social advance since 1946 than it had achieved during the first three decades of its existence. The World Bank, in its report entitled the *Economic Development of Nigeria*, went as far as to assert that 'in less than ten years (i.e. between 1946 and 1953) the economy has grown and strengthened to such an extent that it bears little resemblance to the pre-war economy'.[1] This view is no doubt due to the fact that until the estimates of Nigeria's national income were first published in 1953,[2] only the basic features of the country's economy were known. It was not until ten years after the pioneering work of Prest and Stewart, which covered only one year, 1950/1, that national income estimates covering the period 1950 to 1957 were published,[3] and estimates of the annual rate of growth in the country's gross domestic product are now available from 1950 onwards. But the lack of data about the country's national income between 1914 and 1950 renders unsubstantiated the assertion that more rapid advance had been made during the post-World War Two years than during the preceding years. Any such comparison must take into account the 1930s Great Depression, which affected the Nigerian economy as adversely as it did the economies of most other countries, and the war years between 1939 and 1945 when normal economic activities were disrupted.

[1] International Bank for Reconstruction and Development, *The Economic Development of Nigeria* (Lagos: Government Printer, 1954), p. 6.
[2] A. R. Prest and I. G. Stewart, *The National Income of Nigeria, 1950–51* (London: HMSO, 1953).
[3] P. N. C. Okigbo, *Nigerian National Accounts, 1950–57* (Federal Ministry of Economic Development, Lagos, 1962).

The foundations of the Nigerian economy could be said to have been laid between 1900 and 1929, when the present structure of the economy took shape. During this period, an extensive railway system linked the North with the East and West; new cash crops such as groundnuts, cocoa, rubber, and cotton were introduced, which helped to bring the peasant into the money economy; and

TABLE 2.3 *Volume of principal export products, selected years, 1900–66*

(In long tons)

Years	Cocoa	Palm Kernels	Palm Oil	Ground Nuts	Tin Metal and Ore	Rubber
1900	202	85,624	45,508	599	—	1,271
1910	2,932	172,907	76,851	995	735	1,176
1920	17,155	207,010	84,856	45,409	7,913	492
1930	52,331	260,022	135,801	146,471	12,067	2,177
1940	89,737	235,521	132,723	169,480	14,843	2,902
1947	110,793	316,376	125,954	255,866	14,090	7,445
1953	104,617	402,872	201,345	326,725	12,136	21,260
1959	142,800	430,608	163,692	498,228	7,536	53,340
1966	190,000	394,000	143,000	573,000	12,099	70,000

SOURCES: *Nigerian Trade Journal*, various issues (Federal Ministry of Industry, Lagos); *Digest of Statistics*, various issues (Federal Office of Statistics, Lagos); and *Economic Indicators*, various issues (Federal Office of Statistics, Lagos).

minerals, principally tin and coal, were discovered and exploited. In view of these developments, it is not surprising that export volume and value increased dramatically during this period, as Tables 2.3 and 2.4 indicate. With the rise in the volume and value of exports came a rise in the volume and value of imports.

The prolonged period of stagnation in the Nigerian economy during the thirties and in 1939–45 was followed by a resumption of rapid economic progress immediately after World War Two. This was initiated by conscious development-oriented govern-

TABLE 2.4 *Value of principal export products, selected years,*
1900–66

(£'000s)

Years	Cocoa	Palm Kernels	Palm Oil	Ground Nuts	Tin Metal and Ore	Rubber
1900	9	834	681	4	—	186
1910	101	2,451	1,742	9	77	312
1920	1,238	4,948	4,677	1,120	1,786	57
1930	1,756	3,679	3,250	2,196	1,373	150
1940	1,583	1,500	1,099	1,476	2,727	265
1947	10,650	9,491	5,038	6,397	4,091	677
1953	24,858	22,185	13,020	24,928	7,078	3,287
1959	38,292	25,920	13,752	27,516	4,212	11,604
1966	28,260	22,430	10,962	40,815	15,466	11,474

SOURCES: *Nigerian Trade Journal,* various issues (Federal Ministry
of Trade and Industry, Lagos); *Digest of Statistics,* various issues
(Federal Office of Statistics, Lagos); and *Economic Indicators,* various
issues (Federal Office of Statistics, Lagos).

ment policies.[1] The post-war and Korean war booms in the world
markets for primary products further stimulated economic
development. Thus it can be argued that what happened to the
Nigerian economy after World War Two was merely a resumption
of economic development after a prolonged period of stagnation
between 1929 and 1945.

Table 2.5 shows the rate of growth of Nigeria's gross domestic
product from 1950/1 to 1965/6. During this period, Nigeria's
Gross Domestic Product grew at an annual average rate of 4·5 per
cent. This is indeed an unusually good rate of growth, but Nigeria,
in spite of this, is still a very poor country. With a population
variously estimated at between forty and fifty-five million,[2] the
country has one of the lowest per capita incomes in the world.

[1] In 1946, a *Ten-Year Plan of Development and Welfare in Nigeria*
(Sessional Paper No. 24 of 1945) was launched with a total capital
expenditure of £53·33 million.
[2] Population figures in a country like Nigeria are highly suspect. The
unreliability of the Nigerian figures has been increased rather than

TABLE 2.5 *Gross domestic product at factor cost and at 1957 prices, fiscal years 1950–66*

Fiscal Year	GDP (£ millions)	Percentage Change
1950	688·7	—
1951	741·4	7·6
1952	793·5	7·0
1953	811·6	2·3
1954	872·1	7·4
1955	895·2	2·6
1956	873·7	−2·4
1957	910·0	4·1
1958	900·0	−1·1
1959	938·5	4·3
1960	981·3	4·6
1961	1,014·0	3·3
1962	1,072·3	5·7
1963	1,162·1	8·4
1964	1,233·6	6·1
1965	1,310·9	6·3
1966	1,398·2	6·7

SOURCE: For 1950 to 1957, P. N. C. Okigbo, *Nigerian National Accounts*, Lagos: Federal Ministry of Economic Development (n.d.); and, for 1958 to 1966, the Federal Office of Statistics, Lagos.

A striking feature of the Nigerian economy is the relatively little change which has taken place in its structure since 1950/1.

diminished by the 1962 and 1963 census counts which are believed to have been grossly inflated for political reasons. Officially, the country's population is, according to the 1963 Census, 55·7 million. The results of the census however led to fierce controversy and inter-regional acrimony. The estimated population of Nigeria up to the eve of the 1962 and the 1963 Censuses was 36·5 million. The estimate was based on the United Nations formula for calculating the rate of growth of population. This formula is $Pc = Po (1 + r)^u$, where Pc = present population; Po = population last recorded; r = rate of population growth; and u = number of years between last census and the present one. The assumed rate of population growth for Nigeria, r, was two per cent per annum.

Primary production—agriculture, livestock, fishing, and forestry—still contributes more than three fifths of the GDP. Manufacturing activity (including public utilities) represents less than five per cent of the total national output.

Another significant feature of the Nigerian economy is the relatively small proportion of the country's economic activity geared towards the export market. Agricultural production for local consumption accounts for eighty per cent of total agricultural output. Although export crops only account for about twenty per cent of total agricultural production, they take on a dual significance which is out of proportion to their share of the GDP. They are the principal earners of foreign exchange and one of the most important sources of government revenue through export and produce sales taxes. Taxes on export crops have accounted for between one eighth and one fifth of the total tax revenues of all the governments of the federation. In the early fifties, when the world demand for export crops was strong and their prices in the world market correspondingly high, export taxes represented one third of total tax revenue.

Yet another feature of the Nigerian economy of particular importance to this study is its great regional diversity in level of development and per capita income. The importance of having estimates (however rough) of national accounting data by regions was recognised by Prest and Stewart during their investigation of the national income of Nigeria. As they rightly argued, the federal nature of the Nigerian constitution 'raises a host of financial issues such as the most equitable basis of central government taxes and disbursements among the three political regions, which can be settled much more reasonably once there is a rough knowledge of the relative incomes of the three regions'.[1]

It is difficult to estimate regional GDP in a country where there is considerable inter-regional trade and movement of labour, and where politically separate units are integrated economic units. Lagos, the federal capital, is economically integrated with the Western Region, and the gross product of Southern Cameroons (when it was part of Nigeria) could not be separated from that of

[1] Prest and Stewart, op. cit., p. 22.

Eastern Nigeria. There are also immense difficulties in deriving a regional breakdown of such activities as distribution, transport, and communication, which account for about one sixth of the GDP.

Since 1951, a number of attempts have been made to estimate the GDP of each of the component parts of the Nigerian federation. P. N. C. Okigbo in *Nigerian National Accounts, 1950–57*, attempted a regional breakdown of the Nigerian GDP,[1] and some of the regional governments have computed their own estimates of their region's share of the GDP.[2] These estimates have tended to vary because of differences in the basis of computing the regional share of some activities, principally communication, transport, and distribution. On the physical output side, there is no difficulty in estimating the regional share of the total, since the national estimates were derived from regional data. Physical output, however, accounts for only three quarters of the total GDP. Estimates for the regional shares of the GDP for selected years shown in Table 2.6 have been derived from Appendix D.[3]

Although the data for regional shares of the GDP shown in Table 2.6 should be regarded only as approximations, the general picture is quite clear. Between 1950/1 and 1964/5, the Northern Region slightly increased its relative share of the GDP. From 44·1 per cent of the GDP in 1950/1, the North accounted for 46·5 and 45·5 per cent in 1959/60 and 1964/5 respectively. On the other hand, the Eastern Region's share fell from 25·9 per cent to 20·7 per cent during the same period. One factor responsible for the decrease in the percentage share of the East was the loss of the Southern Cameroon in 1960. The Western Region share (including the Mid-West) fell slightly from thirty per cent in 1950/1 to 27·1

[1] See chapter 9.
[2] Only the Northern region has published its estimates of the region's share in the GDP. See chapter 5 of *The Industrial Potentialities of Northern Nigeria* published by the region's Ministry of Trade and Industry, Kaduna.
[3] The Appendix owes much to the work of Dr R. O. Teriba in his unpublished thesis for the degree of Ph.D. from the University of Manchester entitled *Western Nigeria: Public Sector and Economic Development* (1965).

TABLE 2.6 *Gross domestic product (at factor cost) by regions, selected years*

Regions	Regional Share of GDP (£m)	Regional Share (per cent)	Estimated Regional Population (million)	Estimated Regional Population (per cent)	Regional per capita GDP (£)
1950/51					
North	304·3	44·1	16·8	53·9	18·0
East	178·1	25·9	8·0	25·6	22·0
West	206·3	30·0	6·4	20·5	32·0
Lagos	—	—	—	—	—
Total: Federation of Nigeria	688·7	100·0	31·2	100·0	22·0
1959/60					
North	436·3	46·5	19·5	54·1	22·0
East	210·3	22·4	9·1	25·3	23·0
West	241·1	25·7	7·0	19·5	34·0
Lagos	50·8	5·4	0·4	1·1	117·0
Total: Federation of Nigeria	938·5	100·0	36·0	100·0	26·0
1964/5					
North	562·7	45·5	29·8	53·5	19·0
East	256·6	20·7	12·4	22·3	20·0
West	255·6	20·7	10·3	18·4	25·0
Mid-West	79·4	6·4	2·5	4·6	31·0
Lagos	82·0	6·7	0·7	1·2	123·0
Total: Federation of Nigeria	1,236·3	100·0	55·7	100·0	22·0

N.B.: (1) Eastern Region includes the Southern Cameroons for the years 1950/1 and 1959/60; Western Region includes Lagos for 1950/1 and the Mid-Western Region for 1950/1 and 1959/60.
(2) Figures for GDP are at 1957/8 constant prices. See Appendix D for the basis of the regional breakdown of the GDP.
(3) The population figures used in 1950/1 are those of the 1952/3 census, while the figures for 1959/60 are estimates based on the 1952/3 figures at an assumed growth rate of two per cent per annum. The population growth rate in the federal territory of Lagos for

per cent in 1964/5. The rate of growth of the GDP in the North has outstripped the national average by a wide margin.

Regional diversity is also pronounced in the types of export and food crops produced. Although Nigeria as a whole is not dependent, like many underdeveloped countries, on just one or two export crops for its foreign exchange earnings, each region depends predominantly on one or two crops. From Table 2.7, it will be seen that, with the exception of palm kernels, each of the Nigerian exports is produced primarily by one region—cocoa by the West, palm oil by the East, groundnuts and seed cotton by the North, and rubber by the Mid-West. These crops account for over ninety per cent of the country's agricultural exports, or for about fifty per cent of its total domestic exports.

From the point of view of federal finance, the significance of regional specialisation in the production of export crops is great. As will be seen in subsequent chapters, jurisdiction over export taxation has remained the responsibility of the federal government. However, the revenues derived from export taxes are received by the regions, and are distributed on the basis of regional production. The importance of this to regional-federal finances is crucial.

There are also considerable regional variations in the production of mineral and mineral oils, the revenues from which are again vitally important to the regional and federal government. Nigeria's most important mineral, tin, is produced in the North; Nigeria's petroleum is obtained from Eastern and Mid-Western Nigeria.

Before concluding this chapter, it is necessary to examine briefly the relative importance of the public sector in the economy. The role of governments in the economic development of underdeveloped countries has received considerable attention since the end of World War Two. But it is possible to exaggerate the im-

1959/60 is estimated at four per cent per annum. The population figures for 1964/5 are those of the 1963 Census. See footnote 2, p. 36.

SOURCES: Prest and Stewart; op. cit.; Okigbo, op. cit.; Northern Nigeria Ministry of Trade and Industry, *The Industrial Potentialities of Northern Nigeria* (Kaduna, 1965); and R. O. Teriba, *Western Nigeria: Public Sector and Economic Development* (unpublished Ph.D. thesis), University of Manchester, 1965.

TABLE 2.7 *Produce purchased by marketing boards, selected years*

(in '000 tons)

	Crop Years*					
	1950/1†	1956/7	1958/9	1959/60	1961/2	1962/3
Cocoa						
Western Region	n.a.	128	132	146	186	n.a.
Total	110	131	134	149	191	175
Palm Oil						
Eastern Region	n.a.	162	167	170	161	123
Total	167	184	184	190	173	130
Palm Kernels						
Eastern Region	n.a.	211	211	212	208	169
Western Region	n.a.	235	226	198	201	174
Total	381	461	455	428	430	358
Groundnuts						
Northern Region	143	358	533	445	686	866
Total	143	358	533	445	686	866
Seed Cotton						
Northern Region	42	73	87	86	83	143
Total	42	74	89	89	83	143

* Crop Years are the buying seasons of the marketing boards as follows:

Cocoa   September to August
Palm products   January to December
Groundnuts   November to May
Seed cotton   Northern Region, November to March
    Western Region, March to June

† Totals include the Southern Cameroons, but they are excluded from subsequent years.

SOURCES: Regional Marketing Boards' *Annual Reports*; and *Annual Digest of Statistics* (Federal Office of Statistics, Lagos).

portance of the public sector in the economies of these countries, for relative shares of government revenue in the national income of these countries tend to be low.

During the past decade especially, the relationship between the per capita GDP and the levels and patterns of public revenue and expenditure in underdeveloped and developed countries has been a special concern of economists.[1] One conclusion which has emerged from these studies is that there is a positive correlation between per capita income and the government share of the GDP. From a low per capita income to a middle per capita income, the share of government increases rapidly relatively to increase in per capita income while the rate of change lessens with movements to high per capita income: the income elasticity of government expenditure and revenue is greater than one during the initial phases of development.[2]

Why the government's share in the GDP increases as a country moves from a low to a middle income is not difficult to perceive. Low-income countries lack an adequate supply of social overhead capital. Investments in this sector are customarily now undertaken by most governments and these involve heavy capital expenditure and rapidly increasing annual recurrent expenditures. This sector also has a high capital-output ratio. It is also generally agreed that increased urbanisation and the disappearance of the extended family system and its informal social security are two other concomitants of economic development. These developments require increased public expenditures to provide the urban populations with, at least, minimum levels of social security, unemployment

[1] The principal studies are those of A. M. Martin and W. A. Lewis, 'Patterns of Public Revenue and Expenditure', *The Manchester School of Economic and Social Studies*, September 1956; H. T. Oshima, 'Share of Government in Gross National Product for Various Countries', *American Economic Review*, vol. XLVII, No. 3, June 1957; and J. G. Williamson, 'Public Expenditure and Revenue: An International Comparison', *The Manchester School of Economic and Social Studies*, vol. XXIX, 1961; and Richard S. Thorn, 'The Evolution of Public Finances During Economic Development', *The Manchester School of Economic and Social Studies*, vol. XXXV, No. 1, January 1967, pp. 19–53.

[2] J. G. Williamson, loc. cit., pp. 44–50.

insurance, and 'a complex cosmopolitan political machine to replace the family and village functions'.[1] Finally, economic development tends to bring about changes in social values and a demand for both qualitative and quantitative improvements in government services. All these account for an increasing share of government in the GDP as economic development takes place.

As Table 2.8 indicates, Nigeria is not an exception to this trend.

TABLE 2.8 *Nigerian government revenue as a proportion of GDP, 1955–66*

Fiscal Year	GDP at Factor Cost (Current Prices) (£ million)	Nigerian Government Revenue (£ million)	Revenue as a Percentage of GDP
1955/6	827·5	67·1	8·1
1956/7	870·6	81·7	9·4
1957/8	910·0	81·6	9·0
1958/9	864·9	90·2	10·4
1959/60	903·0	101·2	11·0
1960/1	918·9	125·1	13·6
1961/2	1,049·2	130·9	12·5
1962/3	1,147·6	135·8	11·8
1963/4	1,208·3	146·2	12·1
1964/5	1,219·1	175·1	14·3
1965/6	1,310·9	198·2	14·4

SOURCES: *Annual Abstract of Statistics*, various years (Federal Office of Statistics, Lagos); and *Economic Indicators*, vol. 3, No. 3, March 1967 (Federal Office of Statistics, Lagos).

The government's share of the GDP which was below seven per cent in the early 1950s, has increased substantially between 1955 and 1966. It rose from 8·1 per cent in 1955/6 to 14·4 per cent in 1965/6. Figure 2 shows the rates of growth of public expenditure, revenue, and GDP during the same period. Both public expenditures and revenues have grown at a much faster rate than the GDP.

[1] Ibid., p. 47.

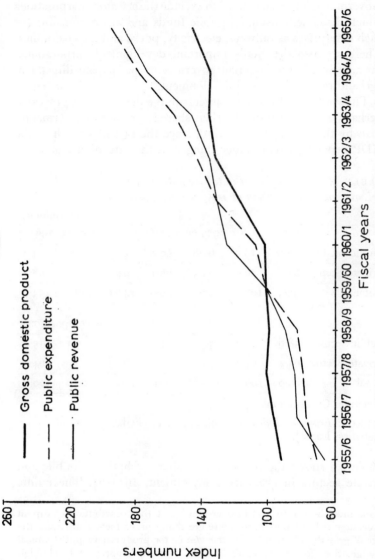

FIGURE 2 *Annual rates of growth in Nigeria's GDP, public expenditure and revenue, 1955–66*

Government has been defined to exclude the statutory corporations which disburse substantial public funds and are responsible for such enterprises as railways, electricity, ports, and the coal mines. There are also the vitally important development corporations, through which the Nigerian governments participate directly in agricultural and industrial development.

The vital role of the governments in the development process is perhaps better illustrated by their share in gross capital formation than by their share in the GDP, since the rate of growth in the GDP depends, among other things, on the rate of investment.[1]

TABLE 2.9 *Gross fixed capital formation by the public and private sectors in Nigeria at 1957/8 prices, 1957–64*

(£ million)

	1957/8	1958/9	1959/60	1960/1	1961/2	1962/3	1963/4
Public Sector*	38·2	49·5	63·8	60·8	55·5	55·0	54·8
Private Sector	61·1	59·0	63·5	66·1	84·6	82·1	98·2
Total	99·3	108·5	127·3	126·9	140·1	137·1	153·0

(Percentage composition)

Public Sector*	38·6	45·6	50·2	47·8	39·6	40·1	35·8
Private Sector	61·4	54·4	49·8	52·2	60·4	59·9	64·2
Total	100·0	100·0	100·0	100·0	100·0	100·0	100·0

*Includes Corporations

SOURCE: *Economic Indicators*, vol. 2, No. 11 (Federal Office of Statistics, Lagos).

Table 2.9 shows the proportionate share of both the public and private sectors in gross fixed investment, 1957–64. The public

[1] One must be careful not to over-emphasise the contribution of capital to economic development, for there are many other factors affecting the rate of growth. These include *inter alia* factor-productivity and technical change. See, for example, Richard R. Nelson, 'Aggregate Production Functions and Medium-Range Growth Projections', *American Economic Review*, vol. LIV, No. 5, September 1964.

sector, which includes the public corporations in this case, has been responsible for an average of 42·5 per cent per annum of the gross capital formation in Nigeria during these seven years, while the annual average during the preceding six years of 1951–7 was only 33·6 per cent. Under the first National Development Plan, 1962–8, and the guideposts to the Second National Development Plan, the public sector plays a still more important role in capital formation. Sixty-seven per cent of the total planned fixed investment is expected to come from the public sector. This increasing importance of the public sector is further proof of the importance of federal finance to Nigeria's economic development.

As we saw in chapter 2, the jurisdiction of the 1922 Constitution was limited to the South. As the legislative council set up under that constitution did not legislate for the northern provinces, more than half the population of Nigeria, occupying over three quarters of its total area, was without a legislative assembly. Even the western and eastern provinces, within the assembly's sphere, were inadequately represented. It was in order to provide Nigeria with a country-wide constitutional framework and a fully representative legislative body that the colonial administration initiated constitutional reforms in 1946.[1]

Under the 1946 Constitution, popularly known as the Richards Constitution after the then Governor of Nigeria, Sir Arthur Richards (later Lord Milverton), a legislative council was set up for the whole of the country. Regional councils were also provided for the three groups of provinces as a 'counterpart in the constitutional sphere'.[2] The regional councils[3] were given some measure of financial responsibility as stated in the Governor's Despatch to the Secretary of State for the Colonies:

---

[1] The Constitution came into effect on 1 January 1947.
[2] *Political and Constitutional Future of Nigeria*, Governor of Nigeria's Despatch to the Secretary of State for the Colonies dated 6 December 1944: Sessional Paper No. 4 of 1945 (Lagos: Government Printer), p. 2.
[3] The Northern Regional Council was bicameral (a House of Chiefs and a House of Assembly) while the Eastern and Western Regional Councils were unicameral.

'I propose to devolve upon the Regional Councils a large measure of financial responsibility. Each would have its own regional
budget, on which would be borne the cost of government services
in the region, including the salaries of government personnel. The
only exception would be the cost within the region of services
declared to be central services such as railway, posts and telegraphs, income tax, and audit which would continue to be carried
on the Central Estimates as at present, together with the central
organisation of government, the headquarters and central staff of
all departments and such charges as interest on public debt,
pensions, etc. Regional revenue would consist in the first place of
the share of the direct tax at present payable to the central government together with any receipts from fees, licences, etc. which
might be allotted to the regional budgets, and in the second place
of annual block grants from central revenue.'[1]

A memorandum giving in greater detail the Governor's proposals for the financial procedure of regional councils and their relations with the legislative council on matters of finance was attached
to the Despatch. These proposals later became Section 52 of the
1946 Constitution.[2]

Sir Sydney Phillipson, then Financial Secretary to the Nigeria
government, was appointed sole Fiscal Commissioner to work out
inter alia the details of the financial arrangements under the constitution in the light of the policy statement of the Governor. It is
the purpose of this chapter to discuss the report of the Phillipson
Commission, examine its major recommendations, and appraise
the performance of the fiscal system during the four-year period
(1948–52) that the constitution was in operation. The importance
of this Commission lies in the fact that its recommendations, which
were subsequently accepted with some modifications, marked the
genesis of federal finance in Nigeria.

[1] op. cit., footnote 2, p.5.
[2] Issued as *Nigeria (Legislative Council) Order-in-Council 1946* on
2 August 1946.

Fiscal arrangements under the Richards Constitution

Since the broad outline of the new fiscal system had been worked out by the Governor in his Constitutional Despatch and incorporated into the 1946 Constitution, the main task of the Phillipson Commission was to develop the detailed implications of this fiscal plan. The Commissioner was enjoined by his terms of reference 'to study comprehensively and make recommendations regarding the problems of the administrative and financial procedure to be adopted under the new constitution'.[1]

In the memorandum on financial procedure annexed to the Constitutional Despatch, two types of regional revenue were identified. According to the memorandum:
'the revenue side of regional budgets would show revenue divided into two heads:

(a) The revenue estimated to be derived from the regional councils' share of the direct tax . . . plus any other revenue from fees, licences, etc. declared to be regional.

(b) The block grant from central revenue.'[2]

The first type of regional revenue was termed 'declared revenue', while the second was called 'non-declared revenue'. It was now left to the Commissioner to develop (1) the criteria for declaring revenue as regional; (2) the basis for determining the size of block grants from central revenue; and (3) the formula for allocating these grants among the regions. The Commissioner recommended two principles for defining regional revenues. The first of these was that the revenue must be identifiable within the region and locally collected by regional authorities. In addition to the government's share of revenue from direct taxes, which were collected by native authorities under the Direct Taxation Ordinance, other regional revenues were receipts from licences, mining rents, fees of courts and offices, rent from government property, and earnings

[1] Sir Sydney Phillipson's report is entitled *Administrative and Financial Procedure under the new Constitution: Financial Relations between the Government of Nigeria and the Native Administration, 1946* (Lagos: Government Printer, 1946).

[2] *Political and Constitutional Future of Nigeria* (Sessional Paper No. 4 of 1945).

from government departments. These revenue sources also satisfied the second of the Commissioner's principles, which was that
such revenues (i.e. declared revenues) must be revenues in respect of which no national or important considerations of policy
are likely to arise.

In respect of the non-declared revenue, two questions were also
posed. First, how was the government to determine the aggregate
of such revenues, since they were to be the basis of the government's grants to the regions: should the central government have
complete freedom in fixing the amount of the grants, or should
there be some guiding principles? And, once the aggregate had
been decided, on what basis was it to be allocated among the three
regional authorities?

The answer to the first question was fairly straightforward.
Since the new constitution was not a federal but a unitary one
(although certain political, administrative, and financial modifications of a devolutionary kind had been introduced), and since
therefore the fiscal supremacy of the central government was un-
challenged, no problem of central-regional fiscal equity had yet
arisen. This supremacy of the central government was enhanced
by the fact that the regional councils possessed no legal powers of
appropriating revenue for regional expenditures. Instead, all
revenues available for regional purposes were voted to the regions
by the Nigerian Legislative Council.

In other words, the position of the regional authorities was
analogous to that of a 'housekeeper', who was provided from time
to time with a variable amount for running the house to the best
advantage possible. It was entirely for the 'householder' (the
central government) to determine what amount should be made
available at any given time for maintaining the household. The
formula derived by the Commissioner for determining the aggregate of declared regional revenue was in close keeping with the
spirit of a housekeeper–householder relationship.[1]

[1] This analogy was used by Sir Sydney Phillipson in his report (p. 10) to
show the limited though important financial responsibility of the regional
councils. Although he did not refer to it again in working out his revenue
allocation formula, he no doubt had it very much in mind.

The formula for deriving the total amount available as central grants to regional authorities may be stated as follows:[1]

$$A = R—(g+s+r)—E$$

where A = total central grants available for regional allocation (non-declared regional revenue)

R = total Nigerian revenue

g = grants received under the Colonial Development and Welfare Act

s = amount set aside as estimated surplus

r = aggregate of total declared regional revenues

E = total recurrent expenditure of the central government (i.e. excluding expenditures on Colonial Development and Welfare Schemes).

Thus, the 'householder' not only provided for his own expenditures first, but also made due allowance for a budget surplus before allocating the balance remaining among his three 'housekeepers'.

While it was relatively easy to derive a formula for determining the total grant available for allocation to the regions, it was not so easy to work out the formula for sharing this total grant among the three regional authorities. It was in his endeavour to derive such a formula that the Commissioner had to grapple squarely with some of the major problems of federal finance—particularly the problems of inter-state or inter-regional fiscal equity and of balanced national development. It is because the principles advanced and discussed at great length in this report and the formula which emerged from the discussion had so great an impact on the subsequent discussions of inter-regional fiscal relationships in the following years, that this period should be regarded as marking the beginning of federal finance in Nigeria.

In his Constitutional Despatch, the Governor had envisaged the setting up of a committee to consider whether legislative powers should be devolved upon the regional councils.[2] In view of this

[1] This formula is the same as that on p. 148 of the Phillipson Report, but recast, and with single letters used to represent each item in preference to Sir Sydney Phillipson's descriptive symbols.

[2] *Political and Constitutional Future of Nigeria*, p. 4.

statement, the Commissioner assumed that the 'regions will, in due course, acquire a large measure of fiscal autonomy appropriating their own proper revenues for their own proper purposes'.[1]

The Commissioner accordingly proceeded to discuss two conflicting principles of inter-state federal-fiscal relationships—allocation of revenue on the basis of derivation, and allocation on the basis of what he called 'even progress'. Given the likely development of regional fiscal autonomy, he argued that it was desirable to inculcate in the regional councils a sense of financial responsibility; that they should be trained in the art of cutting their coat according to their cloth. The scale of expenditure for regional purposes in each region ought therefore to be related to the amount which that region was contributing to the revenue of Nigeria as a whole. Through this derivation principle, each region would receive, in addition to the full amount of its share of the declared regional revenues, a block grant from non-declared revenues in strict proportion to the contribution which that region had made to other revenues.

However, to have strictly applied this principle would have made poor regions poorer and rich regions richer. While this might inculcate a sense of financial responsibility and thereby facilitate further devolution of financial powers, the Commissioner recognised also that it would tend to keep a poor region 'in a humiliating position of dependence'.[2]

Fortunately, the principle of 'even progress' did not have this disadvantage. The Commissioner saw that if 'progress was even over the whole country, and the standard of living and the degree of civilisation throughout the country was raised to a generally equal level',[3] the unity of Nigeria would be better preserved and cemented. Nevertheless, because of unreliable statistical data on the relative well-being of each region, and because the Commissioner considered the assumption of financial responsibility by the regions as of paramount importance ('its recognition indeed seems an essential condition of political training at the regional level and

[1] ibid., p. 12.
[2] ibid., p. 21.
[3] ibid., p. 20.

thus of further political progress'[1]), he chose to allocate the non-declared revenues on the basis of derivation.

Before discussing the formula for allocation based on the derivation principle, as well as the modification and conditions attached to the application of this formula, it is worth noting that the Commissioner considered a third alternative—that of using population as the basis of allocation. In fact, as he acknowledged in his report, he had favoured the population principle on the *a priori* grounds that population seemed to him the 'best available measure of human needs'[2] and, additionally, that it was simple and easy to understand. He did not adopt this principle, however, and offered no explanation. Still feeling the necessity to give greater financial responsibility to the regions themselves, the Commissioner also rejected empowering the Governor of Nigeria with the right to allocate available non-declared revenue according to his judgement of regional need.

It was in his attempt to formulate the regional derivation formula that the Commissioner was faced with the stark realities of inadequate statistical data, and of the difficulties within a national economy of knowing with any reliable degree of accuracy what has been derived from each region. These are difficulties which were to plague subsequent fiscal commissions, and which even today still bedevil the Nigerian fiscal system. Since the three main components of the non-declared revenues were revenues from export duties, import and excise duties, and company tax, it is not surprising that the Commissioner found the quantification of the derivation principle a most difficult exercise.[3] All he did,

[1] ibid., p. 21.
[2] ibid., p. 21.
[3] It should be pointed out that although the Commissioner showed some equations at p. 148 of his report, these were not derivation formulae but equations showing the total revenue of each of the regions. For instance, the equation for Northern Region is as follows:

$$\text{Total Northern Region revenue} = \frac{A \times Dr}{100} + Rn,$$

where 'A' represents total available non-declared revenue, 'Dr' represents regional derivation from non-declared revenue stated in a percentage, and 'Rn' represents the Northern Region's own declared revenue. To find the

and all subsequent fiscal commissioners were able to do, was merely to pull a formula out of their magic bags.

Thus the Commissioner concluded that on the 'best information at present available, the relative proportions, expressed as percentages, contributed by the three regions to Nigerian revenues not declared regional' were: Northern Region, forty-six per cent; Western Region, thirty per cent; and Eastern Region, twenty-four per cent.[1] Once the amount available for regional allocation from non-declared revenues had been determined, it would be allocated to the regions in the proportions stated above.

Having given what he considered the relative regional contributions to the non-declared revenues, the Commissioner compared these with the relative total expenditure on regional services. He found in 1946/7 fiscal year that the recurrent government expenditures for regional services were thirty-six per cent, twenty-six per cent, and thirty-eight per cent respectively for the North, West, and East, figures differing from the percentages of forty-six, thirty, and twenty-four which he had calculated to be the regions' contributions to non-declared revenues.

These differences in relative regional contribution to total revenue were further accentuated when account was taken of total revenues regionally derived (including the declared revenues and the native authorities' share of the direct tax). These contributions were fifty-one per cent, twenty-seven per cent, and twenty-two per cent for the North, West and East respectively. This meant that while the Northern Region contributed the most to total revenue, and had the largest population (fifty-nine per cent of the total), it received only thirty-six per cent of government expenditure. Public spending in the North relative to public expenditure in the other regions was the lowest either on an aggregate or on a per capita basis. On the other hand, the East, which contributed least to total revenue, received the largest relative government expendi-

total revenue due to any region, one needs to be able to know the quantitative value of 'Dr'—otherwise one has an equation with two unknowns. Unfortunately, the Commissioner did not indicate the formula or equation he used to derive 'Dr'.

[1] *Political and Constitutional Future of Nigeria*, p. 149.

ture on regional services. The Western Region contributed to total revenue about as much as it received from government expenditure on regional services.

But in spite of this imbalance between relative regional contributions to total revenue and government expenditure on regional services in the North and the East, the Commissioner was unable to recommend that the allocation formula be followed immediately. He realised that it would not be possible to achieve a position in which the relative regional revenue contributions corresponded to the relative expenditures on regional services without disrupting services in the Eastern Region. Accordingly, he recommended that his ratios should be regarded as 'ideal' percentages in the direction to which revenue allocations should move.

For the financial year 1948/9 (the first fiscal year when the financial provisions of the new constitution were operative), he recommended that available non-declared revenues should be allocated in such a way that together with the declared revenues, sufficient resources would be available to each region to maintain existing levels of government services (other than capital works) and to meet the cost of normal and mainly unavoidable expansion of services. The capital programme, he suggested, should be 'moderately adjusted, if practicable, with reference to the need for giving the Northern Region a share less disproportionate to its contribution to the non-declared revenues of Nigeria'.[1]

The Commissioner recommended that a Revenue Allocation Board be set up, consisting of the Chief Secretary to the Government of Nigeria as Chairman, the three Regional Chief Commissioners or their representatives, the Financial Secretary as Deputy Chairman, the Development Secretary, the Commissioner of the Colony, and the Accountant-General, and the Principal Assistant Secretary (Finance) as Secretary. This board would make recommendations to the government on the allocation of available non-declared revenue during each financial year subsequent to 1948/9. The Financial Secretary would submit to the Board 'a reasoned memorandum of proposals for their consideration'[2] showing clearly

[1] ibid., p. 25.
[2] ibid., p. 26.

how much revenue the Board proposed to reserve for financing Nigerian (as distinct from regional) expenditures.

It was the objective of the Board to ensure:

'. . . as soon as may be, but in any event within five years, a position in which the expenditure on regional purposes within a region is proportionate to the relative contribution made by that region to the total of the non-declared revenues of Nigeria. A principal function of the Board will be thus to make proposals for drawing closer, year by year, to this objective and any proposal designed to further that purpose, not excluding new measures of taxation, will be within the Board's competence.'[1]

In order to provide the necessary statistical material for determining this allocation, the Departments of Customs and Inland Revenue were to prepare regional accounts in respect of import duties and income tax for both individuals and companies.

Thus, the Commissioner, who had earlier strongly favoured allocating revenue strictly on the derivation principle as an essential condition of political training at the regional level, and as a means of training regional councils 'to learn to cut their coats according to their cloth', found himself recommending a revenue allocation based on the level of existing regional services with due allowance being made for reasonable expansion. Strict adherence to the derivation principle had become relegated from an immediate objective to an ultimate objective over a five-year period. And as it happened, the fiscal arrangements proposed by the Commissioner were in operation for only four years.

Evolving the fiscal system: 1914–26 compared with 1948–52

We shall, in the next section, appraise the effect of this new fiscal arrangement on the transfer of financial resources from the Nigerian government to the regional authorities and on the allocation of these resources among the regional authorities. Its impact on regional development and the attendant problem of inter-regional fiscal equity will also be considered. But before doing so, it is appropriate to compare the salient features of the new system

[1] ibid., pp. 26 and 27.

with those of the financial arrangement which was operative from 1914 to 1926. Perhaps the most significant contrast which one can make between the two periods is that amalgamation brought about only limited centralisation, while the 1946 Constitution led to a limited decentralisation after a prolonged phase of complete centralisation in all spheres of governmental activities. During both periods, the conception which prevailed as far as the fiscal system was concerned was that Nigerian revenues constituted 'a single fund to meet the aggregate expenditure'[1] of the central and regional authorities.

Between 1914 and 1926, each government prepared its own annual budget of revenues and expenditures for approval and incorporation into the general budget. This same arrangement was introduced under section 52 of the 1946 Constitution, requesting from each regional council its annual estimates of expenditures and a statement of its apportioned or assigned revenues.[2] The Governor had the power to approve these estimates with or without amendments. When approved, the regional estimates were then laid on the table of the legislative council on the first day of its budget meeting. Thus, but for the existence of regional councils, the fiscal system which was in operation from 1948 to 1952 was quite similar to that which was introduced after the 1914 amalgamation.

The similarity is even more marked when one compares the heads of revenues and expenditures of the central and regional authorities during the two periods. What came to be known as 'declared revenue' were the traditional revenue sources of the Northern and Southern Nigeria governments from 1914 to 1926. And the classification of services and works into central and regional under the 1948–52 fiscal system was more or less the same as the division of functions between the central government and the governments of the North and South during the 1914–26 period.

However, the similarity between the two systems should not be exaggerated. The post-amalgamation financial arrangements ap-

[1] *Amalgamation Report*, p. 45.
[2] *Nigeria (Legislative Council) Order-in-Council, 1946.*

pear to have been shaped more by practical convenience than by logic. There was no attempt to relate the expenditure of the governments to the revenues shown as severally belonging to each. There was also no attempt to apportion revenue. The central government simply took over the one most important source of revenue—customs—and although this had serious consequences on the revenue position of the government of the Colony and Protectorate of Southern Nigeria no one really bothered to impute revenues to each group of provinces with a view to determining, even on paper, whether or not any particular administration was living beyond its means. Nor was there much logic in the allocation of functions during the earlier period. For instance, although the central government assumed revenue from customs, the Departments of Customs and Marine continued to be entirely under the Colony and Protectorate of Southern Provinces: the expenditures of these departments were charged against the South.[1]

Given the philosophy of the man who effected the amalgamation and his strong views against centralisation, the post-amalgamation period could not but have retained some of the features of dualism which belonged to the pre-amalgamation period. The departments of the governments of the North and South were separate and independent of each other and of the central departments, whose heads were no more than coordinators providing technical advice to the Governor. Thus, the dualistic system which existed during the first twelve years after amalgamation really had little or nothing in common with the system introduced under the 1946 Constitution. Although that constitution provided for some measure of devolution to the regional authorities, it in no way reversed the process of administrative and departmental unification which had taken place in the twenties and thirties.

[1] There are indeed many more curious features in the post-amalgamation financial arrangements. The expenditures under Public Works were divided between the two provincial administrations. Thus, the impression is created that the Central Government had no expenditures under Public Works. The Printing Department was exclusively under the Southern estimates of expenditures. The North continued to receive the imperial grants directly.

Central and regional finances, 1948–52

This section will now discuss the operation of the fiscal system during the four years it was in operation; its main effects on the finances of the regional and central governments; and the anomalies which subsequent fiscal commissions tried to improve.

Table 3.1 compares the allocation of funds between the central government and the regional authorities during these four years. It will be seen from this table that large though the revenues available to the three regions were, they were dwarfed by the proportion of total revenue which was retained by the Nigerian government for expenditures on Nigerian services. This proportion averaged seventy-five per cent per annum. This is not surprising, since under the Phillipson formula the central government had first claim to the non-declared revenue. Since Nigeria was not a federation, there could be no objection from the regions. Under a federal constitution this kind of arrangement would be clearly inappropriate.

The main attention and interest during this period was accordingly on inter-regional rather than on central-regional fiscal equity. Attention may now be given to the extent to which the regional allocation of non-declared revenues deviated from the 'ideal' derivation percentages.

As Tables 3.2 and 3.3 indicate, there was considerable divergence between the actual allocations and the recommended derivative allocations. The Northern Region received substantially much less allocation than its derivative share, while the Eastern Region received substantially much more. The Western Region at first received less proportionate allocation than its derivative share, although the gap between its derivative proportionate share and its actual allocation diminished over the years, from 5·9 per cent in 1948/9 to 0·3 per cent in 1951/2.

Thus, throughout these four years the Phillipson recommendation for regional financial responsibility was not achieved. The East remained consistently a 'deficit' region, while the North, and to some extent the West, remained 'surplus' regions. As was to be expected, this phenomenon featured prominently in political discussions and led to much inter-regional misunderstanding and

TABLE 3.1 *Central-regional revenue, 1948–52*

Fiscal Year	Total Nigerian Government Revenues*	Revenues Declared Regional	Revenues Allocated to the Regions from Non-declared Revenues	Total Revenues	Regional Revenues as a percentage of Nigerian Revenues	Revenues Allocated to the Regions as a percentage of Nigerian Government Revenues
	(£'000)	(£'000)	(£'000)	(£'000)		
1948/9	22,001	981	4,495	5,476	24·9	20·4
1949/50	28,145	1,009	6,128	7,137	25·3	21·8
1950/1	28,523	1,056	6,992	8,048	28·2	24·5
1951/2	47,828	1,056	8,268	9,324	19·5	17·2

*Exclusive of grants from the Colonial Development Welfare Funds, which averaged about £2·22 million per annum.

SOURCES: Calculated from Table 1, chapter IV of S. A. Aluko, *Federal Finance and Economic Development in Nigeria* (unpublished Ph.D. thesis, London University, June 1959); *Digest of Statistics*, Federal Office of Statistics, Lagos, several issues; *Reports of Accountant-General*, 1948/9 to 1951/2.

TABLE 3.2 *Share of non-declared regional revenue compared with recommended regional share based on derivation**

(in percentages)

Regions	1948-9		1949-50		1950-1		1951-2	
	Recom-mended Allocation	Actual Allocation	Recom-mended Allocation	Actual Allocation	Recom-mended Allocation	Actual Allocation	Recom-mended Allocation	Actual Allocation
Northern Region	43·9	40·7	45·0	34·8	41·7	36·6	41·7	36·0
Western Region	30·6	24·7	29·0	28·1	27·5	27·2	27·5	27·2
Eastern Region	25·5	34·6	26·0	37·1	30·9	36·2	30·9	36·8
Total	100·0	100·0	100·0	100·0	100·0*	100·0	100·0*	100·0

* the figures do not add up to 100 because of rounding.

SOURCES: S. A. Aluko, op. cit. Table I, p. 144; *Report of the Commission on Revenue Allocation, 1951* (Government Printer, Lagos), Appendix, pp. 178-84.

* Since the derivative percentage shares of the Regions from the allocated non-declared revenue were calculated annually by the Government Statistician from returns submitted by major importers and exporters, they differed from the Phillipson's percentages of forty-six, thirty and twenty-four for North, West and East respectively. The Phillipson percentages were themselves derived from the 1946/7 figures.

friction. The belief was generally held at both official and political levels that the East was being developed at the expense of the

TABLE 3.3 *Proportionate regional share of colonial development and welfare grants and total regional financial resources, 1948–52*

(in percentages)

Regions	1948/9 A	1948/9 B	1949/50 A	1949/50 B	1950/51 A	1950/51 B	1951/2 A	1951/2 B
Northern Region	43·0	44·4	42·0	38·7	45·0	39·0	40·0	40·0
Western Region	23·0	24·0	22·0	26·6	25·0	27·0	31·0	27·6
Eastern Region	34·0	31·6	36·0	34·7	30·0	34·0	29·0	32·4
Total	100·0	100·0	100·0	100·0	100·0	100·0	100·0	100·0

A Proportionate regional allocation of Colonial Development and Welfare Grants
B Proportionate regional share of all revenues (declared and non-declared revenues and grants from CDW)
SOURCE: S. A. Aluko, op. cit., Table 1, p. 144.

North. Sir Arthur Richards, the architect of the 1946 Constitution, expressed it this way:

'I found that the North, which pays its taxes almost as obediently as people do in England, and which contributes more than any other section of Nigeria to the general revenue, is the part of Nigeria which had the least spent on it by the Central Government. The Eastern Provinces, the part of Nigeria which is most vocal and which clamours and calls for more education and for more of everything is the part which contributes less than the other two regions to the general revenue, and it is also the part upon which the Government has been spending most.'[1]

[1] *Address by His Excellency Sir Arthur Richards, G.C.M.G., Governor and Commander-in-Chief of Nigeria, at a meeting of the Colonial Affairs Study Group of the Empire Parliamentary Association, 28th January 1947*, issued under the authority of the Empire and Parliamentary Association, UK Branch, pp. 10–11.

A critique of the derivation principle

Although the Nigerian government laid emphasis throughout this period on the financial unity of the central and regional authorities, and was unable to adopt the derivation principle, this principle later assumed so much importance in the evolution of federal finance in Nigeria that the remainder of this chapter will be devoted to examining it in greater detail, showing some of its inherent difficulties under a federal system.

As noted above, the 1946 Constitution classified regional revenues into two broad categories—declared regional revenues and grants from available non-declared revenues. It was this second broad category which raised the problem of equity, particularly as the principle of derivation applied to its allocation.

In a federation, the basis of allocating nationally-collected taxes is more often than not a reflection of the type of federation in operation. In a closely-knit federation, the basis for allocating nationally-collected taxes among the constituent parts of the federation is very much like the basis of transferring resources from the central government to the local authorities in a unitary state—the guiding criteria being need and equalisation. But in a loose federation, emphasis will tend to gravitate toward the derivative principle. This principle, which applies the extreme view that the revenues from nationally-collected taxes be returned to the region in which they are raised, cannot reduce geographical inequalities. Fully implemented, the principle leaves the distribution of income in a federation 'identical to that in a "Balkan" area of independent unitary countries'.[1]

The derivation principle has therefore proved attractive in 'loose' federations 'where the regions have little sense of national unity or common citizenship'.[2] But no matter how attractive the principle is, its unqualified use brings more problems than it solves, particularly the problem of equity. A revenue allocation system based on derivation requires a considerable degree of pre-

[1] Anthony Scott, 'The Economic Goals of Federal Finance', *Public Finance* No. 3, 1964, p. 252.
[2] ibid., p. 252.

cision in the collection and analysis of statistical data. And such data must constantly be reviewed and up-dated, since patterns of consumption and production change over time. Thus, the un-qualified application of the derivation principle in a country like Nigeria, where statistical data are far from reliable, is bound to lead to an unfair distribution of resources.

There is another reason why an unqualified use of the derivative principle would lead to unfair treatment. Assume a customs union of two members, Y and Z. Assume also that country Y before union was producing goods which were sold to Z, and that the government of Z had been imposing customs duties on the goods. With the formation of the customs union, the import duties would be abolished. Both the people of Y and those of Z would benefit from the abolition of duties, the former because the abolition of duties on their goods would lead to larger sales at lower prices, and the latter because the cheaper goods would lead to increased economic welfare. However, the government of Z would lose revenue, and under a strict application of the derivation principle it would have no claim for compensation for the loss. This hypothetical example is relevant to the Nigerian situation immediately after amalgamation, which in removing all trade barriers brought substantial economic benefits to both parts of the country. The revenues from customs, which formerly had belonged to the government of Southern Nigeria, were transferred to the new central government. The application of the derivation principle, if it is to be equitable, must take into account the actual distribution of revenue before the union, or its probable distribution if the union were dissolved. And in the particular conditions of Nigeria, the dissolution of the country, or the reversion to pre-1914 arrangements, would adversely affect the revenue position of the North.

Since the derivation principle was used for allocating the grants from non-declared revenues, consideration should be given to the main sources of this revenue, and the way the principle was applied in each case. The most important sources were import duties, export duties, excise duties, and the companies tax. These four revenue sources accounted for sixty-five per cent of total Nigeria revenue (including revenue declared regional) in 1948/9.

And of the total non-declared revenue, they accounted for about ninety-five per cent during the same year.

Revenues from import and excise duties constituted, on the average, three fifths of the total non-declared revenue, and about two fifths of the total Nigerian revenue throughout the period 1948–52. These revenues were therefore by far the most important of the non-declared revenues, and the basis of calculating the regional distribution of imports would be very crucial to the over-all fairness of the application of the derivation principle. But the official calculation of the regional distribution of imports was based on the returns of imports submitted by associations of importers for the year 1946, and no attempt was made between 1948 and 1952 to revise these figures. Secondly, these returns did not cover the whole range of imports, but were confined only to five items— tobacco, cotton piece goods, spirits, salt, and petrol. The proportion in which these five imports were stated to be divided among the three regions is as shown in Table 3.4.

TABLE 3.4 *Regional distribution of imports (1946 returns)*

Items	North	West*	East
		(in percentages)	
Tobacco (non-manufactured)	—	30	70
Cotton piece goods	40	35	25
Spirits	10	45	45
Salt	$51\frac{1}{2}$	23	$25\frac{1}{2}$
Petrol	$38\frac{1}{2}$	$47\frac{1}{2}$	$14\frac{1}{2}$

* Lagos and Colony included in the Western Region's figures

SOURCE: *Report of the Commission on Revenue Allocation, 1951* (Government Printer, Lagos), Table XII, p. 59.

The regional distribution of other items was assumed to be the average of the regional distribution of cotton piece goods and salt. It was also assumed that fifteen per cent of the Western Region's share was attributed to Lagos Colony. Accordingly, the percentage distribution of revenue from import duties according to this process was:

North	West (excluding Colony)	East	Lagos
35	29	31	5

The pitfalls in these calculations are many. Not only was the range of items used very limited, but the selection of the items was also biased in favour of some regions. For instance, the percentages of tobacco consumption shown in Table 3.4 were derived from the consumption of non-manufactured tobacco only. But whereas seventy per cent of non-manufactured tobacco was consumed in the East, the North consumed forty-eight per cent of home-produced cigarettes, while the West (excluding Lagos) and the East consumed thirty-nine and thirteen per cent respectively. Moreover, no account was taken of imported cigarettes. These were left among the other commodities to be divided according to the cotton-salt ratio without due regard to regional variations in the consumption pattern of imported cigarettes.

In order to be fair to all the regions, therefore, account should have been taken of all types of tobacco consumption. Instead, what was done in the official calculations 'was to take special account of those forms of consumption which have Northern and Eastern biases, but to take no special account of the consumption which has a Western bias'.[1] According to the 1951 Fiscal Commission, a correction of this error, without changing any of the other figures in the official calculations had considerable effect on the 1946 attribution of revenue from import duties, as follows:

	North	West (including Lagos)	East
Official percentages	35	34	31
Revised by correction in tobacco consumption	29	41	30
Revised for changed system of attributing remaining imports	24	45	31

[1] *Report of the Commission on Revenue Allocation, 1951* (Lagos: Government Printer), p. 60.

The distribution of revenue from the other imports by this cotton-salt proportion favoured the most populous region, since the use of basic commodities is directly related to population. Moreover, no account was taken of home-produced cotton goods. It would also have been more reasonable to treat petrol, lubricating oil, motor vehicles, tyres and tubes, as luxury goods instead of treating them according to the cotton-salt commodity ratio.

The 1951 Fiscal Commission calculated that if revenues from other duties were allocated on the basis of the average regional distribution for the five commodities, including imported and home-produced cigarettes, the proportionate regional share of import duties would have been twenty-four, forty-five and thirty-one per cent, for the North, West, and East respectively. There would have been a decrease of as much as eleven per cent in the share of the Northern Region from import duty revenue, and since the import duty percentages played so large a part in the final calculation of the regional 'ideal percentages', these final figures would have been seriously changed.

All of this demonstrates the danger and the inherent weakness of depending on the derivative principle, particularly with inadequate and unreliable statistical data for the regional distribution of imports. It also demonstrates the need to recalculate these figures annually with a view to correcting at least some of the inaccuracies.

The derivative principle is, on the other hand, more accurately applied to export taxes, since each of the main export crops is derived almost wholly from one region. The only exceptions are palm products (oil palm and palm kernels), but a special investigation was made for the purposes of calculating the ideal regional percentages for these products.

As far as the companies tax was concerned, two of the main sources of the tax—profits on tin mining and on the Cameroons Development Corporation—were easily attributable to the regions; the former to the North and the latter to the East. But the third source of the companies tax—the source that accounted for the bulk of revenue—was from profits of the various trading corporations. These were attributed to the regions in the proportions in which import and export trade was attributed to them. This tax was therefore open to the same objections and criticisms in its allocation among the regions as the allocation of import tax revenue discussed above.

Conclusions

It may be seen from the foregoing discussion that apart from the theoretical limitations of a general application of the derivative principle as the basis of allocating nationally-collected taxes, the percentage derivations contained in the Phillipson Report were so misleading that their application would have led to serious consequences. But the prominence which was given to the principle and the so-called 'ideal percentages' resulted in considerable inter-regional misunderstanding and friction and raised difficulties for subsequent fiscal commissions. The governments of the North and West became firm and relentless advocates of the application of the principle.

This commitment to the principle of derivation and to the belief that the East had been developed at the expense of the other regions, particularly of the North, was so firm that the 1951 Fiscal Commission was enjoined to investigate whether any particular region had in the past been unfairly treated in the allocation of revenue and if so, to recommend what compensation should be made to such a region.[1] The Fiscal Commission of 1953 was even more circumscribed; it was asked to recommend changes in the fiscal system which would have regard to the 'importance of ensuring that the total revenues available to Nigeria are allocated in such a way that the principle of derivation is followed to the fullest degree'.[2]

Sir Sydney Phillipson's most enduring contribution to the development of federal finance in Nigeria would therefore appear to lie in his advocating that revenue allocation should ultimately conform to the principle of derivation.

[1] ibid., p. 5.
[2] A. L. Chick, *Report of Fiscal Commissioner on Financial Effects of Proposed New Constitutional Arrangements* (Lagos: Government Printer, 1953), p. 1.

The constitutional changes which came into operation in January 1952 marked the first decisive step toward federalism in Nigeria. These changes were preceded by a series of review conferences during 1949 and 1950 during which Nigerians were asked to make recommendations as to the constitutional changes which they considered desirable and feasible. It is not surprising that only the leaders of the Northern Region made specific recommendations about revenue allocation. They had by this time come to believe firmly that their region had been discriminated against under the fiscal arrangements that had operated since amalgamation. They resented the failure of the Nigerian government to adhere to the derivative principle in the allocation of revenue under the Richards Constitution. And when that constitution was to be reviewed, they saw this as their opportunity to establish a more equitable system of revenue allocation. Accordingly, they included in their proposals for the review of the 1946 Constitution concrete suggestions on revenue allocation.[1]

Two criteria were recommended by the North as the basis for allocating revenue among the regions—derivation and need, with population being the indicator of need. It was suggested by the region that the full amount of those revenues declared regional should continue to be allocated to the regions on the derivative principle, while grants from the non-declared revenues should be

[1] *Nigeria Review of the Constitution* (*Regional Recommendations*) (Lagos: Government Printer, 1949).

allocated on a per capita basis rather than on the basis of proportionate regional contribution to these other revenues. It was also suggested that the allocation of grants from Nigerian loan funds should be on a population basis.

In the face of the strong feeling in the North about the revenue allocation system and the region's specific recommendations about the future basis for allocating revenue, it was not surprising that the all-Nigeria General Conference[1] on the Review of the Constitution which met in January 1950 recommended that:

'. . . an expert and independent enquiry should be undertaken in consultation with all concerned, to submit proposals to the Governor-in-Council for division of revenue over a period of five years between the three regions and central Nigerian services in order to achieve in that time a progressively more equitable division of revenue as between the three separate Regions and the Centre.'[2]

The conference further recommended that should investigation by the expert commission prove that one region has been unfairly treated during the past years, that region should be given a block grant as compensation for what it had lost.

Although the feeling of inequitable regional allocation of revenue and expenditure which had been engendered by the Phillipson Report and the official public pronouncements were the primary reasons for the above recommendation, there was no doubt that the appointment of a commission would have been necessary, in any event, by the proposed constitutional changes. The regional councils were to become 'housekeepers' rather than 'householders', with specific legislative powers, and the regional executive councils

[1] The review of the 1946 Constitution began at the village level and went up hierarchically to the district, divisional, provincial, and regional levels, culminating in an all-Nigeria General Conference held in Ibadan in 1950. Almost all the recommendations of this conference were accepted by the Governor, and it was from this that the 1951 Constitution was drawn. This unique process of bringing about constitutional changes has been described as the 'most thorough democratic experience in African history' (*African Affairs*, vol. 48, No. 192, July 1949, p. 182).

[2] *Proceedings of the General Conference* (Lagos: Government Printer, 1950), p. 239.

were to be established with responsibility, even if limited, for economic and social policy.

Such constitutional arrangements would necessitate separate and independent regional budgets and therefore a large measure of regional fiscal autonomy. Thus, even if there were no disputes about the fairness or unfairness of the past system of revenue allocation, the proposed constitutional changes called for a review of the fiscal system so that the revenue allocation system and the distribution of tax powers would reflect the increased constitutional status of the regions.

By June 1950, an expert Commission had been appointed[1] with the terms of reference exactly as recommended by the conference. The appointment of this commission together with the proposed constitutional changes marked the first decisive step toward the development of federal finance in Nigeria. This step was to be followed three years later by another fiscal commission—the Chick Commission—whose report made federal finance a reality in Nigeria. It is the purpose of this chapter to discuss the Hicks-Phillipson Commission with a view to determining its permanent contribution to the evolution of federal finance in the country.

First moves: quasi-federalism, 1952-4

The most important and lasting contribution of the Hicks-Phillipson Commission in the development of federal finance in Nigeria may be summarised under three main headings: (1) its rejection of the derivative principle as the sole or most important basis for allocating revenue among the regions; (2) its discussion of some of the general principles of federal finance in their application

---

[1] The Commission was composed of Dr J. R. Hicks, F.B.A., Fellow of Nuffield College, Oxford, Mr D. A. Skelton, Assistant Deputy Minister of Trade and Commerce to the Government of Canada, and Sir Sydney Phillipson. Mr Skelton was subsequently drowned whilst sailing in Lagos harbour. The work of the Commission therefore devolved on Professor Hicks and Sir Sydney Phillipson. The Commission's Report, *Report of the Commission on Revenue Allocation* (Lagos: Government Printer, 1951), is henceforth referred to as the Hicks-Phillipson Report and the commission itself as the Hicks-Phillipson Commission.

to Nigeria; and (3) its advocacy of a system of revenue allocation based on the adoption of not just one but a number of criteria which together would ensure 'justice, liberty, fraternity, and efficiency'. As the Commission stated, whilst

'. . . fairness is a matter of the greatest importance it is not the only thing to look for. Equality of Justice is only one of the aims of a good constitutional system, even in its financial aspects; the claims of Liberty and Fraternity must not be forgotten. . . . A federation consists of a group of governments which have got to work together; but they have not only got to work together, they must also (over a considerable part of the field) be able to work separately. It is important that they should have the Liberty to work separately where they need to do so; and some degree of financial liberty is necessary for the purpose. Without such liberty they cannot be expected to cooperate smoothly, in the way Fraternity requires. . . . And in addition, we need also to pay attention to the demands of Efficiency. A poor country can afford waste even less than a rich country; to give free rein to all the things which may be politically desirable is inevitably expensive, and a poor country cannot afford a government of more than very moderate cost.'[1]

To satisfy these four criteria of liberty, justice, fraternity, and efficiency, the Commission advanced four general principles of federal finance as the basis of revenue allocation: the principle of independent revenue; of derivation; of need; and of national interest.

The principle of independent revenue favours the transfer of specific tax powers to the regional governments. Thus the regions would, for the first time, have powers to impose specific taxes. The Commission argued that to give the regional governments independent tax revenue of their own, over which they would have full control, was desirable both in the interests of regional autonomy and regional financial responsibility—both objectives being consistent with the increased constitutional status of the regions under the 1951 Constitution.

But such regional taxes must satisfy four basic conditions. First, they must be clearly localised within the separate regions; second,

[1] Hicks-Phillipson Report, p. 45.

regional taxes must have stable revenue yields; third, they must be inexpensive to administer; and fourth, they must not hinder or endanger national interest and policy.

The first condition is to ensure that a regional tax be paid by the people living within the region or by businesses operating within that region. This eliminated the company tax, since this levy was borne by a few large companies which operated in more than one region. Revenue from company tax in 1950/1 accounted for seventeen per cent of the total revenue.

The second condition, requiring stability in revenue yields, is to ensure regional finances against marked annual or cyclical variations. 'It is more important for regional taxes to be steady than for central taxes'[1] the Commission observed. While this would mean that central revenues would be more buoyant than local revenues in terms of rapid development, it would also mean that during a recession the main shock would be borne by the central government with its greater financial strength, instead of falling upon lesser and weaker governments. It is much easier for the central government to obtain external aid and to resort to deficit financing in an emergency than it is for a regional government. This requirement for regional revenue stability would dispose of export duties (which in 1950/1 accounted for another seventeen per cent of the total revenue), because by their very nature export tax yields are elastic with respect to changes in the world prices of export products.

The third condition, economy of tax collection, would disqualify import duties from becoming regional taxes. While it is true that import duties are universally imposed by the central government in order to minimise the cost of collection, to ease and to create an effective national commercial policy, the overwhelming importance of revenue from these duties would mean a severe restriction in the scope of regional finance. In 1950/1, about sixty per cent of total revenue was derived from import duties.

Given these restrictions, therefore, the taxes excluded from regional jurisdiction are those which in 1950/1 accounted for about ninety-four per cent of total revenue. In fact, the Commission was left with only taxes already declared regional under the Richards

[1] ibid., p. 50.

Constitution. But even then, these taxes which qualified for regional jurisdiction (principally direct taxes; the jangali tax; motor, liquor, and other licences) still presented some problems.

First, the Commission found that those taxes which met the requirements for regional jurisdiction were invariably also those which met the requirements for local jurisdiction. Taxes which are appropriate as regional taxes and do not also satisfy the conditions for local taxes were indeed hard to find. In Nigeria, in particular, the direct tax (levied under the Direct Tax Ordinance) had been the main source of local revenue, with the central government being content to receive a small share of its proceeds in order to maintain the tradition that it was a central rather than a local tax. Making this tax regional was therefore of little consequence from a revenue point of view. Native authorities would continue to take the lion's share of the proceeds. Any reduction in the share of the local authorities would only mean a corresponding increase in grants which would have to be paid to them.

Secondly, the total revenues which the regions would derive from these regional taxes would indeed be very miserable. It has already been mentioned that the taxes which qualified for regional jurisdiction under the Commission's criteria accounted for only six per cent of total revenue in 1950/1. Table 4.1 shows the relative share of these taxes in the revenue structure of the regions.

Although the Commission held the view that revenue from motor licences could be considerably increased by charging higher licensing fees, it had no illusions whatsoever about the potentiality of declared revenues even if they became regional revenues. In order therefore to provide substantial independent tax revenues for the regional governments,[1] the Commission had to look for other sources of independent revenues. It rejected regional jurisdiction of independent revenues. It rejected regional jurisdiction over a general sales tax because it 'would be administratively impracticable', and 'the costs of collection would be too heavy'.[2]

[1] The Commission thought that a regional government should have direct control over at least twenty-five per cent of its revenue. Significantly, it failed to achieve this objective through its recommendations.
[2] Hicks-Phillipson Report, p. 52.

TABLE 4.1 *Proportionate shares of declared regional revenue in total regional revenue, 1948/9 and 1951/2*

	1948/9 North	West	East	1951/2 North	West	East
(a) Total Regional Revenue (£m)	2·37	1·33	1·77	3·73	2·48	3·12
(b) Revenue Declared Regional (£m)	0·54	0·22	0·22	0·59	0·24	0·23
(b) as a percentage of (a)	22·8	16·5	12·4	15·8	9·7	7·4

SOURCE: Calculated from *Estimates of Nigeria*, 1948/9 and 1951/2 and from the *Accountant-General's Reports*, 1948/9 and 1951/2.

It recommended that the customs duty on motor fuel should be replaced by a sales tax on petrol which should become a regional tax.[1]

The Commission favoured a regional sales tax on petrol because such a tax would be easy to organise: the importation of petrol into Nigeria was in the hands of a small number of large and responsible companies. The tax also satisfied the four criteria for regional taxes established by the Commission. In addition, two new taxes—a tax on entertainment (including racing) and a tax on kolanuts (by the Northern government)—were suggested as other possible regional taxes. The Commission also recommended a more intensive utilisation of stamp duties for revenue purposes.

But in spite of these proposals, the Commission realised that sufficient revenue could not be raised from regional taxes alone, and that the regions would have to rely on grants from the centre for most of their revenue. Such grants, the Commission maintained, should reflect the national aspect of the federation rather than the 'aspect of diversity and separateness'. The other three principles were then used to determine the nature, scope, and magnitude of these grants. The Commission, while not in favour of the use of the principle of derivation as the only basis of transferring resources from the centre to the regions, was not opposed

[1] This tax would be confined to motor spirit only. It would not extend to lubricating oils or to fuel oils, e.g., kerosene.

to its selective use. As was shown in the preceding chapter, allocating the proceeds of any tax among the regions in the proportions to which the people of the regions have contributed to the tax requires a high degree of precision, and if revenues from a large number of taxes ('non-declared revenues') are to be allocated on the basis of this principle, very complicated and expensive enquiries would have to be made from year to year in order to ensure equity in distribution. The derivative principle would thus be difficult to apply if the taxes chosen were not capable of being accurately identified according to each region.

It is therefore preferable, the Hicks-Phillipson Commission contended, to confine the use of this principle to such taxes as can be so allocated with simplicity and certainty. The Commission identified tobacco taxes as conforming to these conditions, and recommended that half of the revenues from these taxes should be allocated among the regions on the basis of derivation.

The relative importance of revenues from tobacco taxes (about a quarter of the total revenue from customs) was no doubt also another factor which made their choice an obvious one for allocation to the regions. The recommendation that only half the proceeds of the taxes should be allocated among the regions was based on the belief that to allow the regions the whole of the proceeds of tobacco taxes would favour Western Region more than it would the other regions. The derivative proportion was a relationship of 2 : 6 : 3 for the North, West, and East respectively. This allocation, the Commission maintained, would upset the balance between the regions, and would also frustrate the balance among the principles of revenue allocation it was trying to apply.

Both the principles of independent revenue and of derivation depended on the taxpaying ability of the regions, and this in turn depended on their relative wealth. The two principles therefore favoured the West in their application, since it was the most developed region. And while both principles satisfied in large measure the needs for justice and liberty in the fiscal system, it was left to the principle of need to provide for the requirements of fraternity.

Arguing that the simplest interpretation of allocation according

D

to need is allocation based on population (since, in the absence of other information, the needs of different people may be assumed to be equal), the Commission suggested that some part of the allocation of revenue should be made in accordance with population. The Commission recognised other criteria for ascertaining need, such as relative poverty and special geographical difficulties like sparsity of population in the North and density of population in the East, but maintained that these refinements could not be considered in Nigeria because of a lack of statistical data and the low level of development. The Commission accordingly recommended that the central government should give a capitation grant to the regional governments in proportion to the population of the respective regions. Even this population variable had to be confined to adult male taxpayers in each region because of a lack of reliable census data. The Commission did not recommend a specific rate of capitation grant.

Finally, in regard to the principle of national interest, the Commission suggested central government grants for two specific regional services—education and police—which in its opinion were of high social importance and required some measure of national direction. These grants would be one hundred per cent of regional expenditures, and in addition a grant of fifty per cent would be given for expenditures of native administration police.

These then were the main features of the fiscal system recommended by the Commission. Under this system, the regional governments would have complete control over regional taxes, including the petrol tax; they would receive fifty per cent of the revenue from taxes on tobacco and cigarettes to be allocated on the basis of derivation; they would obtain a substantial amount, to be determined from time to time by the central government, in the form of capitation grants based on the number of adult male taxpayers in each region; and finally, they would receive specific grants toward regional expenditures on education and the police.

The Commission also made two important recommendations which, although having no immediate financial implications, were of great importance as far as the evolution of federal finance was concerned. These were the introduction of a uniform system of

income taxation throughout Nigeria by the central government and the establishment of a Nigeria Loan Commission to consider and formulate future loan policies for the central and regional governments.

Consideration should now be given to the second part of the Commission's terms of reference, which is the issue of whether any region had been unfairly treated in the past in the allocation of revenues and expenditures. Since the problem of inter-regional fiscal equity loomed large in the evolution of federal finance in Nigeria, subsequent fiscal commissions were faced with the same issue.

As was pointed out in chapter 2, the fiscal justification for the amalgamation of Northern and Southern Nigeria in 1914 was the financial difficulties of the government of the Protectorate of Northern Nigeria. Until the amalgamation, Northern Nigeria had been dependent on outside assistance in order to balance its budget, despite the considerable effort made to raise revenue internally by the imposition of direct taxes.

Only about seven per cent of the revenue from customs accruing to the government of the Colony and Protectorate of Southern Nigeria was imputed to the North. Thus, whereas the average annual revenue from customs collected at the ports of Southern Nigeria between 1908 and 1913 was £1·37 million, only £0·07 million was allocated to the North annually. With amalgamation in 1914, however, all revenue from customs accrued to the Nigerian government, with the result that during the post-amalgamation years it was the budget of the government of the South that was persistently in deficit. Had the two parts of Nigeria been federated in 1914 rather than amalgamated, and had the revenues of the new federation been allocated on the derivative principle, the relative pre-amalgamation (federation) budgetary position of the North and South would have been maintained. Thus, if a judgement were to be made on the basis of the relative budgetary positions of the North and South during the pre-amalgamation period, the verdict on the allegation of unfair treatment of the North would have been one of not proven. But as the Commission rightly observed, a problem of equity or fairness can

TABLE 4.2 *The financing of per capita public expenditures in the regions, 1948/9–1950/1*

(in pence)

	1948–9			1949–50			1950–1		
	North	West	East	North	West	East	North	West	East
1 Total Public Expenditure in the Regions*	83	128	99	97	143	114	112	174	128
2 Grants from Non-declared Revenue	32	66	71	36	74	78	43	84	88
3 Expenditure Finances from Local Sources (1)—(2)	51	62	28	61	69	36	69	90	40
4 (3) as a Percentage of (1)	61	47	28	63	48	31	61	52	31

* These figures are net central government education grants to voluntary agencies. As these agencies were operating rather extensively in the West and the East, but less in the North, the inclusion of education grants would further reduce the relative contribution to total expenditures of the East particularly, and the West.

SOURCE: Table X, p. 44 of the Hicks-Phillipson Report.

scarcely arise as between political entities until such political entities have come into existence.

Arguing that the derivation principle is not the only principle by which to judge the case of 'unfair treatment' among component parts of a federation, the Hicks-Phillipson Commission used other tests, principally the per capita revenue effort and the relative under-capitalisation of the regions to determine the principle of need. In seven tables, two of which are reproduced here, the Commission showed (Table 4.2) that while the North enjoyed the lowest per capita public expenditures in spite of its relatively high tax effort, the East, whose tax effort was much lower, enjoyed a much higher per capita expenditure. The cumulative effect of the low level of public expenditure in the North is the dearth of social overheads. Table 4.3 compares some of the facilities existing in the three regions in 1951.

TABLE 4.3 *Some overhead facilities in the regions per million of estimated population, 1951*

	North	West	East
Hospital beds	215	235	590
Dispensaries	24	41	49
Primary schools	106	821	654
Secondary schools	0·4	6	20
Teacher training institutions	2	6	9
Approximate road mileage	1,000	1,400	1,250
Approximate mileage of tarred roads	16	108	47

SOURCE: Table XVII, p. 73 of the Hicks-Phillipson Report.

Thus, the North was worse off than the other two regions in respect of each of the facilities shown in Table 4.3, indeed very much worse off in such cases as primary and secondary schools, teacher training institutions, and mileage of tarred roads. Under-expenditure in the past inevitably results in under-equipment in the present. On the grounds of need, the Commission therefore recommended that a special once-for-all grant of not more than £2 million should be paid to the North by the central government

from its general revenue balance, to assist that region in making up
for its relative shortage of overhead facilities.

Fiscal system under the 1951 Constitution

Before discussing the reception given to the proposals of the
Hicks-Phillipson Commission and their effects on the finances of
the central and regional governments, note should be taken of
some of the relevant features of the 1951 Constitution within whose
framework the proposed fiscal system was to operate. It will be
recalled that the establishment of the Commission was recommended by the General Conference on the Review of the 1946
Constitution even before the details of the new constitution had
been finally settled. The Commission had therefore to proceed
with its work on the basis of the broad agreement reached that the
regions would be granted increased autonomy entailing legislative
and executive powers within the framework of a united Nigeria.
The Commission assumed on this basis that a federal constitution
with a strong central government but powerful regional authorities
was in the offing, and proceeded, quite logically, to discuss the
problems of revenue allocation and of sharing tax powers as if
Nigeria were a federal country.

In fact, however, the 1951 Constitution[1] established a quasi-
federal rather than a truly federal system of government. Although
it did convert the regional councils from consultative to legislative
assemblies with powers to enact laws on specific matters[2] which
greatly increased regional autonomy, and although regional cabinets with a majority membership of Nigerian ministers were set up
alongside with a central cabinet in which Nigerian ministers were
also in the majority, the powers of both the regional legislatures
and cabinets (executive councils) were considerably circumscribed.
No bill passed by a regional legislature could become law until it

[1] The *Nigerian (Constitution) Order-in-Council, 1951,* No. 1172 of 1951,
made on 29 June 1951, published in the *Nigeria Gazette*, vol. 38, No. 35,
of 6 July 1951. The Constitution came into operation on 1 January 1952.
[2] See Appendix B on the allocation of functions between the Central and
Regional legislatures under the 1951 Constitution.

had been submitted for the approval of the Governor. If he had an objection to a bill it automatically lapsed. In other words, the regions were not coordinate but subordinate authorities to the central government in both legislative and executive powers.

But in spite of these constitutional limitations on the powers of the regions, the 1951 Constitution was still a significant advance, and provided the regions with expanded responsibilities. They ceased to be 'housekeepers' and became 'householders' in respect of the functions within their competence. The limited federal nature of the constitution necessitated the rejection or modification of some of the recommendations of the Hicks-Phillipson Commission. For example, the Commission had proposed independent regional revenue which should be handed over to complete regional control. But some of the revenues which had been declared regional under the 1946 Constitution did not come under the jurisdiction of the regional legislatures under the 1951 Constitution. A notable example was revenue from the licensing of vehicles and drivers, of which the Commission had made specific mention. It was the view of the Nigerian government[1] that to give the regions power to legislate in vehicle licensing would not be in the public interest, since it could result in the creation of three different systems of road standards and worthiness. This, the Governor maintained, would be a retrograde measure creating many difficulties and disadvantages without any compensating advantages. It was therefore decided that legislation governing the licensing of vehicles should continue to be central government responsibility while the regional authorities would have power to establish the fees charged for licences.

The same procedure was also followed with regard to direct taxation. It was the official view that granting this power to regional legislatures would inevitably lead to such administrative complexities as taxation agreements between regions. The Commission's recommendation that a regional sales tax should replace customs duties on motor spirit, although supported in principle, was also

[1] As stated in the Governor's Dispatch of 15 October 1951 to the Secretary of State for the Colonies (published in *Nigeria Gazette Extraordinary*, vol. 38, No. 65, of 7 December 1951).

found impracticable. Central government control over the taxation of motor spirit was retained, but it was agreed that revenues accruing therefrom should be allocated to the region in proportion to regional consumption. While the Commission's suggestion that the regions should have control over the taxing of entertainment (including horse racing) was accepted, the other remaining taxes proposed for regional control—the kola-nut tax and stamp duties —were rejected.

The net effect of all this was that under the new fiscal system as promulgated by the *Nigeria (Revenue Allocation) Order-in-Council, 1951*,[1] the regional legislatures were given few powers of taxation of their own. They were only empowered to levy an entertainment tax and impose a sales tax on the distribution of motor spirit. Such a sales tax, if levied, would be additional to, rather than a substitute for, the import duties on motor spirit.

The suggestion of the Commission for the establishment of a Loans Commission on which the regions would be represented was also rejected on the grounds that the recommendation 'was made at a time when the exact shape of the Nigerian Executive had still to be defined in a Constitutional Instrument. . . . In this field, policy can be settled with due regard to regional interests in a manner much less complicated. . . .'[2]

The other proposals of the Commission were accepted and incorporated in the revenue allocation order.[3]

[1] No. 2127 of 1951 (published in the *Nigeria Gazette*, vol. 38, No. 65, of 7 December 1951).
[2] Governor's Dispatch, loc. cit.
[3] It is worth noting that a committee which the General Conference on the Review of the 1946 Constitution had set up to consider the report of the Hicks-Phillipson Commission suggested two major changes which the Governor was unable to support and which were rejected by the Secretary of State for the Colonies. The Committee had suggested that the whole of the revenue (and not merely the fifty per cent proposed by the Commission) from duties on tobacco and cigarettes should be given to the regions in accordance with the principle of derivation. They also suggested that the once-for-all special grant to Northern Nigeria should be increased from £2 million (recommended by the Commission) to £3 million. Their first suggestion was based on the need to give the regions more resources to enable them to provide more services to their people so that 'popular

Central-regional finances, 1952-4

In examining the probable effects of their proposals on regional finances, the Hicks-Phillipson Commission noted that the fiscal system envisaged in their report would work to everyone's satisfaction only if Nigerian revenues increased commensurate to a rapid rate of development. 'If there is no more [revenue] to be divided than there has been in the past', the Commission observed, 'no change in financial arrangements can prevent there being a great deal of trouble ahead.' For if the Northern share was to grow relatively to the Eastern share, the East would have to receive less revenue. Until there was a rapid expansion of Nigerian revenues the Northern Region would be unable to pay for its services, and would not be able to gain appreciably. This, of course, would create serious difficulties for Nigeria as a whole.

To estimate the effect of its proposals on regional finances, the Commission attempted a recalculation of regional estimates of revenue for the year 1950/1 based on its proposals. The central government, however, had been empowered to establish the rate of the capitation grant, and as a result it was not easy to anticipate the amounts of the grants. But this exercise of calculating the probable effects of the proposals on regional finances indirectly helped to indicate the range of capitation grant which the central government should make.

Table 4.4 shows that both the North and the West would be better off under the proposed scheme than under the existing arrangements, but the East would be worse off, with a deficit of £280,000. And as far as all the regions were concerned, their net gain would amount to only £15,000. Different assumptions about the rates of capitation grants would, however, have different effects on the finances of the regions and the net resources transferred from the centre to the regions, as Table 4.5 indicates. It will be

government might thereby be made a success'. Their second suggestion was made in order that the development of the North might accelerate faster than the Commission thought necessary. Because both suggestions would upset the balance among the regions as well as the balance among the principles laid down by the Commission, the Governor was unable to support them.

TABLE 4.4 *Estimated effect of the Hicks-Phillipson Commission Allocation Plan on regional budgets if operative in fiscal year 1950/1*

(£'000s)

Proposed Resources for Regional Allocation	North	West	East
Petrol tax	175	385	140
Fifty per cent of tobacco taxes	345	977	501
Capitation grant at 9s	1,652	490	633
Education grants	218	681	646
Police grant (regional expenditures)	201	396	346
Police grant (fifty per cent of Native Administration expenditures)	153	48	—
Total estimated regional allocation under the plan	2,744	2,977	2,266
Actual regional allocation from non-declared revenue, 1950/1	2,492	2,932	2,546
Probable net effect (+ or −) of the plan on regional finances	+252	+45	−280

N.B.: The figures for the West include allocations which would have been due to Lagos and the Colony had they been constituted into a separate region rather than being merged with the West.

SOURCE: Table XXV of the Hicks-Phillipson Report, pp. 141–2.

seen from this table that the Eastern Region would not break even until the capitation rate had reached 13s, by which time a net sum of £1,247,000 would have been transferred from the centre to the regions.

How did this scheme work out in practice during the financial years in which it was in operation, 1952/3 and 1953/4? Tables 4.6 to 4.9 provide relevant data on central and regional finances during these two years.

As it was intended by the Commission, regional finances were much strengthened under the new system of allocation. The regional governments absorbed a much larger proportion of total Nigerian revenue. Whereas in 1951/2 the regional governments

TABLE 4.5 *Effects of the different rates of capitation on the finances of the regional and central governments*

(£'000s)

| Rate of Capitation (Shillings) | Surpluses (+) or Deficits (−) | | | |
	North	West	East	Centre
9	+252	+45	−280	−17
10	+433	+100	−210	−323
11	+616	+165	−140	−641
12	+799	+210	−70	−939
13	+982	+265	0	−1,247

SOURCE: Hicks-Phillipson Report, Table XXVI, p. 142.

received only 17·2 per cent of total central government revenue through grants, in 1952/3 they received 25·8 per cent, even though central revenue increased between the two years by 0·4 per cent (Table 4.9). On the whole, the regions faired much better than had been expected by the Commission, mainly because revenue from the tobacco taxes more than doubled the Commission's estimates, but the central government established a lower capitation grant—11s per adult male taxpayer—which was less than the Commission had anticipated.[1]

But in spite of this increase in the financial strength of the regions, the central government still, as under the old system, retained the major share of Nigerian revenue for its own use, and financial control remained firmly in its hands.

Although most of the revenue allocations that had to be made to the regions under the new system were constitutionally fixed, the central government not only had power to fix (and vary) the rates of taxes on the commodities from which the regions derived their revenue, but also was empowered to fix the rates of the capitation grants. The revenues from these grants alone accounted for about a quarter of the total regional grants and allocations. The rates and variations of these grants therefore affected the finances of the regions appreciably.

[1] *Revenue allocation (Capitation Rate) Order (No. 2 of 1952), Official Gazette*, vol. 39, No. 2, of 3 January 1952.

TABLE 4.6 *Regional finances, 1952–4*

(£'000s)

	1952/3			1953/4		
	North	West	East	North	West	East
(a) REGIONAL GRANTS AND ALLOCATIONS						
(i) Allocation of revenues from duties on motor spirits	294	600	256	353	739	335
(ii) Allocation of revenues from duties on tobacco and cigarettes	1,159	1,844	1,264	829	1,642	830
(iii) Capitation grants	2,036	629	746	2,063	630	761
(iv) Education grants	344	837	965	506	1,383	1,423
(v) Police grants	461	515	440	484	593	475
TOTAL GRANTS AND ALLOCATIONS FROM THE CENTRE	4,294	4,425	3,671	4,235	4,987	3,824
(b) INDEPENDENT REGIONAL REVENUE	888	625	540	1,546	1,717	950
TOTAL RECURRENT REVENUE	5,182	5,050	4,211	5,781	6,704	4,774
(c) UNDER-DEVELOPMENT GRANT	2,000*	—	—	—	—	—
(d) SPECIAL GRANTS†	1,358	618	519	557	603	574
TOTAL REGIONAL FINANCE	8,540	5,668	4,730	6,338	7,307	5,348
(e) REGIONAL EXPENDITURE	4,955	4,757	4,322	6,055	6,528	4,736
(f) BUDGET SURPLUS OR DEFICIT	+3,585	+911	+408	+283	+779	+612

* This was actually paid before the commencement of the 1952/3 financial year.

† These include Colonial Development and Welfare Grants, specific grants for meeting increases in wages and salaries as approved by the Central government at the beginning of this period, a grant for the West in respect of services previously provided by the government in the municipality of Lagos, but which, because of the merger of Lagos with the West, were transferred to the West.

SOURCES: *Accountant-General's Report; Estimates; Nigerian Gazettes;* and *Digest of Statistics*, 1952–4.

TABLE 4.7 *Hypothetical comparison of relative regional shares of federal grants and allocation under the Hicks-Phillipson and the Phillipson recommendations, 1952–4*

(£'000s)

	1952/3			1953/4		
	North	West	East	North	West	East
(a) Actual regional allocation of federal grants (under the Hicks-Phillipson Plan)	4,294	4,425	3,671	4,235	4,987	3,824
(b) Hypothetical regional allocation of federal grants on the Phillipson (1946) Plan*	4,708	3,370	4,312	4,957	3,549	4,540
(c) Surplus or Deficit ((a)—(b))	−414	+1,055	−641	−722	+1,438	−716

* The percentages used in working out these hypothetical allocations were the actual percentages used in allocating the available non-declared revenue in 1951/2, i.e., 38 per cent, 27·2 per cent and 34·8 per cent for the North, West and East respectively.

SOURCE: Central and Regional Governments' *Estimates*, 1952/3 and 1953/4.

TABLE 4.8 *Proportionate regional shares of central allocations and grants, 1951–4*

	1951/2	1952/3	1953/4
North	38·0	33·8	32·4
West	27·2	35·7	38·2
East	34·8	29·6	29·3
Total	100·0	100·0*	100·0*

* Figures do not add up to 100 per cent because of rounding.

SOURCE: Central and Regional Governments' *Estimates*, 1951–4.

TABLE 4.9 *Central and regional governments' revenue, 1951–4*

(£'000s)

	1951/2	1952/3	1953/4
(a) Gross central government revenue (exclusive of grants under CD and W)*	47,828	48,003	56,229
(b) Total regional allocations and grants (exclusive of regional share of grants under CD and W)	8,268	12,390	13,046
(c) Net central government revenue (retained for Central expenditure ((a)—(b)))	38,560	35,613	42,183
(d) Regional government revenues (including central government allocations and grants)	9,324	14,443	17,259
(e) Proportionate share of total regional revenue in gross central revenue ((d) as a percentage of (a))	19·2	30·8	30·7
(f) Proportionate share of regional allocations and grants in gross central revenue ((b) as a percentage of (a))	17·2	25·8	23·2
(g) Regional revenue as a percentage of net central revenue ((d) as a percentage of (c))	25·5	40·5	40·9

* CD and W = Colonial Development and Welfare.

SOURCES: *Accountant-General's Reports*, 1951/2, 1952/3 and 1953/4; and Regional Governments' *Estimates* 1951–4.

It has been noted that by the time the recommendations of the Hicks-Phillipson Commission had been implemented, the most important suggestions about regional tax powers aimed at granting the regions a larger measure of financial autonomy had been whittled down. The result was that independent revenues accounted for only about one fifth of total regional revenues during 1951/2 and 1952/3. Thus, financial autonomy for the regions, which was expected to accompany the emergence of federal finance, still remained a future prospect rather than a reality.

With regard to inter-regional fiscal relationships, the balance between the regions which the Commission sought to establish was found very difficult to accomplish due to unexpectedly large revenue receipts from tobacco taxes, and capitation grants too low to equalise regional fiscal variances. It became the West and not the North, as the Commission had computed, which received the largest share of the central government's allocations and grants (Table 4.8). The West received this advantage because of the merger of the capital city of Lagos to it. Lagos, because it is Nigeria's capital city, its chief port, and the centre of economic activities, had the highest per capita consumption of commodities like petrol and tobacco, which accordingly were included in the figures for the Western Region.

Conclusions

It is not surprising that the fiscal system under the 1951 Constitution did not confer on the regions a greater degree of financial autonomy. To do so would have resulted in a financial arrangement in advance of the letter and spirit of the Constitution. Although the regions in particular, and the country as a whole, achieved an appreciable constitutional advance in 1951, the new constitutional provisions were far from federal. The regional authorities were still subordinate to the central government; in exercising their executive authority the regions were subjected to central government control, and as far as legislation was concerned, all regional bills had to receive the prior approval of the Governor of Nigeria before they could be submitted for royal assent. Most of the powers were still retained by the centre—the exceptions being listed in the schedule to the constitution[1]—but the central legislature could delegate additional functions to the regions should it so desire.

Election to the central legislature was not direct: members were elected from the regional legislatures. Some members therefore belonged to two legislative assemblies. In view of this relationship between the central and the regional legislatures, and between

[1] See Appendix B for the allocation of functions under the 1951 Constitution.

regional and central executives, and in view also of the financial relationship which was promulgated under and in accordance with the Constitution, one may, using the term of A. H. Birch, say that the form of government introduced was more like a system of 'democratic centralism' than a federal system.[1]

In a country with the size and diversity of Nigeria, coupled with the intense regional loyalty and rivalry of the people, it is not surprising that the 1951 Constitution was short-lived. Although in its formal structure constitutional power was still firmly with the central legislature and executive, political power and influence resided in the regions.[2] Also the new ministers, both regional and central, impatiently discovered that they had influence and prestige but little power and responsibility. They were expected to execute collective government policy, but could not exercise individual responsibility and power.

The regions were not completely satisfied with the system of revenue allocation under the Constitution. They found the limitations on their taxing power irksome, and desirous as they were to provide more social services for their people, they discovered that the constraints imposed on their taxing powers made the realisation of their plans difficult. As far as inter-regional fiscal relationships were concerned, the Western Region, while admitting that the Hicks-Phillipson Commission was much fairer to it than the Phillipson Commission, was of the view that it was still not obtaining its fair share of the national revenue because of the relatively small weight given to the principle of derivation.[3] Thus, even

[1] *Federalism, Finance and Social Legislation* (Oxford: Clarendon Press, 1955), p. 297.

[2] All of the leaders of the three political parties in power in the regions preferred regional ministries to central ones. The central government, which consisted of four ministers from each region, was politically less important than the regional executive. Central ministers, who were nominees of the parties in power in the regions, had to refer matters to their leaders who were regional ministers.

[3] The political party then in power in Western Nigeria, the Action Group, while supporting the derivation was disturbed by the inequity caused by the unreliable and restricted data used by Sir Sydney Phillipson in the 'ideal percentages'. The Action Group leaders were also angry with the central government for rejecting the recommendation of the Committee of

before the subsequent constitutional and political crisis, the system of revenue allocation had begun to break down.

The statutory grants to the regions had to be augmented by special grants in order that the regions might be able to pay for their services, particularly for the increase in salaries and wages which was granted to civil servants in 1952. Other special grants were made to the regions to compensate for the difference between the estimated revenue from import and excise duties on tobacco and the actual revenue resulting from this source. The revenue from tobacco duties was grossly over-estimated in 1952/3 and since the regions had based their estimates of expenditure on estimates of revenue, the central government had to give them special grants to prevent a curtailment of regional services.

Another development which led to the breakdown of the carefully balanced fiscal system which the Hicks-Phillipson Commission sought so hard to establish was the imposition by two of the Sixteen that the whole revenue (and not fifty per cent) from tobacco duties should be allocated to the regions on the derivation principle. See, for example, a pamphlet entitled *Commentary on Chick's Report* (Lagos: Amalgamated Press of Nigeria Ltd.), written by the Action Group. One of the leaders of the Action Group, who was then the regional Minister of Education, was no doubt voicing the resentment of Western Nigerian leaders when he said during a debate on revenue from tobacco duties on 21 August 1952: 'We believe that the Western Region contributes a very substantial amount to the Central coffers. At the beginning of the review of the Constitution the belief of the Northern Region was that they contributed fifty per cent to the Nigerian revenue. The Revenue Allocation Commission has shown that this is not the case, and that the Western Region does contribute a very substantial amount to the Central revenue but what does the Western Region receive from this revenue?' On the recommendations of the Committee of Sixteen rejected by the old government, he thought that 'Government had treated the representatives of the people with utter disrespect'. After remarking that the Western Region had not been fairly treated in the past, he added: 'it was revealing to know that when Sir Sydney Phillipson made his recommendation he forgot to add a very significant portion of tax on tobacco to the Western Region, a sum which was so large on arithmetical calculation . . . as to rob the Western Region of almost all of what was essentially her due.' He ended by suggesting that a new revenue allocation formula should be considered. (*House of Representatives Debates, First Session*, 14–22 August 1952, pp. 327–30.)

three regional governments of a sales tax on export produce. This was a development that the Commission neither could have foreseen nor would have approved of in view of the importance which it had attached to regional revenues being as stable as possible. However, the three regional governments, because of the increasing need for more revenue, decided to impose sales tax on export produce a year after the introduction of the new fiscal arrangement.[1] For political reasons, the Eastern Region government could not proceed with this tax measure, but both the Northern and the Western Region governments imposed the tax with effect from 1 April 1953. The produce sale tax,[2] which was levied on the main export crops, was voted for a single year in the first instance but was subsequently renewed until it became a permanent feature of the fiscal system in the West and North.

It will be seen from the foregoing analysis that although the immediate reason for the 1954 constitutional change was a political crisis in the eastern and central legislatures,[3] there were fiscal causes of the failure of the 1951 Constitution as well. After two years of operating under the new system of revenue allocation, it was realised that 'democratic centralism' would have to give way to

[1] Since it was only the central legislature which could impose a tax on exports, the regional legislatures had to request the Governor to introduce these measures.

[2] The rates were £1 per ton on groundnut, palm kernel, and palm oil; £4 per ton on cocoa; 10s per ton on beni seed; 2s 6d per ton on soya beans; and one tenth of a penny per pound on cotton.

[3] In the Eastern Region, the members of the legislature, having lost confidence in the regional executive, nevertheless found it impossible to remove the ministers as they were unable to obtain the two-thirds majority of all members prescribed by the Constitution. It was also discovered that there was no provision for the dissolution of the regional House of Assembly. In the House of Representatives a crisis developed through a motion brought up by a member from the Western Region requesting self-government for Nigeria in 1956. The Action Group central ministers resigned because of a decision of the Council of Ministers that central ministers should not take part in the debate on the motion. And when a Northern Region representative attempted to kill the motion before it had been debated by the House, all the representatives from the West and most of the representatives from the East walked out of the House.

federalism in the country's constitutional arrangement if the various parts of Nigeria were to remain together. The fiscal arrangement would have to give more independent tax powers to the regions. The crisis of 1953 provided an opportunity for the review of the Constitution, and for the emergence of a federal system of government with a federal fiscal arrangement.

5 Operation of federal finance in Nigeria: first phase

Emergence of federal finance

As a result of the political and constitutional crisis of 1953, many observers in both Nigeria and Great Britain came to the view that any new constitution for Nigeria must provide for a larger measure of autonomy for the regions than the 1951 Constitution allowed. The leaders of both the West and the East strongly advocated a federal constitution with the regions completely autonomous in those functions which were within their jurisdiction.

In a statement in the House of Commons on the crisis, the Secretary of State for the Colonies said:[1]

'Her Majesty's Government in the United Kingdom considers that the constitution will have to be re-drawn to provide for greater regional autonomy and for the removal of powers of intervention by the centre in matters which can, without detriment to other regions, be placed entirely within regional competence.'

The Northern Region, whose leaders were particularly bitter about the crisis,[2] went much further than the Secretary of State for the Colonies in a remarkable motion passed by the Northern

[1] Statement by Mr Oliver Lyttelton in the House of Commons, 21 May 1953.
[2] The leader of the Northern representatives, the Sardauna of Sokoto, had, after the walk-out of the Eastern and Western representatives, remarked that 'the mistake of 1914 has come to light'. *House of Representatives Debates*, vol. II, 1 April 1953, p. 1053. He was referring to the amalgamation of Northern and Southern Nigeria.

House of Assembly.[1] According to this resolution, Nigeria should become a confederation or customs union. Each region would be given complete legislative and executive autonomy with respect to all matters except defence, external affairs, customs, and West African research institutions. There would be no central executive or policy-making body for the whole of the country, but a non-political central agency at a 'neutral place preferably Lagos'. Common services like the railways, electricity, ports, coal mining, and air services would be organised on an inter-regional basis and administered by public corporations largely managed by experts.

As regards the fiscal system, all revenues, except customs revenue, would be levied and collected by the regional governments. Customs duties would be collected at the ports by the central agency and paid to each region on the derivative basis, and the administration of the customs would be so organised as to ensure that goods consigned to each region were separately cleared and charged duty. Thus under this rather extreme proposal, Nigeria would become a confederation of three countries. Had this proposal been accepted, the Nigerian confederation would have been without parallel in the modern world.

This Northern proposal[2] was as unworkable as it was curious. Due to the free movement of goods and services between the regions, it would have been, even with the best of expertise, impossible to identify at the time of importation the region in which the actual consumption of all the imported goods would take place. The Hicks-Phillipson Commission chose tobacco and petrol as the two items whose region of consumption could, with some reorganisation and improvement in the data collection process, be easily identified.[3]

[1] Northern Regional Legislature, *House of Assembly Debates, Second Session*, 18, 22 and 23 May 1953.
[2] It became widely known as the 'Eight-Point Plan'. It is significant that a similar proposal was put forward by the Eastern Region in 1966 as the only solution to the political crisis which has faced the country since January 1966.
[3] The Financial Secretary to the Government, in a speech in the House of Representatives on 21 August 1952, had to admit that this could not be a precise calculation. Speaking about the consumption of tobacco, he said

The proposal was curious because one would not have thought that the North would propose a system of revenue allocation based entirely or even partially on the principle of derivation. The North, being both poor and populous, should in its own interest have preferred allocation according to need by means of capitation grants. As noted earlier, this had been the proposal of the Northern delegation to the 1950 Constitution Review Conference. The Northern leaders were no doubt too angry with their southern compatriots to consider in full the implications of their proposals.

It was in this mood that Nigeria went into conference in July and August of 1953,[1] and again in January and February 1954[2] to produce its first federal constitution. The North was persuaded to give up its plan for confederation, and a new federal constitution came into effect on 1 October 1954.[3]

Whereas the 1951 Constitution had given Nigeria a powerful central government, with the regional governments dependent on its favours, the 1954 Constitution reversed the situation. A federal government with specific subjects assigned to it was established, while the regional governments were assigned residual functions.[4] The federal government became responsible for external relations (including foreign trade), principal internal communications, banking, mining, the incorporation of companies operating throughout Nigeria, and certain existing central institutions. The list of exclusive legislative powers of the central government was indeed short and specific. The concurrent legislative list included important items like industrial development, power, scientific and

'it is now known, for example, that the company [the Nigerian Tobacco Company Ltd.—Nigeria's sole manufacturer of cigarettes] sold cigarettes in Sokoto, Northern Nigeria, which were later shipped and sold in Ibadan'.

[1] *Report of the Conference on the Nigerian Conference*, London, 1953, Cmd. 8934.

[2] *Report by the Resumed Conference on the Nigerian Constitution* (Lagos: Government Printer, 1954).

[3] *The Nigerian (Constitution) Order in Council, 1954*, No. 1146 of 1954.

[4] See Appendix B for the exclusive federal and concurrent legislative lists as contained in the First Schedule of the *Nigeria (Constitution) Order in Council, 1954*.

industrial research, and higher education. On the whole the central government was left with greatly reduced powers. As if to emphasise the reduced status and power of the central government and to underscore the large degree of regional autonomy, Nigeria officially came to be called the Federation of Nigeria.

Since financial power in government is the ultimate power, the constitutional conference agreed to the appointment of a fiscal commission, whose sole member was Sir Louis Chick, which would recommend a revenue allocation system that would reflect the proposed federal arrangement. In its terms of reference, the Commission was asked, *inter alia*:

'(1) To assess the effect on the public expenditure of Nigeria as a whole of the re-allocation of functions between the Centre and the Regions . . . and in particular to estimate, after taking account of any transfer of physical assets and liabilities involved, the net cost of—

(a) Central services;

(b) the services remaining to be undertaken by the Regions.

(2) In the light of (1) above . . . to enquire how the revenues available, or to be made available, to the regions and to the centre can best be collected and distributed, having regard on the one hand to the need to provide to the regions and the centre an adequate measure of fiscal autonomy within their own sphere of government and, on the other hand, to the importance of ensuring that the total revenues available to Nigeria are allocated in such a way that the principle of derivation is followed to the fullest degree compatible with meeting the reasonable needs of the centre and each of the regions.[1]

While it is obvious that a federal system of government must have a federal financial system, the Chick Fiscal Commission was not called upon to devise one. Instead, the Commission was speci-

---

[1] Sir Louis Chick, K.B.E., was appointed as the Commissioner. His report is entitled *The Report of Fiscal Commissioner on Financial Effects of Proposed New Constitutional Arrangements* (Lagos: Government Printer, 1953). Henceforth, this Commission will be referred to simply as the Chick Fiscal Commission and its report as the Chick Fiscal Commission Report.

fically enjoined to have regard '. . . to the importance of ensuring that the total revenues available to Nigeria are allocated in such a way that the principle of derivation is followed to the fullest degree compatible with meeting of the reasonable needs of the Centre and each of the Regions'. Not only, therefore, did the new constitutional proposals call for radical changes in the fiscal system based on the recommendations of the Hicks-Phillipson Commission, but the terms of reference of the Chick Fiscal Commission were framed in such a way as to make such radical changes inevitable. The Commission had to lean heavily on the principle of derivation.

The Commissioner, however, interpreted his terms of reference rather broadly. His view was that only the revenue collected by the federal government in excess of its own needs should be allocated to the regions in accordance with the principle of derivation. This view was based on three main reasons. First, he argued that if the federal government was to be independent of the regional governments within its own sphere, and also coordinate with them, it must have its own revenues. He accordingly rejected the suggestion that all revenues should be allocated to the regions, with the federal government making a levy on the regional governments within an agreed maximum for the funds it needed to discharge its responsibilities. Secondly, he maintained that as the economic development of Nigeria would depend in a large measure upon the financial resources of the federal government, its 'reasonable needs' must be:

'. . . viewed generously and its present reserves must not be distributed lavishly to the regions. While it is true that the expensive social services are to be a regional responsibility, it is also true that the main immediate need in the field of economic development is the improvement and extension of the country's road, railway, post and telecommunications facilities.'[1]

These services were to be federal responsibilities, and their improvement and further development would involve very large capital expenditures, part of which would have to be financed from loans. The financial strength of the federal government, he concluded, would be 'a weighty factor in determining the amounts

[1] Chick Fiscal Commission Report, p. 10.

and terms of loans', especially if such loans were to be obtained from external sources. Finally, he argued that if the federal government was to be in a position to assist any regional government which might find itself in serious financial difficulty beyond its control (due, for example, to crop failures), the 'reasonable needs' of the federal government must be interpreted generously. 'The federal government would be failing in its duty if it were not able to assist a regional government in such circumstances.'[1]

The revenue allocation system which was recommended by the Chick Fiscal Commission and which was subsequently accepted and incorporated in the 1954 Constitution for the Federation of Nigeria is tabulated in Table 5.1. As this table indicates, the tax powers of the federal government were still substantial. In fact, they remained much as they had been under the 1951 Constitution. Jurisdiction over import and export taxes and mining royalties as well as the collection of the revenues from these taxes remained a federal responsibility. The Commission recommended that excise duties should be a federal subject because of the difficulties likely to arise from different regional rates of excise duties. With regard to the income tax, since the jurisdiction over 'incorporated companies operating throughout Nigeria' was exclusively a federal matter, it was logical for the taxation of the companies also to be a federal subject so that there could be a uniform level of company tax throughout Nigeria. The Commissioner supported federal jurisdiction over personal income taxation also on the grounds that it was desirable that there should be a uniform level of taxation on personal incomes in order that the free flow of capital and labour might not be impeded. The experience in other federations had shown, he argued, that where tax jurisdiction over personal income was left to regional or state governments, the federal government had later been compelled to assume jurisdiction.

The difference between the federal fiscal system which emerged in 1954 and the fiscal systems in existence during the period of 'democratic centralism' of 1952–4 and the period of devolution of financial responsibility to the regional governments of 1948–52 did not lie in any marked change in central/regional tax powers. The

[1] ibid., p. 10.

TABLE 5.1 *Nigeria's federal fiscal system under the 1954 Constitution*

Tax	Jurisdiction (Federal or Regional)	Formula for the Allocation of the Proceeds from the Taxes
(a) IMPORT AND EXCISE TAXES		
(i) Import and excise duties on tobacco (manufactured and unmanufactured).	Federal both in the fixing of rates and in the collection of revenue.	Fifty per cent was retained by the federal government for its own use; remaining fifty per cent was allocated to the regions in accordance with regional consumption.
(ii) Import duty on motor spirit.	Federal both in the fixing of rates and in the collection of revenue.	All of the proceeds were allocated to the regions in accordance with regional consumption.
(iii) Import duties on goods other than tobacco and motor spirit.	Federal both in the fixing of rates and in the collection of revenue.	Fifty per cent was retained by the federal government; the remaining fifty per cent was allocated to the regions in the following proportions: North, thirty per cent; East, thirty per cent; West, forty per cent.
(b) EXPORT TAXES		
(i) All export duties on produce other than hides and skins.	Federal both in the fixing of rates and in the collection of revenue.	Fifty per cent of the proceeds was retained by the federal government; the remaining fifty per cent of the revenue from the duty on each kind of export produce was allocated among the regional governments in proportion to purchases made in each region. For this purpose, purchases made in Lagos were deemed to have been made in the Western Region.

Tax	Jurisdiction (Federal or Regional)	Formula for the Allocation of the proceeds from the taxes
(ii) Export tax on hides and skins.	Federal both in the fixing of the rates of tax and in the collection of the revenue.	Fifty per cent of the proceeds was retained by the federal government and the remaining fifty per cent was allocated to the North.
(c) INCOME TAX		
(i) Direct tax (under the direct taxation ordinance)	Regional both in the fixing of rates and in the collection of the revenue.	Proceeds shared between the regional governments and the native authorities and local governments of the region as decided by the regional governments.
(ii) Personal income tax (under the income tax ordinance).	Federal both in the fixing of the rates and in the collection of the revenue.	Proceeds of the tax collected from persons with incomes of less than £150 (mainly Nigerians in Lagos who did not come under the Direct Taxation Ordinance) were retained by the federal government; proceeds of the tax on persons with incomes of over £150 were allocated to the regional governments on the basis of the residence of the taxpayers, with the federal government retaining the proceeds of the tax from Lagos taxpayers.
(iii) Company tax	Federal both in the fixing of rates and in the collection of revenue.	Proceeds were retained in full by the federal government.
(d) MINING ROYALTIES	Federal both in the fixing of the rates and in the collection of revenue.	Allocated in full to the region from which the mineral was extracted.

Tax	Jurisdiction (Federal or Regional)	Formula for the Allocation of the proceeds from the taxes
(e) OTHER ITEMS OF REVENUE		
(i) Fees, earnings of government departments and revenue from government property.	Federal and regional both in the fixing of rates and in the collection of revenue.	Fees relating to regional subjects accrued to regional governments (with the federal government being treated as a regional government in respect of Lagos); earnings of government departments and revenue from government property accrued to the governments operating the department or owning the property.
(ii) Profits from the West African Currency Board.		Retained in full by the federal government.

SOURCES: *Nigeria (Constitution) Order-in-Council, 1954*; Chick Fiscal Commission Report, 1953.

central authorities retained jurisdiction over the most important taxes in Nigeria. The radical changes which occurred in 1954 were in the system of allocation.

Partly because of the great change in the constitutional position of the regions and partly because the regions were anxious to reduce the financial resources of the federal government to the minimum so that they could have a much larger share, the financial strength of the centre was much weaker after 1 October 1954 than it had been previously. This was a trend which was given impetus by the 1946 Constitution, which encouraged 'regionalism', and which reached its climax in 1954 when Nigeria became a federation with residual powers in regional hands and with the federal government left with only specific and limited functions. Had the Chick Fiscal Commission not interpreted its terms of reference generously in favour of the federal government, the financial position of that government would have been even more limited.

It is not the emergence of federalism *per se* that led to the reduced financial strength of the centre vis-à-vis the regions: rather it was the ambivalent attitude of the architects of Nigerian federation, who appeared more interested in drawing up a charter for regional obscurantism than in a fiscal system designed for economy, efficiency, and equity. The Fiscal Commissioner, in regard to his first term of reference enjoining him to 'assess the effect on the public expenditure of Nigeria as a whole of the re-allocation of functions between the centre and the regions', came to the conclusion that 'the net effect of the re-allocation of functions on the regional expenditure estimates' was small, except in the case of the North, because the additional expenditure imposed on the regional budgets by the re-allocation of functions is largely offset by the transfer of expenditure on the Nigeria Police Force to the federal government[1] and by the transfer of Western Region expenditures in respect of Lagos to the federal government.[2] Had the Nigerian leaders wanted to do so there was no reason why the federal government could not have retained the same financial strength as the old central government, thereby enhancing its ability to ensure balanced national development and promote national standards.

The significant impact of the new fiscal system on the finances of the federal government is perhaps best illustrated by considering statistics for regional revenue allocation during the 1954/5 financial year—the transitional year from the old to the new system. The revenue estimates had been prepared for the full year on the basis of the old system of allocation, but when the new constitution

[1] ibid., p. 7, para. 27.
[2] Under the 1954 Constitution, the municipality of Lagos was constitutionally separated from the Western Region and federalised. It will be remembered that it had been merged with that region under the 1951 Constitution. The merger of Lagos with the West, or its federalisation, was one of the most critical issues before the 1953 Constitutional Review Conference. Nigerian leaders were divided on the issue, with the Northern and Eastern leaders favouring the existing arrangement. Her Majesty's Government decided in favour of making Lagos a federal territory, constitutionally independent of any region. (See the *Report of the Conference on the Nigerian Constitution*, London: Cmd. 8934, 1953).

TABLE 5.2 *Comparison of approved 1954/5 estimates of revenue allocation to the regions with the revised estimates of revenue allocation for the same year*

	Approved Estimates of Revenue Allocation, 1954/5 (Prepared under the 1951 Revenue Allocation System)			Revised Estimate of Revenue Allocation 1954/5 (Prepared under the Revenue Allocation System operating under the 1954 Constitution)		
	North	West ($£$'000)	East	North	West ($£$'000)	East
Tobacco duties	914	1,839	813	735	1,700	842
Motor spirit import duty	315	668	277	369	782	316
Import duties—other	—	—	—	1,253	1,671	1,212
Excise duties—beer	—	—	—	5	17	8
Export duties	—	—	—	1,035	2,784	510
Income tax	—	—	—	210	105	66
Mining rents and royalties	—	—	—	789	—	—
Capitation grant	2,118	652	764	1,060	362	382
Education grant	600	1,490	1,658	300	750	829
Police grant	555	678	574	293	337	290
Transferred service grant	—	200	—	—	58	—
	4,502	5,527	4,086	6,049	8,566	4,455

SOURCE: Federal and regional government's *Estimates*, 1954/5.

became operative on 1 October 1954 the estimates of revenue had to be recast to allow for revenue to be allocated during the remaining half of the year under the new system. As Table 5.2 shows, the revenue allocation for that year increased from £14·1 million to £19·1 million, even though the new system operated for only half the year. All the regions received additional revenue, fifty-four per cent going to the West, followed by thirty-four per cent and nine per cent to the North and East respectively. The result was that there was an increased revenue disparity among the regions as the following indexes show:

	North	West	East
Original revenue allocations, 1954-5 (North=100)	100	123	91
Revised allocations based on the new constitution for the second half of the year (North=100)	100	158	73

Since the new allocation system was so unfavourable to the East, the Commissioner recommended that constitutionally-prescribed grants of £500,000 and £250,000 be made to that region in the first two years of the operation of the new constitution, i.e. in 1954/5 and 1955/6.

One of the consequences of the replacement of *ad hoc* grants based on expenditure with statutory payments based on revenue and derivation was that the regional governments would share in the improvement in federal revenues resulting from development, or would bear part of the burden of a decline following a fall in the value of Nigeria's foreign trade. Regional finances thus became exposed to fluctuations in Nigeria's prosperity. The Commissioner recommended, however, that in case a regional government found itself in serious financial difficulty through causes beyond its control, the federal government should be empowered to make grants out of its own revenue and at its discretion.

Other recommendations of the Commissioner which are of interest include one on budgetary and accounting procedures (that the capital budget should be shown separately from the recurrent budget), and another on inter-governmental charges for services rendered and goods supplied. The Commissioner also recommended that the governments' imports should not be exempted from duties. Finally, he recommended that £7 million out of the total reserves of the federal government should be allocated to the regions in proportion of 3 : 2 : 2 for the North, West, and East respectively.

The Hicks-Phillipson Commission had advanced its proposals to 'serve as a financial basis for the common life of the regions of Nigeria for many years to come'. The Commission had believed that its plan was one which would accommodate itself to growth, and which would 'go on producing a fairer distribution than there is at present'. It attempted to advance a plan that would provide for a 'fair spreading of the general revenues of Nigeria over the three regions so as to keep these differences (in social and economic development) within reasonable bounds'.[1] The fiscal system set up in accordance with the Hicks-Phillipson Commission's recommendations broke down after a few months, however, and was completely replaced by a new and radically different system after two years: nevertheless, the ideas of the Commission still remain and have dominated all subsequent discussions on federal finance in Nigeria.

In contrast, the Chick Commission Plan was not intended to last longer than two years, since the 1953 and 1954 constitutional conferences had decided that a further review of the Constitution (and inevitably the fiscal system) should take place not later than August 1956. Given this understanding, therefore, and also the specific emphasis on regional fiscal autonomy and an allocation system based primarily on derivation, the Chick Fiscal Commission had proposed a temporary plan intended to meet a particular situation. While the Hicks-Phillipson Commission based its proposals on the premise that the three regions could equalise their wealth, the Chick Fiscal Commission accepted regional disparity and this disparity was further accentuated by the regionalisation of the marketing boards and the division of their reserves among the regions. It is appropriate now to examine the fiscal implications of regionalising the marketing boards before studying the impact of the new federal and budgetary system of 1955–9.

Fiscal implications of regionalising the marketing boards

Of greater fiscal significance than the allocation of tax revenue on the derivation principle was the decision of the 1953 Constitutional Conference to regionalise the marketing boards and divide their reserves between the regions. This decision, together with the new system of revenue allocation, gave the regions not only fiscal

Hicks-Phillipson Commission Report, p. 149.

autonomy, but also financial predominance over the federal government. In regard to inter-regional fiscal relationships, the regional control of the finances of the marketing boards accentuated regional disparity in financial resources.

The stabilisation activities of the marketing boards have been extensively discussed in economic literature,[1] but stabilisation has never constituted the sole responsibility of marketing boards, particularly the Nigerian ones. The preoccupation of economists with the stabilisation role of the marketing boards has led, until recently, to inadequate attention being given to their more important function of providing financial resources for economic development.[2]

One of the most important institutional developments affecting fiscal policy in Nigeria is the marketing arrangements for the country's exports. By the end of World War Two, three of the principal export products of Nigeria (cocoa, palm products, and groundnuts) had been subjected to statutory marketing by the West African Produce Control Board. Between 1946 (for cocoa) and 1949 (for other products) the activities of this board in Nigeria had been transferred to four Nigerian commodity boards—for cocoa, oil palm produce, groundnuts, and cotton.

The primary responsibility of the West African Produce Con-

---

[1] See especially P. T. Bauer, *West African Trade. A Study of Competition, Oligopoly and Monopoly in a Changing Economy* (London: Cambridge University Press, 1954, reissued with a new preface by Routledge and Kegan Paul, 1963); P. T. Bauer and F. W. Paish, 'The Reduction of Fluctuations in the Income of Primary Producers', *Economic Journal*, December 1952; Polly Hill, 'Fluctuations in Incomes of Primary Producers', *Economic Journal*, June 1953; P. Ady, 'Fluctuations in Incomes of Primary Producers: A Comment', *Economic Journal*, September 1953; Milton Friedman, 'The Fluctuations in Incomes of Primary Producers, a Critical Comment', *Economic Journal*, December 1954; B. M. Niculescu, 'Fluctuations in Incomes of Primary Producers, Further Comments', *Economic Journal*, December 1954; G. H. Helleiner, 'The Fiscal Role of the Marketing Boards in Nigerian Economic Development, 1947–1961', *Economic Journal*, September 1964; and 'Marketing Board and Domestic Stabilisation in Nigeria', *The Review of Economics and Statistics*, February 1966.

[2] G. H. Helleiner, loc. cit., p. 582.

E

trol Board was the maintenance of the West African cocoa industry
'at a time when the normal operations of the market would undoubtedly have ruined it'.[1] This is because it had become evident
to the British government that the 'merchant firms were unable,
in view of the uncertainty of disposal, to undertake the risk involved in purchasing the entire crops'.[2] The producer price
policy of the Board was decided not with reference to the price
which the Board realised from the sale of the products in the world
market, but with reference to what was considered sufficient to
maintain the industry and the producer prices considered sufficient
to maintain the world market prices. The objectives of the British
government as executed by the Board have been summarised by
Charlotte Leubuscher as giving the colonial governments a firmer
grip on the territories; enabling them to control purchasing power
and keep down inflation; and using the producer prices as an
instrument for encouraging or discouraging particular lines of
production.[3]

It is thus evident that price stabilisation was not the primary
objective of the British government during the war years when the
marketing of the produce was brought under control. The setting
up of the Nigerian Commodity Marketing Boards between 1946
and 1949 was preceded by a change of policy. These boards were
to act as agents or trustees for the producers. By fixing a steady
buying price in advance of the sale of each season's crop, the boards
would cut the link between the price of cocoa in West Africa and
the day-to-day price on the world market. Accordingly, in some
seasons when world prices were high, the prices paid to producers
were less than the average realised on overseas sales. The boards
would, on such occasions, show a 'surplus'. In other seasons world
prices would be below the prices paid to producers, and on these
occasions the boards would take a loss which would be financed

---

[1] *Report on Cocoa Control in West Africa, 1939–1943, and Statement on
Future Policy*, Cmd. 6554, 1944, p. 7, para. 25.
[2] ibid., p. 2, para. 3.
[3] Charlotte Leubuscher, *Bulk Buying from the Colonies* (London: Oxford
University Press, for Royal Institute of International Affairs, 1956),
p. 11.

from the surpluses accruing in years of high world prices.[1] But the boards were also empowered to allocate their funds for other purposes of general benefit to the cocoa producers and the industry, such as research, disease eradication and rehabilitation, the amelioration of indebtedness, the encouragement of cooperation, and the provision of other amenities and facilities to producers.[2]

The Nigerian Commodity Marketing Boards, accepting as their task the stabilisation of producer prices, followed a conservative price policy and allocated most of their annual surpluses to building up their reserves which were mostly invested abroad in British government and Commonwealth securities. Each of the boards, with the exception of the Cotton Marketing Board, adopted a common policy in allocating surplus funds among their three main objectives: seventy per cent was set aside for price stabilisation, 22·5 per cent for development purposes, and 7·5 per cent for research.

Thus, at the time that the 1953 Constitutional Conference placed the marketing boards under regional control, with their assets distributed on the basis of derivation, a sum of £75·5 million had been accumulated by all the boards. The resumed conference on the Nigerian Constitution held in Lagos in January and February of 1954 agreed to the regional distribution of the reserves as shown in Table 5.3.

Of the amount allocated to the Eastern Region, little was available for development purposes, since a sum of £12·5 million was to be treated as first-line reserves to be kept in liquid form for use in price stabilisation. On the other hand, the Western Region, which received most of the total reserves, needed to set aside only about one fifth as first-line reserve and could use the balance.

Not only did the distribution of the reserves of the marketing boards enhance the financial autonomy of the regions, but it widened even further the inter-regional disparity in financial resources. More important, the setting up of regional marketing

[1] *Statement of the Policy Proposed for the Future Marketing of Nigerian Oils, Oilseeds and Cotton*, Cmd. 6950, 1946, p. 8.
[2] ibid., p. 6, para. 15.

TABLE 5.3 *Regional distribution of marketing boards' reserves*

(£ million)

	Total Allocated by the Resumed Conference	Recommended Utilisation by the 1954 World Bank Mission	
		First-line Reserves	Second-line Working Capital
Northern Region	24·8	4·6	20·2
Western Region	34·4	7·6	26·8
Eastern Region	15·1	12·5	2·6
Southern Cameroons	1·2	0·4	0·8
Total	75·5	25·1	50·4

SOURCE: Report by the *Resumed Conference on the Nigerian Constitution*, 1954, p. 73.

boards in 1956 gave the regional governments a most important fiscal weapon. The regional boards have since become so closely integrated as to be veritable departments of the regional governments. The decisions as to producer prices, rates of produce sales tax, and the allocation of the boards' surpluses among loans, grants, and direct expenditure by the boards themselves, are, in effect, made by the regional governments.

Federal and regional finances, 1955–9

This section is concerned with the quantum of financial resources which became available to the federal and regional governments under the Chick Fiscal Commission's recommendations between 1955 and 1959. The problems posed by the operation of federal finance during these and subsequent years will be examined and discussed in further detail in chapters 7 and 8.

Table 5.4 shows the great change in federal-regional fiscal relationships during this period. The change is even more striking when the table is compared with Table 4.9. Whereas in 1951/2 and in 1952/3 regional revenue was only twenty-four per cent and

TABLE 5.4 *Federal and regional recurrent revenues, 1955–9*

(£ million)

Financial Year	Net Federal Government Revenue	Total Regional Government Revenue	Northern Region Government Revenue	Western Region Government Revenue	Eastern Region Government Revenue
1955/6	34·10	33·05	11·67	12·37	9·01
1956/7	41·52	40·24	13·60	14·77	11·87
1957/8	40·92	40·71	13·05	14·96	12·70
1958/9	45·22	44·24	15·03	15·90	13·31

SOURCE: *Annual Abstract of Statistics*, various years (Federal Office of Statistics, Lagos).

forty per cent of the central government revenue, under the 1954 fiscal system the federal and regional governments shared the total current revenue resources of Nigeria on about a fifty-fifty basis. The relative financial strength of the regions is demonstrated by Tables 5.5 through 5.7.

As we have already pointed out, the regionalisation of the marketing boards gave the regions tremendous fiscal powers. Not only were they given the power to fix producer prices and to impose produce sales tax but they could also use the reserves of the boards without restriction. The regions did not have to depend on conventional current revenue alone. These powers limited the export tax jurisdiction of the federal government and posed grave problems for Nigerian fiscal policy.

The Northern Region's total current revenue from 1955 to 1959 was £53·36 million. Its total current receipts, however, amounted to £65·20 million during the same period, the difference resulting from the transfer of resources from the marketing board (Table 5.5). About a tenth of the total recurrent and capital receipts in the North came from its marketing board.

The fiscal importance of the marketing board to the government of Western Nigeria is clear from Table 5.6. About a fifth of the region's total financial resources between 1955 and 1959 came from the Board. However, as far as the Eastern Region is con-

TABLE 5·5 *Northern regional finances, 1955–9*

(£ million)

Source	1955/6	1956/7	1957/8	1958/9	Total 1955–9	Percent- ages
1 Independent regional revenues	4·95	5·77	5·20	6·86	22·78	31·8
2 Statutory payments from federal government revenue	6·73	7·83	7·85	8·17	30·58	42·6
(a) TOTAL RECURRENT REVENUES	11·68	13·60	13·05	15·03	53·36	74·4
3 Marketing Boards' loans and grants	—	2·50	2·50	2·00	7·00	9·8
4 Transfer from Consolidated Revenue Fund	—	4·00	0·50	—	4·50	6·3
5 Others	—	0·03	0·01	0·30	0·34	0·5
(b) TOTAL RECURRENT AND CAPITAL RECEIPTS	11·68	20·13	16·06	17·33	65·20	91·0
6 Federal grants and loans	—	—	—	—	—	—
7 External grants and loans	2·08	1·70	1·27	1·34	6·39	8·9
(c) TOTAL REGIONAL REVENUES	13·76	21·83	17·33	18·67	71·59	100·0*

* Figures do not add up to 100 because of rounding.

SOURCES: *Annual Abstract of Statistics*, various years (Federal Office of Statistics, Lagos); *Official Gazettes*; and Federal and Regional Governments' *Estimates*, 1955–9.

TABLE 5.6 *Western regional finances, 1955–9*

(£ million)

Source	1955/6	1956/7	1957/8	1958/9	Total 1955–9	Percentages
1 Independent regional revenues	1·80	3·32	2·63	2·40	10·15	11·1
2 Statutory payments from federal government revenue	10·57	11·45	12·33	13·50	47·85	52·3
(a) TOTAL RECURRENT REVENUES	12·37	14·77	14·96	15·90	58·00	63·4
3 Marketing Boards' loans and grants	0·50	20·75	0·75	—	22·00	24·9
4 Transfer from Consolidated Revenue Fund	—	5·38	1·00	—	6·38	7·0
5 Others	—	0·52	0·33	0·85	1·70	1·8
(b) TOTAL RECURRENT AND CAPITAL RECEIPTS	12·87	41·42	17·04	16·75	88·08	97·1
6 Federal grants and loans	—	1·00	—	—	1·00	1·1
7 External grants and loans	1·51	—	0·02	0·05	1·58	1·7
(c) TOTAL REGIONAL FINANCES	14·38	42·42	17·06	16·80	90·66	100·0*

* Figures do not add up to 100 because of rounding.

SOURCES: *Annual Abstract of Statistics*, various years (Federal Office of Statistics, Lagos); *Western Nigeria Statistical Bulletin*, various years (Ministry of Economic Planning, Ibadan).

TABLE 5·7 *Eastern regional finances, 1955-9*

(£ million)

Source	1955/6	1956/7	1957/8	1958/9	Total 1955-9	Percentages
1 Independent regional revenues	2·23	4·87	5·51	5·65	18·26	37·4
2 Statutory payments from federal government revenue	5·77	6·90	7·08	7·42	27·17	55·7
(a) TOTAL RECURRENT REVENUE	8·00	11·77	12·59	13·07	45·43	93·1
3 Marketing Boards' loans and grants	0·11	0·10	0·11	0·12	0·44	0·9
4 Transfer from Consolidated Revenue Fund	—	—	0·27	—	0·27	0·6
5 Others	—	—	—	—	—	—
(b) TOTAL RECURRENT AND CAPITAL RECEIPTS	8·11	11·87	12·97	13·19	46·14	94·6
6 Federal grants and loans	0·90	—	—	0·12	1·02	2·1
7 External grants and loans	—	0·31	0·40	0·91	1·62	3·3
(c) TOTAL REGIONAL FINANCES	9·01	12·18	13·37	14·22	48·78	100·0

SOURCES: *Estimates of the Eastern Regional Government, 1955-9; Annual Abstract of Statistics*, various years (Federal Office of Statistics, Lagos).

cerned, the regionalisation of the marketing board did not confer appreciable financial benefits. Throughout the four fiscal years under examination, the Eastern Nigeria government received only £0·4 million from the Eastern Nigeria Marketing Board (Table 5.7). In fact, the government of that region was unable to balance its recurrent budget during the 1957/7 and 1957/8 fiscal years, and it was only able to do so in 1955/6 because of the grant of £0·9 million which the Chick Fiscal Commission recommended should be paid by the federal government.

Thus the new fiscal arrangement accentuated regional financial disparity (1) by making available to the regions part of the proceeds of the export tax on the derivation principle; (2) by transferring the control of marketing boards to the regional governments; and (3) by giving the regions half the revenue from import duties on all goods other than tobacco and motor spirit, the whole of the proceeds from import and excise duties on tobacco, and the import duties on motor spirit. While the Eastern Region was having difficulty in balancing its budget even on recurrent account, the Western Region and to some extent the Northern Region were generating surpluses on current account and were receiving substantial amounts from their marketing boards.

The total financial resources available (from all sources) to the Eastern and Northern regional governments were only fifty-three per cent and seventy-eight per cent of those available to the Western Region government from 1955/6 to 1958/9. The following comparison, in indices, of the average annual financial resources available to the regional governments during the fiscal years 1952–4 and 1955–9 shows this disparity most pointedly:

	1952–4 (Annual Average)	1955–9 (Annual Average)
Northern Region government	100	100
Western Region government	87	127
Eastern Region government	68	68

These indices also show the changes in the relative financial position of the regions. Whereas the East's relative position vis-à-vis the North remained the same during the two periods, the West's position changed dramatically.

An appraisal

The Hicks-Phillipson Commission had attempted to advance a fiscal plan which would be applicable for at least a generation. It tried, as stated in the report,

'to draw up a plan which will not only bring about a reasonable redistribution of revenues in the present, but which will serve as a financial basis for the common life of the regions for many years to come. . . . Nigeria with good sense, good management and good luck should be able to grow greatly in wealth and in civilisation even during the next twenty years and certainly during the next fifty but the growth will only be hampered if too much time has to be taken up by constitutional disputes. What we have tried to do is draw a financial plan which will accommodate itself to growth.'[1]

As it turned out, the Hicks-Phillipson plan was short-lived, though the ideas remained. On the other hand, the Chick Fiscal Commission was under no illusion about the permanence of its proposals. The plan was not intended to last for more than a few years; Sir Louis Chick, the sole commissioner, was all too conscious of the temporary nature of his plan.[2]

During the four financial years that Chick's system of revenue allocation was operative, all the regions became disenchanted with the derivation principle: the North with the way it was applied; the West with the fact that it did not go far enough in its application; while the East felt that it should not be applied at all.

The derivation principle, it will be recalled, applied in full to the import duty on motor spirit, to half the proceeds of the import duty on tobacco, to revenue from excise and export duties, and to revenue from all the other import duties. It was the allocation of

[1] Hicks-Phillipson Commission Report, p. 149.
[2] *Report by the Conference in the Nigerian Constitution* (Lagos: Government Printer, 1943), Cmd. 8934, p. 10. The conference agreed to a further review of the Constitution and the fiscal system not later than August 1956, although the review did not take place until May 1957.

the latter duties which caused a great deal of contention, the North and East arguing that these duties favoured the West at their expense. In deriving the formula for the allocation of revenue from the import duties other than tobacco and motor spirit, Sir Louis Chick had drawn upon the calculations made by Prest and Stewart in their study of the national income of Nigeria.[1] The regional breakdown of consumption expenditure on imported goods in 1950/1 had been as follows (in percentages):[2]

Northern Region	Western Region (including Lagos)	Eastern Region (including Southern Cameroons)
27·2	45·4	27·4

The Prest-Stewart calculations had to be altered by Chick in two respects: the former study had not considered tobacco and motor spirit duties separately, and the Lagos consumption of these items had been attributed to the Western Region. The following excerpts from Chick's report show how he adjusted these figures:[3]

'In considering to what extent they should be varied for the purpose of distributing the half import duties which I have recommended should go to the regional governments, it is necessary to bear in mind that, while revenue derived from Lagos is to be federal revenue the federal government's needs will be provided for by the distribution of revenue between the federal government and the regional governments. . . . Consequently, the revenue from those duties attributable to Lagos is available for distribution among the regional governments, including the western regional government. With these considerations in mind and having regard to the fact that no correction is proposed to be made in respect of the motor spirit and tobacco duties, I recommend that the regional governments' 50 per cent share of these import

[1] A. R. Prest and I. G. Stewart, op. cit., p. 63.
[2] Government imports and capital goods were excluded from this calculation, but customs duties and the cost of distributing the goods internally were included.
[3] *Chick Fiscal Commission Report*, pp. 11 and 12.

duties should be distributed in the proportions of 30 per cent to the
Northern Regional Government; 30 per cent to the Eastern
Regional Government; and 40 per cent to the Western Regional
Government.'

Thus, the Commission made a reduction of 5·4 per cent from
the West's share of other import duties to allow for the combined
Lagos elements in other import duties, motor spirit and tobacco
duties. Both the East and the North contended that this deduction
was not adequate, and that the West was therefore receiving more
than its fair share of revenue from other import duties.

A second criticism of the system of revenue allocation was that
the range of independent revenues given to the regions was still
considerably limited. As Table 5.1 indicates, the federal government retained its jurisdiction over all taxes other than those taxes
under the 1946 Constitution which were declared regional. What
had happened since 1952 was that the federal government had been
transferring an increasing proportion of its revenue to the regions,
but the power to tax and to vary the rates of taxes had remained
firmly in its hands. The regional governments found this extremely
irksome, since they had very little room for improving their
financial position by making an extra tax effort. They were, therefore, anxious to increase their tax powers.

The third criticism was the total disregard of the particular
needs of a region compared with its revenue-raising ability. This
is not a necessary result of the derivation principle itself, but of the
extent to which it was carried. The result was, as indicated in the
preceding section, a widening of the gap between the regions—the
West becoming increasingly better off, with the North and the
East, particularly the latter, having difficulties in carrying out their
development programmes. The need to redress the regional imbalance in the allocation of the financial resources was strongly
urged by both the East and the North.

Finally, one of the effects of the Chick Fiscal Commission's plan
was the greatly-increased dependence of the finances of the
regional governments on export trade. The Hicks-Phillipson
Fiscal Commission, on the grounds of stabilising regional finances,
had rejected the regionalisation of export taxes and the sharing of

the proceeds of the tax with the regional governments. Tables 5.8 to 5.10 show the degree of dependence of the regional governments on the export sector for revenue between 1955 and 1959.

In 1955/6, 21·8 per cent of the total finances of the Northern Region government came from the export sector, in the form of export duties, produce sales taxes, and marketing boards' loans and grants. Under the Hicks-Phillipson Commission's scheme, only six per cent of the government's revenue would have come from the export sector in the same year. Between 1955 and 1959, the dependence of the Northern Region government increased from 21·8 to 29·1 per cent.

The Western Region government was of course much more dependent on the export sector than was its Northern counterpart. Taxes on the export sector accounted for 30·6 per cent in 1955/6 and for fifty-eight per cent the following year. These shares fell to 25·5 per cent in 1957/8 and thirty per cent in 1958/9 (Table 5.9). The Eastern Region government depended much less on the taxes on the export sector although they were still quite important. Their proportionate share of the government's revenue averaged about 20·2 per cent per annum during the period (Table 5.10).

Thus a de-stabilising factor was built into the revenue structure of the regional governments. But the emphasis which was placed on the derivation principle as the basis of allocation of revenue did not allow an objective consideration of the problem which this built-in de-stabiliser would sooner or later pose to the regional governments' finances if and when a fall took place in the world prices for export produce. Unfortunately, the downward trend in the world prices for export produce began much sooner than had been anticipated, with serious consequences to the regional governments, particularly the government of the West.

TABLE 5.8 *Degree of dependence of regional finances on export produce: Northern Region, 1955–9*

(£ million)

Fiscal Year	(a) Total Regional Financial Resources	(b) Revenue from Export Duties	(c) Revenue from Produce Sales Taxes	(d) Marketing Boards' Grants and Loans	(e) Total Financial Resources Derived from Export Produce (2+3+4)	(f) Percentage Contribution of Export Produce to Total Regional Financial Resources: (e) as a percentage of (a)
1955/6	13·75	2·16	0·84	—	3·00	21·8
1956/7	19·83	2·37	0·54	2·50	5·41	27·2
1957/8	17·33	1·92	0·21	2·50	4·63	26·7
1958/9	18·40	2·30	1·21	2·00	5·51	29·1

SOURCES: Federal government's *Estimates*, 1955–9; and Northern Region *Official Gazette*, various years.

TABLE 5.9 *Degree of dependence of regional finances on export produce: Western Region, 1955–9*

(£ million)

Fiscal Year	(a) Total Regional Financial Resources	(b) Revenue from Export Duties	(c) Revenue from Produce Sales Taxes	(d) Marketing Boards' Grants and Loans	(e) Total Financial Resources Derived from Export Produce (2+3+4)	(f) Percentage Contribution of Export Produce to Total Regional Financial Resources: (e) as a percentage of (a)
1955/6	14·38	3·28	0·63	0·50	4·41	30·6
1956/7	42·42	2·84	0·82	20·75	24·41	58·0
1957/8	17·06	3·02	0·58	0·75	4·35	25·5
1958/9	17·55	4·15	0·36	0·75	5·26	30·0

SOURCES: Federal government's *Estimates*, 1955–9; and Western Region *Official Gazette*, various years.

TABLE 5.10 *Degree of dependence of regional finances on export produce: Eastern Region, 1955-9*

(£ million)

Fiscal Year	(a) Total Regional Financial Resources	(b) Revenue from Export Duties	(c) Revenue from Produce Sales Taxes	(d) Marketing Boards' Grants and Loans	(e) Total Financial Resources Derived from Export Produce $(2+3+4)$	(f) Percentage Contribution of Export Produce to Total Regional Financial Resources: (e) as a percentage of (a)
1955/6	9·01	1·08	1·04	0·11	2·23	24·7
1956/7	12·18	1·32	1·09	0·10	2·51	20·6
1957/8	13·37	1·24	1·14	0·11	2·49	18·6
1958/9	14·22	1·22	1·10	0·12	2·44	17·0

SOURCES: Federal government's *Estimates*, 1955-9; and Eastern Region *Official Gazette*, various years.

6 Operation of federal finance in Nigeria: second phase

A review of the fiscal system

The disenchantment of the regional governments with the derivation principle, the deficiencies in the application of the principle, particularly as it related to the allocation to the regions of their share of other import duties, and the convening of another constitutional conference in 1957 to review the 1954 Constitution made yet another review of the fiscal system in general and the system of revenue allocation in particular inevitable. One of the decisions of the 1957 Constitutional Conference, therefore, was the appointment of a fiscal commission whose terms of reference, *inter alia*, were:

'To examine the present division of powers to levy taxation in the Federation of Nigeria and the present system of allocation of the revenue thereby derived in the light of:

(i) experience of the system to date;

(ii) the allocation of functions between the governments in the federation as agreed at the present Conference;

(iii) the desirability of securing that the maximum possible proportion of the income of regional governments should be within the exclusive power of those governments to levy and collect, taking into account consideration of national and inter-regional policy;

(iv) in connection with (iii) above, the special problems in the field of indirect taxation as a result of the position of Lagos as federal territory;

(v) insofar as the independent revenues that can be secured for the various governments are insufficient to provide not only for their immediate needs but also for a reasonable degree of expansion, and bearing in mind the federal government's own further needs, the desirability of allocating further federal revenue in accordance with such arrangements as will best serve the overall interests of the federation as a whole.'[1]

The fact that the terms of reference of this Commission[2] were much broader than those of the 1953 Fiscal Commission is conclusive evidence of the disillusionment of the regions with the system of revenue allocation which had operated since October 1954. The Commission, in approaching the term of reference enjoining it to have regard to the 'desirability of securing that the maximum possible proportion of the income of regional governments should be within the exclusive power of those governments to levy and collect', examined the various existing taxes one by one in the light of the paramount need to ensure complete freedom of trade throughout the federation. It found after a most searching analysis that the federal government would have to retain its jurisdiction over import and export taxes and excise duties. The Commission also recommended that the basic jurisdiction to impose general sales taxes should be exclusively federal in the interest of unfettered inter-state trade. The only concession that it made was in respect of produce sales taxes imposed by the regions on the main export crops. The Commission concluded this part of its enquiry by admitting the fact:

'. . . that in Nigeria the major sources of revenue, namely, customs duties (with their complementary excise duties) and taxes on the profits of companies are federal and must inevitably remain federal in any system which recognises the basic realities of a federation. Our task therefore resolves itself into a search for other

---

[1] *Report by the Nigerian Constitutional Conference, 1957*, Cmd. 207, p. 28.
[2] The Commission, consisting of Sir Jeremy Raisman (Chairman) and Professor R. C. Tress (member), is popularly known as the Raisman Commission and will be referred to as such in this book. The Commission's report entitled *Report of the Fiscal Commission* (London: HMSO, 1958), Cmd. 481, will be referred to as the *Raisman Report*.

forms of taxation which can be placed within regional jurisdiction. Such taxes must be administratively practicable without trenching improperly on the federal field and without involving the erection of barriers to inter-regional trade or laying excessive burdens on persons who must live and work in more than one region. We have endeavoured to carry out this task to the best of our ability. The scope for the enlargement of regional jurisdiction may seem disappointingly small.'[1]

Therefore, the Commission had to devise other methods of securing regional autonomy in taxation. With respect to export taxes it recommended that the proceeds should be returned in full to the region of origin. This was a corollary to its recommendation that the regional governments should retain jurisdiction over sales taxes on export crops. Thus, a combination of produce sales taxes (regional jurisdiction), export duties (federal jurisdiction), and regional control of the marketing boards would ensure more than ever before that the regional governments would derive the full benefit from export production within their regions. Although they could not vary the rates of export taxes, they would have complete autonomy in fixing the rates of the produce sales taxes and in deciding what resources the marketing boards should make available to them. Thus, the regional governments would be decisive in fixing producer prices.

The Commission also attempted to meet the requirement of regional fiscal autonomy by recommending regional jurisdiction over sales taxes on motor vehicle fuel. The Eastern Region had, since 1 April 1956, imposed a purchase tax on certain scheduled commodities, including motor vehicle fuel. Since the proceeds of the import duty on motor spirit were, under the Chick system, already being allocated to the regions on the basis of consumption, the granting of jurisdiction to impose sales taxes on motor vehicle fuel would make it possible for each regional government to determine the total tax burden to be borne by the users of motor vehicles in its region.

Thirdly, the Commission rejected the substitution of regional sales taxes for federally-imposed import duties on manufactured

[1] *Raisman Report*, p. 8.

and unmanufactured tobacco and excise duties on tobacco products manufactured in the country. It recommended, instead, that only the proceeds of both import and excise duties should be distributed in full among the regional governments; the federal government would receive the share attributable to consumption in Lagos.

But it is with respect to its recommendation on personal income tax jurisdiction that the Commission made one of the most fundamental changes in the fiscal system of Nigeria. The Hicks-Phillipson Commission had argued very strongly against regional jurisdiction over personal income taxation. After noting that it has been the almost universal experience of all federations for personal income taxation to come, sooner or later, under federal government jurisdiction, the Hicks-Phillipson Commission had argued that on equity, economic, and political grounds it was in the over-riding national interest for jurisdiction over personal income tax to be in the hands of the federal government. The Commission had stated the case as follows:

'A highly progressive income tax is in principle too powerful a fiscal weapon to be wielded by any authority save one which can use it with the maximum degree of responsibility . . . income taxes have deeper implications for policy, both economic and other, than most other taxes have. Their control should therefore rest in that place where these implications can most readily be taken into account.'[1]

The Chick Fiscal Commission had endorsed these views and had recommended a continuation of federal jurisdiction over the personal income tax assessed under the Income Tax Ordinance. However, the proposal of the Hicks-Phillipson Commission for integrating the direct tax system (the fiscal tool of Lugard's system of indirect rule) with the personal income tax system, although accepted in principle, was never implemented, and in 1956 the Eastern Region government imposed an income tax on all Africans in its region. The Western Region followed suit in 1957. Thus, by the time of the Raisman Commission that same year, income tax jurisdiction over Africans outside of Lagos was regional, and revenue from the income tax on non-Africans collected by the

[1] *Hicks-Phillipson Commission Report*, p. 127.

federal government was distributed among the regions on the basis of derivation.

In view of its desire to enlarge as much as possible the fiscal autonomy of the regions, it is not surprising that the Raisman Commission recommended complete regional jurisdiction (African and non-African) over the personal income tax. To support this recommendation, the Commission advanced four reasons: (1) the long tradition of regional jurisdiction over the personal tax levied on Africans; (2) the dependence of native authorities in the North and local government councils in the East and West on revenues from the direct tax; (3) the fact that the regional income tax laws were already in operation in both the East and the West, and that valuable experience had been gained; and (4) that a Nigeria-wide personal income tax system would need an extensive inspectorate which would be beyond the administrative resources of the federal government. The Commission then concluded that regional jurisdiction of personal taxation

'. . . would leave to the regions control of an expanding source of revenue which their local knowledge and the experience already gained would help them to exploit. It would make the best use of the administrative resources available and avoid posing the federal government with difficult staffing problems. Finally, as an instrument of economic control personal income tax carries little weight in the present state of Nigerian development.'[1]

To prevent double taxation from arising, and to ensure uniformity in treatment, the Commission recommended the enactment of an Income Tax Management Act. It also drew attention to the desirability of keeping differences in tax rates and allowances among regions (including Lagos) to a minimum. It further suggested that a region could invite the federal government to exercise over-all jurisdiction in this field within the region's territory if it so wished.

The problem which this change in jurisdiction over the personal income tax has posed is discussed at some length in chapter 8. It is sufficient to note here that the Raisman Fiscal Commission under-estimated the difficulties which the practical application of

[1] *Raisman Report*, p. 19.

regional jurisdiction over personal income tax would face, and tended to exaggerate the problems of leaving it with the federal government. One is tempted to think that the Commission was forced to this situation because, in accordance with its terms of reference, it had to increase the tax jurisdiction of the regional governments as distinct from merely increasing their revenues. After having refused to transfer to regional control customs duties, general sales taxes, excise duties, the company tax, and the taxation of mining and minerals, the Commission found itself unable to deny the regions their jurisdiction over the personal income tax.

One of the noted defects in the 1954 fiscal system was the practical difficulties of applying the derivation principle as far as revenue from 'other' import duties was concerned. Another defect had been the disregard for each region's need in relation to its revenue resources, and the disparity in the rates of development which this had brought about. It is in its solution to these two problems that the Raisman Commission made its most important contribution to Nigeria's federal system of finance.

To avoid a revenue allocation system that depended too much on derivation, and to establish at the same time a system capable of taking into account the differing needs of the regions was the goal of the Commission's Distributable Pool Account, into which would be paid thirty per cent of the revenue from mining rents and royalties and thirty per cent of the revenue from other import duties. The funds in this account would then be allocated on the basis of a formula developed by the Commission using criteria entirely different from the derivation principle.

Under the 1954 fiscal arrangement, revenue from mining rents and royalties had been allocated on the basis of derivation. At that time all royalties were derived from tin and columbite, which were extracted from the Northern Region. But by 1957, when the Raisman Commission was making its enquiries, the prospects of Nigeria becoming a petroleum-producing country had greatly increased. Test production for petroleum had begun in the East, and oil exploration had started in both the North and West.

In view of the uncertainty which still surrounded the production of oil in commercial quantities, the Commission did not think that the region in which oil was found should alone bear all the risk. On the other hand, should oil production result in any one region on a commercial basis, the balance of national development would be upset. Accordingly, the Commission recommended that:

'. . . the government in whose region oil royalties originate should clearly have a significant share in them. Secondly, the federal government ought also to have a share. Besides being responsible for mineral policy, it is likely to be involved in the financing of heavy expenditure in connection with the oil industry. . . . In the interests of balanced development between the regions, we consider it to be essential that, wherever oil royalties may arise, all the regions should have some share.'[1]

Revenue from mining rents and royalties was then to be allocated between the regional government in whose area the mineral or mineral oil existed, the federal government, and the distributable pool in ratios of fifty, twenty, and thirty per cent respectively.

A ratio of seventy per cent to the federal government and thirty per cent to the Distributable Pool Account was recommended for all revenue from import duties other than duties on tobacco, motor spirits (including diesel oil), beer, wines, and potable spirits which the Commission had recommended should be retained in full by the federal government. This 70 : 30 percentage allocation was based on the need to strengthen the finances of the federal government and to provide the regions with another expanding source of revenue. But more important, it was regarded by the Commission as a system devised for allocating federal revenues to the regional governments which would best serve the over-all interests of the federation. This change in the use of the general import duties needs to be noted carefully. 'We would emphasise here,' the Commission wrote, 'that this use of the general import duties is quite distinct from the use made of other import duties in the existing system. The latter was intended to be deployed as a further application of the principle of derivation. Our own principles for the allocation of general import revenue involve a departure from derivation.'

This departure from the derivation principle is even more pro-

[1] ibid., p. 25.

nounced in regard to the formula for allocating the funds in the Distributable Pool Account. The four factors taken into account by the Commission in arriving at the formula were, first, the preservation of *continuity* in government services; second, the *minimum responsibilities* which a government has to meet by virtue of its status as a government; third, *population* as a broad indicator of need, since this determines the scale of the services which each government has to provide; and fourth, the *balanced development* of the federation. On the basis of these criteria, the Commission 'arrived at the following percentages as representing an equitable sharing of the Distributable Pool Account for the immediate years ahead':

	Per cent
Northern Region	40
Western Region	24
Eastern Region	31
Southern Cameroons	5
	100

The Raisman Plan formed the fiscal system of Nigeria from 1 April 1959 until 1 April 1966, when the recommendations of the 1964 Fiscal Review Commission became operative. Between 1959 and 1966 there were only two modifications. In 1961, when the Southern Cameroons opted out of the federation, the funds in the Pool were allocated among the regions according to the following fractions:

Northern Region	*Western Region*	*Eastern Region*
40/95ths	24/95ths	31/95ths

This was because the regions could not agree on a basis for sharing the five per cent which became available after the departure of the Southern Cameroons.

The second modification in the fiscal system took place with effect from 9 August 1963, when a new region—the Mid-West—was created from the Western Region. The West's share in the Pool was divided between it and the new region in the ratio of 3 : 1.

In many respects the Raisman proposals were closer to the Hicks-Phillipson scheme than to the Chick Plan. In fact the four cardinal principles of federal finance enunciated by the Hicks-Phillipson Commission and discarded by the Chick Commission were reinstated by the Raisman Commission. The restoration may not have gone as far as the Hicks-Phillipson Commission would have liked, but given the political, social, and economic changes which had taken place between 1951, when the Hicks-Phillipson Commission sat, and 1958, when the Raisman Commission reported, the restoration of the principles of need and of national interest through the Distributable Pool was no mean achievement.

The only limitation lies in the formula for allocating the funds in the Pool. Of the four factors listed, only the population criterion was quantifiable. Since the Commission could not quantify each of the criteria it was content only to discuss them in a broad general manner. It is apparent that its formula was not objective. As will be explained later, this formula posed a number of important problems in inter-governmental fiscal relations at the regional level.

Within the country's fiscal system, there is provision for periodical reviews, particularly of the composition and allocation of the Distributable Pool. The first fiscal review commission was appointed in 1964. Its recommendations became operative in the 1966/7 fiscal year. This commission and its report will be discussed in the chapter on fiscal adjustment in Nigeria. (Appendix C to this study summarises in broad outline the main changes which have taken place in Nigeria's fiscal system since 1914.)

Federal and regional finances, 1959–66

The recommendations of the Raisman Fiscal Commission became operative with effect from the 1959/60 financial year and lasted until 1965/6 without any substantial changes. Tables 6.2 to 6.7 provide data on the finances of the federal and regional governments during this period.

The Raisman Fiscal Commission made some revenue projections for the years 1959/60 to 1961/2, reproduced in Table 6.4,

TABLE 6.1 *Federal and regional recurrent revenues : the Raisman projections, 1959–62*

(£ million)

Financial Year	Federal Government	Total Regional Government Revenues	Northern Region	Western Region	Eastern Region
1959/60	41·43	42·90	15·22	15·01	12·67
1960/1	43·58	45·02	15·95	15·73	13·34
1961/2	45·62	46·73	16·51	16·24	13·98

SOURCE: *Report of the Fiscal Commission*, Cmd. 481, Appendix F, p. 66.

which proved to be very conservative. The Commission projected that the total recurrent revenues available to the regional governments during this three-year period would be higher than those of the federal government during the same period. It also projected that the North would have slightly more revenue than the West, and that both regions would each have more revenue than the East. Table 6.2 indicates, however, that the revenues of all the governments increased much faster than had been anticipated. Between 1959/60 and 1961/2 the federal government's revenues increased by thirty-one per cent, while the revenues of the governments of the North, West, and East increased by twenty-six, twenty-one, and twenty-nine per cent respectively. The Commission had projected that the federal government's revenue would increase by ten per cent, while those of the Northern, Western and Eastern governments would rise by eight, eight, and ten per cent respectively during the period. Thus, not only did the revenues of all the governments increase faster in absolute terms than was projected by the Commission, but also their rates of growth were higher than estimated.

Between 1962 and 1966, the rates of growth in the revenues of all the governments except the West, both in absolute and relative terms, were even greater than in the preceding three years. The revenues of the federal government increased by forty-three per

TABLE 6.2 *Federal and regional recurrent revenues, 1959–66*

(£ million)

Financial Year	Net Federal Government Revenues	Total Regional Government Revenues	Northern Region Revenues	Western Region Revenues	Eastern Region Revenues	Mid-West Region Revenues
1959/60	50·24	50·95	17·52	18·68	14·75	—
1960/1	70·09	55·03	17·66	20·55	16·82	—
1961/2	65·76	65·14	22·80	23·92	19·08	—
1962/3	66·86	68·94	22·80	24·45	21·69	—
1963/4	75·57	70·66	25·31	19·40	22·18	3·77
1964/5	85·83	89·28	33·46	20·87	26·71	8·24
1965/6	94·30	94·88	32·59	22·39	29·97	9·93

SOURCE: Federal and Regional Governments' *Estimates* and *Official Gazettes*, various years.

cent. Those of the Northern government increased by forty-seven per cent, the Eastern government's increased by fifty-seven per cent. Only the revenue of the West fell, by seven per cent. Figure 3, supplemental to Figure 2, graphically shows this trend in the rates of growth. It also shows that the revenues of all the governments except those of the West have increased faster than the country's GDP.

The two principal factors responsible for these high growth rates in public revenue were the substantial increase in import tariffs imposed during the period and the very rapid development of the oil industry in Nigeria since 1959. One of the reasons given by the Raisman Fiscal Commission for recommending that the rents and royalties on minerals and mineral oil should not be allocated entirely on the basis of derivation was the uncertainty which then surrounded the prospects of producing oil on a commercial basis. But from 1958 to 1966 Nigeria became an important oil-producing country, increasing its tonnage from 229,000 to 20·668 million tons. The fiscal effect of this very rapid growth in oil production was a substantial increase in the revenues available to all the governments, particularly that of the principal oil producing region—the East.

Other financial resources available to all the governments increased during these years. There were loans and grants from the regional marketing boards, transfers from the consolidated revenue fund, grants and loans from the federal government, and external grants and loans. Tables 6.3 to 6.6 show the total finances available to each of the regional governments from 1959/60 to 1965/6. All regions show increases: the total financial resources of the Northern Region increased from £22·96 million in 1959/60 to £41·66 million in 1965/6 (Table 6.3); the Western Region from £22·68 million to £29·82 million (Table 6.4); the Eastern Region increased from £21·07 million to £38·61 million in the same period (Table 6.5); and the Mid-West, too, increased its resources from £3·77 million to £13·46 million between 1963 and 1966 (Table 6.6).

A comparison of Tables 6.3 to 6.5 with Tables 5.5 to 5.7 reveals the significant changes which have taken place in the financial structure of the governments. Three quarters of the total financial

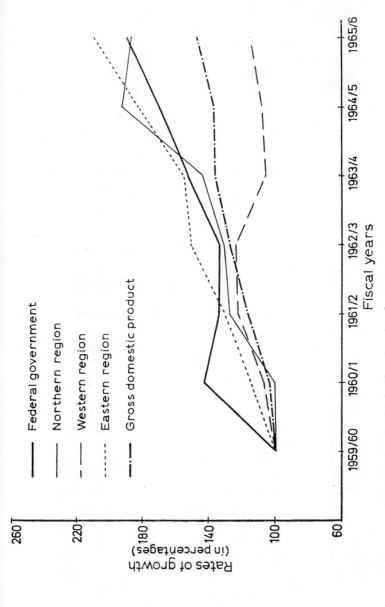

FIGURE 3 *Rates of growth of federal and regional revenues,*
1959–66

TABLE 6.3 *Northern Region finances, 1959–66*

(£ million)

Source	1959/60	1960/1	1961/2	1962/3	1963/4	1964/5	1965/6	Total 1959–66	Per-centages
1 Independent regional revenue	5·62	4·45	5·89	6·81	7·44	8·83	8·71	47·75	20·8
2 Statutory payments from federal government revenue	8·25	7·94	9·76	9·34	11·22	14·72	14·34	75·57	33·0
3 Grants from **distributable** pool	3·65	5·27	6·49	6·65	6·65	9·91	9·54	48·16	21·0
(A) TOTAL RECURRENT REVENUE	17·52	17·66	22·14	22·80	25·31	33·46	32·59	171·48	74·8
4 Marketing board loans and grants	1·00	—	—	—	—	—	—	1·00	0·4
5 Transfer from consolidated revenue fund	1·00	1·50	5·00	3·70	2·13	4·65	7·50	25·48	11·1
6 Others	0·03	0·20	0·36	0·58	0·28	0·75	—	2·20	1·0
(B) TOTAL RECURRENT AND CAPITAL RECEIPTS	19·55	19·36	27·50	27·08	27·72	38·86	40·09	200·16	87·3
7 Federal grants and loans	1·77	6·59	—	3·00	3·67	4·00	1·43	20·46	8·9
8 External grants and loans	1·64	1·64	2·28	0·59	0·15	1·90	0·14	8·34	3·8
(C) TOTAL RECURRENT FINANCES	22·96	27·59	29·78	30·67	31·54	44·76	41·66	228·96	100·0

SOURCES: Northern Nigeria, *Estimates*, various years; Northern Nigeria, *Official Gazette*, various years.

TABLE 6.4 *Western Region finances, 1959–66*

(£ million)

Source	1959/60	1960/1	1961/2	1962/3	1963/4	1964/5	1965/6	Total 1959–66	Percentages
1 Independent regional revenue	4·44	4·55	7·43	7·51	6·30	6·17	7·93	44·45	19·5
2 Statutory payments from federal government revenue	12·05	12·84	13·23	12·95	9·77	10·08	9·83	80·58	35·6
3 Grants from distributable pool	2·19	3·16	3·26	3·99	3·33	4·62	4·63	23·88	11·5
(A) TOTAL RECURRENT REVENUE	18·68	20·55	23·92	24·45	19·40	20·87	22·39	148·91	66·6
4 Marketing board loans and grants	1·00	12·88	4·83 (Dr)	8·36(b)	—	—	1·00	20·22	12·4
5 Transfer from consolidated revenue fund	3·00	—	1·50	4·50	1·90	2·66	0·70	9·70	4·7
6 Others	—	—	3·10(a)	1·03	0·90	0·73	1·36	9·70	4·7
(B) TOTAL RECURRENT AND CAPITAL RECEIPTS	22·68	33·43	23·69	38·34	22·20	24·26	25·45	188·53	88·4
7 Federal grants and loans	—	—	3·12	6·59	5·17	6·24	2·72	21·17	8·1
8 External grants and loans	—	0·27	0·66	—	—	0·45	1·65	3·47	4·5
(C) TOTAL REGIONAL FINANCES	22·68	33·70	26·81	45·59	27·37	30·95	29·82	213·17	100·0*

NOTES: (a) Includes transfers from Revenue Equalisation fund of £3m.
(b) Includes securities worth £6·36m. assigned to the government by the Board.
* Figures do not add up to 100 because of rounding.

SOURCES: Western Nigeria *Estimates*, various years; Western Nigeria *Official Gazette*, various years.

TABLE 6.5 *Eastern Region finances, 1959–66*

(£ million)

Source	1959/60	1960/1	1961/2	1962/3	1963/4	1964/5	1965/6	Total 1959–66	Percentages 1959–66
1 Independent regional revenue	5·68	6·57	7·78	7·66	8·40	8·95	10·24	55·33	26·7
2 Statutory payment from federal government revenue	6·24	6·16	6·83	8·88	8·64	10·09	12·29	66·52	32·0
3 Grants from distributable pool	2·83	4·09	4·47	5·15	5·14	7·67	7·39	29·35	14·1
(A) TOTAL RECURRENT REVENUE	14·75	16·82	19·08	21·69	22·18	26·71	29·92	151·20	72·8
4 Marketing board loans and grants	—	—	4·00	2·00	3·00	2·00	2·00	13·00	6·3
5 Transfer from consolidated revenue fund	4·18	—	—	4·00	2·00	3·00	2·00	15·18	7·3
6 Others	0·46	—	—	1·80	0·19	0·38	0·31	3·14	1·5
(B) TOTAL RECURRENT AND CAPITAL RECEIPTS	19·39	16·82	23·08	29·49	27·37	32·09	34·23	182·52	87·9
7 Federal grants and loans	0·59	—	2·80	2·00	3·00	2·50	2·84	13·73	6·6
8 External grants and loans	1·09	1·72	0·18	0·60	3·60	2·64	1·54	11·37	5·5
(C) TOTAL REGIONAL FINANCES	21·07	18·54	26·06	32·09	33·97	37·23	38·61	207·62	100·0

SOURCE: Regional *Estimates* and *Gazettes*.

TABLE 6.6 *Mid-Western Region finances, 1963–6*

(£ million)

Source	1963/4[a]	1964/5	1965/6	Total 1963–6	Percentages
1 Independent regional revenue	0·63	1·87	1·68	4·18	14·9
2 Statutory payments from federal government revenue	2·48	4·24	4·38	11·10	39·4
3 Grants from distributable pool	0·66	2·13	3·87	6·66	23·7
(A) TOTAL RECURRENT REVENUE	3·77	8·24	9·93	21·94	78·0
4 Marketing board loans and grants	—	0·20	0·05	0·25	0·9
5 Transfer from consolidated revenue fund	—	—	1·30	1·30	4·6
6 Others	—	—	—	—	—
(B) TOTAL RECURRENT AND CAPITAL RECEIPTS	3·77	8·44	11·28	23·49	83·5
7 Federal grants and loans	—	2·50	0·15	3·65	9·1
8 External grants and loans	—	—	2·03[b]	2·03	7·2
(C) TOTAL REGIONAL FINANCES	3·77	10·94	13·46	29·17	100·0*

NOTES: (a) From 9 August 1963 when the new region was created to 31 March 1964.
(b) Of which £1·96 million are loans arising out of contractor finance agreements.
* Figures do not add up to 100 because of rounding.

SOURCES: Mid-Western Nigeria *Estimates*, various years; Mid-Western Nigeria *Official Gazette*, various weeks.

resources of the government of the North were derived from re-current revenue, both in 1955–9 and in 1959–66. But only 0·4 per cent was received by this government from the region's marketing board as against 9·8 per cent between 1959 and 1966. Throughout this second phase of federal finance, the Northern Region govern-ment depended substantially on internal and external loans and grants, accounting for 12·7 per cent on its total resources.

In the Western Region, 67·7 per cent of the government's total financial resources was derived from recurrent revenue (Table 6·4). This is 4·3 per cent more than in the previous period of 1955 to 1959. Marketing board loans and grants, which had contributed about a quarter of total revenues between 1955 and 1959, con-tributed only 12·4 per cent of the revenues of the region in the period from 1959 to 1966. During the earlier period, loans and grants played a very insignificant role in the revenues of the West (2·8 per cent), but in the second period they contributed 11·8 per cent of the region's revenue.

The Eastern Region was less dependent on recurrent revenue between 1959 and 1966 than it had been between 1955 and 1959—72·8 per cent as compared to 93·1 per cent. The Marketing Board contributed substantially more resources during the second period than it was able to do during the first—6·3 per cent as compared to 0·9 per cent. And like the other two regions, the East also increased its dependence on external and internal loans. These rose from 5·4 per cent of total receipts in 1955–9 to 12·1 per cent in 1959–66.

Between 1963 and 1966, the government of the Mid-West derived seventy-eight per cent of its total financial resources from recurrent revenue (Table 6.6). The government of that region has received much less revenue from its marketing board than the other regional governments. This is not surprising, because the marketing board of the new region was not yet in a position to provide the government with grants and loans on a scale compar-able to those of the other regional marketing boards. The Mid-West also depended more on internal and external loans and grants than the other regional governments: loans and grants constituted 16·3 per cent of its total financial resources.

Perhaps the most significant feature of the revenues of the

regional governments during the 1959–66 period is the reduction
in the disparity in regional revenues, as the following indices show:

	Average Annual Financial Resources, 1952–4	Average Annual Financial Resources, 1955–9	Average Annual Financial Resources, 1959–66
Northern Nigeria	100	100	100
Western Nigeria	87	127	99
Eastern Nigeria	68	68	95

This change in the relative position of the regions is remarkable.
The East had improved its relative position, while the West had
lost a large part of its advantage. This was one of the objectives of
the Raisman Fiscal Commission, as the following excerpts from
its report shows:

'. . . it will be seen that our scheme may be expected to provide
increasing revenues in each year for all the Regions save the West.
There is a case for some check in the rate of the expansion of
government services in the West in view of the favourable treatment which the Western Region has enjoyed under the present
allocation system.'[1]

What the Commission had hoped would be merely a temporary
check turned out in reality to be a penalisation of the West. The
abrupt fall in the world price of cocoa during the period adversely
affected the region's finances. The creation of the Mid-West region
at a time when oil began to be produced in commercial quantities
in that area also resulted in the loss of a potentially important
source of revenue. The finances of the region's government became strikingly unstable. Total financial resources that had increased from £22·68 million in 1959/60 to £45·59 million in
1962/3, fell to £27·37 million in the following year. They increased
to £30·95 million in 1964/5, but fell again to £29·82 million in
1965/6.

---

[1] ibid., pp. 32–3.

Federal finance and public expenditure

The problem of federal finance in Nigeria has so far been examined from the point of view of resources; that is, the allocation of tax jurisdiction and the inter-governmental distribution of revenue. Before embarking on a detailed analysis of the specific problems which have arisen as a result of the allocation of the jurisdiction over each tax and the sharing of revenues, the impact of federal finance on public expenditures will be examined briefly in this section.

The two most important factors in determining the level and pattern of public expenditures of each government in a federation are the availability of financial resources and the distribution of functions. Ideally, the functions to be performed by each level of government should either correspond to the tax resources allocated to it or vice versa. In practice, this has not been the case with any of the existing federations of the world. As we saw in chapter 1, there is invariably little correspondence between the assignment of different responsibilities and duties to the federal and regional authorities and their financial resources. More often than not the tax resources sooner or later become inadequate to finance their assigned duties. This asymmetry between functions and resources often leads the lower level of government to transfer some of its functions to the federal government, to borrow to a self-defeating level, to accept financial assistance from the federal government, or, less frequently, to raise taxes to such a level that they begin to have a disincentive effect on output, saving, and investment.

In the light of the experience of the older federations, it is difficult to argue that there are firm guiding principles for the allocation and assignment of governmental responsibilities among the various levels of government in a federation. The criteria of efficiency and economy in the allocation of functions seem always to have been subordinated to political considerations. Yet it is possible to discern some guidelines from experience. First, one of the main reasons for a federation is that the federating units wish to take advantage of economies of scale. Certain functions can be provided more efficiently by the federal government than by the unit governments. The most important of these are national defence, external borrowing, banking and currency, coinage and legal tender, exchange control, and immigration and emigration.

Secondly, there are functions which are more local than national in nature, and which can therefore be more efficiently provided by lower levels of government. The principal ones in this category are services related to agriculture, forestry, fisheries, town and country planning, local government, and public health and sanitation. Yet the benefits of providing some of these services by one state government may extend beyond its borders to the neighbouring states. The existence of benefit spill-overs indicates that the well-being of one community depends to some extent on the public goods provided by its neighbours. In order to ensure that goods or services which have spill-over effects are not provided at less than a level of social optimum, the federal government may direct responsibility for the provision of such goods or services.

Appendix B of this study traces the changes which have taken place in the allocation of functions in Nigeria since 1951, when the constitution was quasi-federal. At that time the regional legislatures were empowered to make laws pertaining to matters enumerated under the second criterion noted above. They also constituted services with spill-over effects. All the other functions not enumerated in the constitution came within the exclusive jurisdiction of the central government.

Since 1954, the residual powers have been vested in the regions, and the exclusive powers of the federal legislature have been enumerated. Almost all of these functions falling within the exclusive federal legislative list are those which come under the first guideline noted above, i.e., functions better provided centrally than regionally because of advantages of economies of scale. In addition there are a number of functions over which both the federal and the regional authorities have concurrent legislative powers. Most of these can be expected to have spill-over effects, and therefore may require central control or arbitration. It should be pointed out that the functions in the exclusive federal list in Nigeria are not substantially different from those in the federal legislative lists of other federations (e.g., USA and Australia) where residual powers lie with the unit governments.

It will be seen from the allocation of functions between the federation and the regions in Nigeria that the governments of the regions are charged with the responsibility of providing social services and of developing agriculture and industry. Thus the responsibility for promoting economic and social development rests with the regions.

Consideration will now be given to the pattern of public expenditures in Nigeria in the light of these considerations. The recurrent expenditures of the federal and regional governments have risen considerably since 1946. Between 1955 and 1966, they rose over 250 per cent (at current prices). The federal government expenditures trebled while the expenditures of the East increased fourfold during the same period. The expenditures of both the North and the West (including the Mid-West) have doubled (see Table 6.7). Between 1950/1 and 1961/2, public expenditures rose from five per cent to about twelve per cent of the GDP. But the public expenditures of the governments of the federation have grown at different rates during this period. Figure 4 shows graphically the rates of growth of recurrent public expenditures of each government of the federation between 1959 and 1966.

The increases in expenditures have of course been made possible by corresponding increases in revenues. But since 1959/60, expenditures have tended to rise faster than revenues and the GDP (Figure 2). Whereas revenues have increased by an average of 9·3 per cent per annum, expenditures have grown at an annual rate of about 12·7 per cent since 1959/60. The fastest-rising element of expenditures has been the internal and external public debt servicing. The next largest absolute increase has been for education. Expenditures on health services, police, security forces, and general administration have also shown major increases.

There are differences in the patterns of expenditure of the federal and regional governments. These are due partly to differences in functions and partly to differences in policies. Responsibility for defence and security belongs exclusively to the federal government, while the regional governments are primarily res-

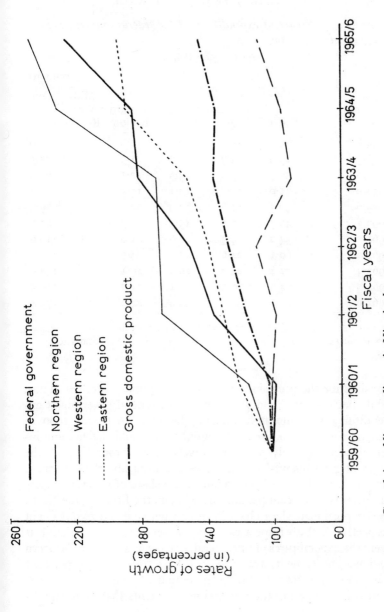

FIGURE 4 *Growth in public expenditures in Nigeria, by governments, 1959–66*

Legend:
- Federal government
- Northern region
- Western region
- Eastern region
- Gross domestic product

Rates of growth (in percentages)

Fiscal years: 1959/60, 1960/1, 1961/2, 1962/3, 1963/4, 1964/5, 1965/6

TABLE 6.7 *Recurrent expenditures of the federal and regional governments, 1955–66*

(at Current Prices)

(£ million)

Financial Year	Federal	Northern Region	Eastern Region	Western Region	Mid-West Region	Total All Govt's
1955/6	29·2	14·9	6·7	12·8	—	63·6
1956/7	25·9	15·7	12·6	11·3	—	65·5
1957/8	30·5	13·5	13·5	12·1	—	69·6
1958/9	35·0	12·8	12·1	13·5	—	73·4
1959/60	40·3	14·6	12·9	22·1	—	89·9
1960/1	40·7	17·0	15·3	22·6	—	95·6
1961/2	54·2	24·3	16·8	21·6	—	116·9
1962/3	60·1	24·6	17·9	24·9	—	127·5
1963/4	72·4	24·7	19·3	19·1	3·4	138·9
1964/5	74·7	30·0	24·1	21·0	6·7	156·5
1965/6	82·6	35·9	24·9	24·2	7·8	175·4

SOURCES: *Annual Abstract of Statistics*, various years; and *Economic Indicators*, various quarters (Federal Office of Statistics, Lagos).

ponsible for the provision of social and economic services. Thus, while between 37·2 and 47·7 per cent of federal government expenditures was allocated annually between 1959 and 1966 to general services, i.e., general administration and defence and internal security, only a comparatively small proportion of the regional governments' expenditures has been absorbed by these activities. In the West the proportionate share of general services has been 15·5 per cent per annum, while in the East and the North the proportionate shares have been 12·7 per cent and 26·9 per cent respectively. With respect to economic services, little variation is seen: the expenditures of the federal, northern, western and eastern regional governments averaged 10·3, 15·4, 16·0, and 7·7 per cent per annum respectively during the period.

It is in comparing the regional governments that more significant differences in the patterns of expenditure can be found. In both the Eastern and Western regions, social services (principally education and health) account for forty to fifty per cent of total expenditures. In the North, they account for about one third of total public expenditures (the federal government's expenditures averaged only 13·4 per cent during this period). Not only are the Eastern and the Western regions more socially advanced than the North, but they have been devoting over two fifths of their annual budgets to education. Since 1955, primary education has been free in the Western region and to a large extent in the Eastern as well.

In addition to both governments devoting a higher proportion of their budgetary resources to education than the North, they have also spent more on a per capita basis. For example, per capita recurrent expenditures on education in 1964/5 in Northern Nigeria was only thirty-one per cent of that of the West and twenty-nine per cent of that of the East. This is also the case with expenditures on public health. Per capita recurrent expenditures on health in the North was thirty-eight per cent of that in the West and forty-four per cent of that in the East in 1964/5.

Partly because of the increasing burden of social services, but also because the revenues of some of the regional governments are no longer as buoyant as they were previously, it has become difficult to have a balanced budget on current account in some of the regions. Between 1962 and 1966, the Western Nigeria government was able to balance its budget only once and the Northern Nigeria government only twice (Table 6.8). Taking the four years together, the recurrent budgets of both governments were in deficit. On the other hand, the Eastern Nigeria government had budget surpluses throughout the period. Thus the Eastern Nigeria government, which had to be given special grants in 1955/6 and 1956/7 before it could balance its budget, had become between 1959 and 1966 the strongest financially of all the regional governments. This is attributable mostly to the discovery of mineral oil in the East, and the precipitous fall in the world prices of the main export crops of both the North and the West.

While some of the regions have had difficulty in balancing their budgets, the federal government has generated a substantial sur-

TABLE 6.8 *Regional governments' budgets, 1962–6*

(£ million)

	1962/3	1963/4	1964/5	1965/6
Northern Nigeria				
Recurrent revenue	22·8	25·3	33·5	32·6
Recurrent expenditure	24·6	24·7	30·0	35·9
Recurrent budget: surplus (+) deficit(−)	−1·8	+0·6	+3·5	−3·3
Western Nigeria				
Recurrent revenue	24·4	19·4	20·9	22·4
Recurrent expenditure	24·9	19·1	21·0	24·2
Recurrent budget: Surplus (+) deficit (−)	−0·5	+0·3	−0·1	−1·8
Eastern Nigeria				
Recurrent revenue	21·7	22·2	26·7	30·0
Recurrent expenditure	17·9	19·3	24·1	24·9
Recurrent budget: surplus (+)	+3·8	+2·9	+2·6	+5·1
Mid-Western Nigeria				
Recurrent revenue	—	3·8	8·2	9·9
Recurrent expenditure	—	3·4	6·7	7·8
Recurrent budget: surplus (+)	—	+0·4	+1·5	+2·1

SOURCE: Derived from Tables 6.3 to 6.7.

plus on current account each year since the second phase of the operation of federal finance. Table 6.9 shows the surpluses generated each year from 1962/3 to 1965/6. These surpluses have resulted in spite of the substantial increases in federal expenditures during the period. It is not surprising, therefore, that the regions have argued that additional financial resources should be transferred from the federal government to them. The view is widely held among the regional governments that the strong financial

TABLE 6.9 *Federal government revenue and expenditure, 1962-6*

(£ million)

	1962/3	1963/4	1964/5	1965/6
Recurrent revenue	69·9	75·6	85·8	94·3
Recurrent expenditure	60·1	72·4	74·4	82·6
Recurrent budget: surplus (+)	+9·8	+3·2	+11·4	+11·7

SOURCE: Derived from Tables 6.2 and 6.7.

position of the federal government has resulted in that government financing low-priority, non-developmental projects while they, through no fault of their own, have been starved of funds with which to finance high-priority developmental projects.

The distribution among the regions of federal government's public expenditures, particularly on capital accounts, has been one of the main causes of federal-regional and inter-regional conflict. Each region has accused the federal government of discriminating against it in the siting of federal projects. The view is widely held in the regions that federal expenditures should be more fairly distributed among them. The most persistent complainants are the West and the East. The West has contended that it has suffered more than any other region from this 'discriminatory' practice of the federal government. On the other hand, the East feels strongly that it has been treated worse than the West in this regard. A recent publication, *The Problem of Nigerian Unity: The Case of Eastern Nigeria*,[1] quoted examples of federal projects located in the North, the West, and Lagos and concluded that 'Easterners have benefited least from the siting and development of national institutions'.[2]

All these charges and counter-charges are reminiscent of similar allegations made in the forties and early fifties by the North and the West that the East was being developed at their expense. In any

[1] Published by the Ministry of Information, Eastern Nigeria, Enugu, 1967.
[2] ibid., p. 13.

case, it is not true that a federal project which is located in a particular region benefits only the people of that region. Most of the
national projects financed by the federal government, such as the
£78 million Kainji hydro-electric project, the iron and steel industry, the Universities of Ibadan and Lagos, etc., are projects
with spill-over effects, and their benefits extend far beyond the
regions in which they are situated. Besides, the federal government
has little choice in the location of some of these projects; considerations such as the availability of raw materials and other co-operant
factors have played a decisive role in their siting.

Even if it can be shown that the federal government has concentrated its development projects in certain regions, would this
necessarily be an undesirable policy in view of the uneven level of
development of the various parts of the federation? Would it not
be better in promoting the unity of the country that the gap between
the levels of development of the different parts of the country be
closed? The main reason why the Hicks-Phillipson Commission
recommended a special grant to the North in 1951 was to facilitate
a rapid development in its productive capacity in order that its
level of development could catch up to those of the other regions.
Although a great measure of success has been achieved during the
past one and a half decades, there is still more to be done to promote balanced national development. It is only the federal government which can reduce the imbalance among the regions, through
its public expenditures policy and by way of grants. As we saw in
chapter 1, it is indeed one of the essential features of federal
finance that the federal government should be able to do this.

Over-all appraisal and conclusions

Between 1946 and 1957, four fiscal commissions of enquiry were
appointed in Nigeria, three of these between 1951 and 1957. These
four commissions developed Nigeria's federal fiscal system. Since
public finance, whether in a federal or unitary state, is a means to
an end and not an end in itself, it is in the light of the goals of public
finance that Nigeria's fiscal system must be appraised. Among the
many goals of public finance, the most important are economic

development, the most efficient allocation of existing resources, the mobilisation of new resources, the redistribution of income, and the promotion of economic stability. As a detailed analysis of Nigeria's individual taxes in the light of the country's fiscal arrangements is undertaken in chapters 7 and 8, the present appraisal will be limited only to an over-all view of the system.

The discussion may be approached from two points of view. First, to what extent is the distribution of tax powers between the federal and the regional governments conducive to the achievement of the goals of public finance, particularly the efficient mobilisation and allocation of resources and the promotion of economic development and stability? Second, to what extent does the system of revenue allocation facilitate income redistribution and equity between the centre and the regions and among the regions? In other words, to what extent does Nigerian federal finance satisfy the essential features of federal finance discussed in chapter 1? The trend in the newer (e.g., India) as well as the older (e.g., USA, Canada, Australia) federations is for financial powers to be centralised in the federal government. This centralisation has been necessitated by a number of factors, the most important of which is the need to give the federal authority adequate fiscal powers to meet the responsibilities and obligations posed by the goals of public finance. The Nigerian fiscal system is no exception to this trend. The most important financial powers, with the exception of jurisdiction over personal income taxation and the marketing boards, lie with the federal authority. In addition, this centralisation of financial powers promotes efficiency and economy in the administration of the tax system. But the exclusion of personal income taxation and the control of the marketing boards from the jurisdiction of the federal government has imposed considerable limitations on the ability of that government to use its tax powers to achieve the goals of public finance.

Indeed, the whole financial arrangements have inhibited the development of an effective, development-oriented national fiscal policy. Where tax powers are federal and the revenues accruing from such taxes are either fully or partially regional, it has not been easy for the federal government to use such taxes as an effective

instrument of fiscal policy without bringing about federal-regional
conflicts. And there have been complaints in the past that the
federal government has not consulted the regions before imposing
a tax or changing the rates of existing taxes. For its part, the federal
government has argued that extensive consultation would endanger
the principle of budgetary secrecy. The result is that the regions
must prepare their budgets for the financial year on the basis of
prevailing federal tax rates. The regions find this budgetary uncertainty irksome.[1]

Every effort was made by the several fiscal commissions to find
adequate independent revenue sources for the regions so as to
reduce their dependence on revenue from federal taxes. But this
has proved to be difficult. The result is that only a small fraction of
the regional governments' revenues is derived from regional taxes,
even with the regionalisation of the income tax. In the 1965/6
financial year, the percentages of revenue obtained from regional
taxes were 26·7, 35·8, 34·2 and 16·7 for the North, West, East, and
Mid-West respectively.

While the federal government has been given constitutional
power to impose certain taxes, the revenue which accrues from
most of them is shared with the regional governments, and in
some cases is allocated entirely among the regional governments.
In the course of evolving a federal fiscal system for Nigeria, the
several fiscal commissions have been guided by various principles
for sharing revenue among the regions. The most important of
these have been the principles of derivation, need, and of national
interest.

By 1957, when the Raisman Fiscal Commission was appointed,
the regional governments had become disenchanted with the
principle of derivation as the primary basis for allocating revenue.
Although it is still the basis for allocating the whole of the revenue
from export taxes and import and excise duties on tobacco,
petroleum and diesel oil, and half the revenue from mining rents
and royalties, the experiences of the past fourteen years (1952–66)
have justified the fears of the Hicks-Phillipson Commission that

[1] For a full discussion of this point, see P.N.C. Okigbo, *Nigerian Public
Finance* (London: Longmans, 1965), pp. 60–75.

only a minimum reliance should be made of the principle.

Fortunately, the establishment of the Distributable Pool Account in 1959, and the allocation of the proceeds of the account on the basis of population and need, has mitigated some of the more deleterious effects of the derivative principle. The account has become the most important source for the redistribution of income among the regions. Between 1959 and 1966 it has contributed an annual average of twenty-one per cent of the recurrent revenue of the North, 23·7 per cent of the Mid-West, and 14·1 per cent of the East. For reasons explained earlier in this chapter, its role in the West has been much more limited. Its contribution in that region has only averaged 11·1 per cent per annum. Thus, through the Distributable Pool Account, resources are transferred from one part of the federation to the other on the basis of need. The broader issues of fiscal adjustments in Nigeria are discussed more completely in chapter 10.

With regard to the operation of the system since 1959, a number of conclusions emerge from the analysis of this chapter. Marked changes have taken place in the relative position of the regional governments. Primarily because of the discovery of mineral oil in commercial quantities in the East, the government of that region has become financially stronger in the 1960s than it was in the 1950s. On the other hand, the Western Region government, whose finances were buoyant in the early fifties, has been unable to balance its recurrent budget during the past four years from 1962 to 1966. The North has also had difficulty in balancing its budget during this period.

Yet the Western Region has made more strenuous efforts in raising revenue from regional and local taxes than the East and the North. For example, in 1965/66, the revenues from purely regional and local taxes were as follows:

North	West	East
£20·20m.	£16·13m.	£14·51m.

On a per capita basis and using the 1963 census figures, the revenue-raising effort of the three major regional governments and their local authorities were as follows:

North	*West*	*East*
£0·68	£1·6	£1·2

Adequacy and elasticity of resources are two of the requirements of federal finance which we mentioned in chapter 1. While the resources of the federal and Eastern Nigeria governments have been more or less adequate and elastic since 1959, those of the Northern and Western Nigeria governments have proved inadequate. Yet because of the built-in inflexibility of Nigeria's fiscal system with fixed percentage distribution of revenue enshrined in the country's constitution, it has not been easy to come to the assistance of needy governments. Although the federal government possesses the power to make grants to the regional governments, it has rarely used it, in spite of the fact that its resources have proved more elastic than the Raisman Fiscal Commission ever thought possible. It is not surprising that in view of the strengthened financial position of the federal government the regions have demanded that additional federal revenue should be transferred to them.

Finally, the Nigerian fiscal system has failed to satisfy the requirement that regional revenues should be as stable as possible. It is more important for local revenue to be stable than for state revenue to be stable and more important for state revenue to be stable than federal revenue. Yet the revenue allocation system has built instability into the finances of the regions because of their dependence on revenue from export duties.

It will thus be seen that Nigeria's fiscal system is defective in many important respects. Before putting forward proposals designed to remove these deficiencies (chapter 11), let us consider in great detail the problems posed to Nigerian federal finance by direct and indirect taxation, loans and public debt policy and the issues of fiscal adjustment.

7 Federal finance and taxation: indirect taxes

The development of the Nigerian tax structure

Since the amalgamation of Nigeria in 1914, government revenues have evolved in virtually the classical pattern of tax structural change during economic development. The traditional direct taxes on persons and wealth, which were the predominant sources of revenue during the first decade or so after amalgamation, have been eclipsed by the rapid growth of foreign trade taxes. Currently, the major taxes in the Nigerian fiscal system, in order of their relative importance as revenue sources, are import duties, export taxes, excise taxes, the personal income tax, and the companies income tax. The traditional direct taxes—community tax in the North, the poll or personal tax in the West, East, and Mid-West, and the cattle tax in both the North and the East—have now become secondary sources of revenue.

The revenues derived by both the federal and regional governments from these taxes between 1961 and 1966 are shown in Table 7.1. The revenue from import duties reached its zenith in the 1964/5 fiscal year. The rapid rise in revenue from this tax since 1950, and particularly since 1958, has been due to two main factors. First, there has been a rapid increase in the volume and value of imports. Between 1958 and 1966, the value of imports has increased by over fifty per cent. Second, higher duties have been imposed on most imports, increasing the tariff rate by about fifty per cent between 1958 and 1966.

On the other hand, revenues from export duties have declined in

TABLE 7.1 *Major tax revenues of the federal and regional governments, 1961–6*

					($£$ million)
	1961/2	1962/3	1963/4	1964/5	1965/6
DIRECT TAXES					
Personal income tax	6·7	9·0	9·5	10·2	13·9
Companies income tax	5·9	5·7	5·6	5·4	7·5
Petroleum profits tax	—	—	—	0·4	1·3
Community tax (a)	1·1	0·5	0·9	0·9	0·8
Cattle tax (b)	0·2	0·3	0·3	0·3	0·3
Produce sales or purchase tax	3·2	3·5	3·5	3·2	3·1
Total revenues from Direct Taxes	17·1	19·0	19·8	20·4	26·9
CUSTOMS AND EXCISES					
Import duties	57·0	60·8	63·4	83·4	74·9
Export duties	13·1	11·8	14·2	14·4	15·9
Excise taxes	6·4	7·1	9·8	13·6	21·6
Total revenues from Customs and Excises	76·5	79·7	87·4	111·4	112·4
TOTAL TAX REVENUES	93·6	98·7	107·2	131·8	139·3

(a) Imposed only in the North.
(b) Imposed only in the North and the East.

SOURCE: Federal and regional governments' *Estimates* and *Official Gazettes*.

relative importance and, for some years, even in absolute terms. A number of factors have caused this decline. First, the rates of the export taxes (ten per cent *ad valorem* for the principal exports) have remained unchanged for many years. Second, the world prices for most Nigerian exports have fallen substantially. And finally, the rapid growth of import-substituting industries has resulted in an increase in the relative importance of excise duties in the tax structure. In fact between 1961 and 1966 revenue from excises increased by 338 per cent, faster than any other source of tax revenue.

Direct taxes have been only slightly income-elastic during the past five or six years. Revenues from them increased by forty-six per cent between 1961 and 1966 as compared to an increase of thirty-seven per cent in the GDP. The traditional direct taxes, particularly the cattle and community taxes, have been income-inelastic during this five-year period. The companies income tax has also been income-inelastic. Revenue from this tax increased by only twenty-seven per cent between 1961 and 1966. This is due primarily to the generous concessions granted to private and public companies as an incentive to investment.

As is shown in Table 7.2, direct taxes contribute on an average annual basis less than one fifth of total tax revenues and thirteen per cent of total recurrent revenues. On the other hand, revenues from customs and excise duties account for about four fifths of total tax revenues and three fifths of total recurrent revenues. In the aggregate, tax revenues account for an average of about three quarters of the annual revenues, while non-tax revenues, which are principally derived from mining rents and royalties and motor vehicle licences, account for the remaining one quarter.

Although all the governments of the federation are overwhelmingly dependent on revenues from customs and excise, the degree of dependence varies from government to government. As the federal government does not share in the revenue from export taxes, its main source of revenue is import duties. Among the regions, the North, West, and Mid-West are much more dependent on revenue from import and export duties than is the East. The two major sources of revenue for the Eastern Region government are import duties and the personal income tax.

Table 7.3 shows the relative importance of the three major taxes to each of the governments and the extent to which fiscal power has been concentrated in the hands of the federal government. The two federal taxes, import and export duties, account on the average for over four fifths of the revenue of all the regional governments except for the East, where it accounts for an average of 55·8 per cent per annum of that government's total revenue.

TABLE 7.2 *Revenue structure of the federal and regional governments, 1961/2 and 1964/5*

	(In percentages)	
	1961/2	1964/5
Direct taxes as a percentage of total tax revenues	18·2	19·0
Direct taxes as a percentage of total recurrent revenues	13·0	13·6
Customs and excise duties as a percentage of total tax revenues	81·8	82·0
Revenue from customs and excise duties as a percentage of total recurrent revenues	59·0	62·3
Total tax revenues as a percentage of total recurrent revenues	72·0	75·9

SOURCE: Derived from Tables 6.2 and 7.1.

TABLE 7.3 *Federal and regional revenues from import, export and personal income taxes, annual averages, 1963–6*

	(In percentages)				
	Federal Gov't.	Northern Gov't.	Western Gov't.	Eastern Gov't.	Mid-West Gov't.
Import duties	58·0	44·0	42·0	45·4	67·0
Export duties	—	28·0	29·0	10·4	29·0
Personal income tax	3·0	10·0	10·5	17·0	0·7
Total	61·0	82·0	81·5	72·8	96·7

SOURCES: Federal and regional governments' *Estimates* and *Official Gazettes*, 1963–6.

(The major export of the East is oil palm produce, the price of which has fallen more than that of cocoa in the West and groundnuts in the North.) This centralisation of fiscal power, while very real in the case of import and excise duties, is much less so with regard to export taxes, since marketing boards are under regional control, and these boards can and have used their monopsonistic position.

Given the past performance of the tax system, what are the likely trends? Although tax revenues will probably continue to be buoyant, it is unlikely that the tax system as a whole will be as income-elastic in the next five to ten years as it has been in the past. Import revenues would appear to have reached their zenith in 1964/5. Revenues from export taxes are not likely to be more productive in the foreseeable future than they have been in the immediate past. The most income-elastic tax revenues in the future are therefore likely to be excises, the companies income tax (once the tax holidays are over), and the petroleum profits tax. Excises first yielded revenue only in the 1964/5 financial year. The following year, the revenue had increased threefold. Given more efficient tax administration, the personal income tax could also become more income-elastic. If one excludes revenues from petroleum (rents and royalties), the elasticity of the tax system is probably not much more than unity. Revenues from royalties on petroleum will probably rise very rapidly in the future. Together with revenues from the petroleum profits tax, they are likely to transform the character of the revenue system in the latter part of the 1960s.

In the remainder of this chapter and in the next chapter, some of the problems which have been encountered in the utilisation of each of the major taxes both as revenue raisers and as tools of economic control will be discussed. These problems will also be viewed in the light of the federal nature of the fiscal system of the country.

Export taxation

It has been shown in chapter 2 that over half the country's GDP is derived from agricultural production. However, only a relatively small proportion of the country's agricultural production is exported. Production for domestic consumption accounts for some eighty per cent of total agricultural output. Production for export accounts for the balance and is only about one twelfth of the GDP,

The importance of primary produce for export lies in the fact that they are the principal source of earning foreign exchange and a major source of government revenue (Table 7.4). During the Korean War boom, when the world prices for primary products were relatively high, exports accounted for almost one quarter of total government revenue: although their proportionate share in total revenue has been downward since then, they are still a major source of government revenue—about one tenth (Table 7.1).

TABLE 7.4 *Value of major export commodities 1963, 1965 and 1966*

Commodity	1963		1965		1966	
	Value (£m)	Percent-age of Total Exports	Value (£m)	Percent-age of Total Exports	Value (£m)	Percent-age of Total Exports
Groundnuts and groundnut oil and cake	45·88	24·8	47·81	18·1	55·20	19·9
Cocoa	32·36	17·5	42·69	16·1	28·25	10·1
Palm oil	9·37	5·1	13·59	5·2	11·00	3·9
Palm kernels	20·82	11·3	26·54	10·1	22·43	8·1
Rubber	11·77	6·4	10·99	4·2	11·50	4·1
Cotton	10·95	5·9	3·30	1·3	3·35	1·2
Timber and plywood	7·84	4·2	6·41	2·4	6·80	2·4
Crude petroleum	20·14	10·9	68·01	25·8	91·97	33·1
Total major commodities	159·13	86·1	219·34	83·2	230·50	82·8
Other commodities	25·70	13·9	43·99	16·8	48·20	17·2
TOTAL DOMESTIC EXPORTS	184·83	100·0	263·33	100·0	278·70	100·0

SOURCE: *Review of External Trade*, Statistical Studies FOS 1965 P(1) and 1967 P(1), 1964 and 1966 (Lagos, Federal Office of Statistics).

Another feature of agricultural production for exports particularly relevant to a discussion of the problem of export taxation is the concentration of each of the major crops in a particular region (Table 2.7). One region is dominant in the production of one or the other of the major export crops: the West, cocoa; the East, oil palm; the North, groundnuts and seed cotton; and the Mid-West, rubber. The only exception is palm kernel, whose total production is more or less evenly shared by the East and the West.

Export duties are a federal tax, but the revenue therefrom is regional. Although *ad valorem* duties and specific duties are both used in Nigeria, the major export crops—groundnuts, groundnut cake and oil, cocoa, palm oil, palm kernels, raw and seed cotton, and rubber—bear *ad valorem* duties of ten per cent.[1] Two of the remaining major exports crops, hides and timber and wood, have specific rates: £22 a ton in the case of hides, and 3d per cubic foot in the case of timber and wood.

In addition to export duties, produce sales (or purchase) taxes are imposed on the export crops by the regions. Although produce sales taxes are purely a regional tax, all the regions have established the same rates—a good example of inter-governmental cooperation in the fiscal field.[2] The current rates of the produce sales taxes are as follows:

Cocoa	£4 per ton
Palm oil	£1 per ton
Palm kernels	£1 per ton
Groundnuts	£1 per ton
Soya beans	2s 6d per ton
Cotton	one tenth of a penny per lb
Rubber	one quarter of a penny per lb

[1] Paste rubber, as an exception, is charged only five per cent export tax. The duties on crepe and raw rubber are ten per cent.
[2] Although the general sales tax or purchase tax is in the exclusive federal legislative list, sales or purchase taxes on produce, hides and skins, motor spirit, and diesel oil are excluded from the federal list and are regional taxes.

Thus, export crops bear two types of taxes—export duties and produce sales tax. All the exports bearing produce sales taxes are marketed through the marketing boards.

The advantages and disadvangages of export taxation are well known. Export taxes are easy to collect, particularly in Nigeria, where the most important crops are marketed through marketing boards. If an exporting country is in a monopolistic position, and if the demand is inelastic, it can pass on to foreigners the whole or a large part of the tax. However, in none of the crops exported by Nigeria does this condition prevail. The incidence of the tax, therefore, probably falls for the most part on the producers. Also, it is argued that export taxation acts as a supplement to the income tax, since the latter is so difficult to assess and collect in underdeveloped countries. But export taxation only taxes output not consumed internally. This argument, therefore, has little validity. Finally, it is argued that export taxes may serve as a tax on windfall gains due to higher world prices or a bumper output caused by favourable weather conditions. This argument, while persuasive with respect to higher earnings caused by these two factors, loses its validity when increased output is the result of better productive effort and initiative.[1]

On the other hand, export taxation, by discriminating against non-exported commodities, affects the allocation of resources. It diverts output either to the home market or to illicit channels of export. It also shifts production to home-consumed commodities.[2]

[1] cf., A. R. Prest, *Public Finance in Under-Developed Countries* (London: Weidenfeld and Nicolson, 1963), where these arguments are developed at length. See also P. T. Bauer and B. S. Yamey, *The Economics of Under-Developed Countries* (Nisbet and Cambridge University Press, 1957); R. Nurkse, 'Trade Fluctuations and Buffer Policies of Low Income Countries', *Kyklos*, 1958; G. K. Helleiner, 'The Fiscal Role of the Marketing Boards in Nigerian Economic Development, 1947–1961', *Economic Journal*, September 1964, pp. 582–610; and G. K. Helleiner, 'Marketing Boards and Domestic Stabilisation in Nigeria', *Review of Economics and Statistics*, February 1966, vol. XLVIII, No. 1, pp. 69–78.
[2] It should be noted that the supply elasticities for agriculture in Nigeria are subject to some uncertainty. The substitution effect (higher relative prices for effort relative to leisure) would be expected to reduce effort and output. On the other hand, the income effect would work in the opposite

Export taxation probably reduces saving more than consumption. In a country where farming is a peasant industry, and where credit facilities are extremely limited, the importance of private savings for new investment cannot be overemphasised. The arguments that farmers have a low marginal propensity to save are not supported by recent evidence showing increases in agricultural output during the past six decades or so due more to the individual efforts of farmers and their investment than to public investment (see Table 2.3, p. 35).

Thus, there are strong arguments both on economic and equity grounds against export taxation. However the principal concern here is its role in Nigerian federal finance. Since 1954, when revenue from export taxes came to be shared among the regions on the basis of the derivation of the crops, this tax has created instability in regional finances. Export duties are primarily *ad valorem* duties, and revenues from them have been subject to the vagaries of world prices for primary produce. Revenues have declined with the fall in the world market prices and despite some price recovery in the last two or three years are still below the 1959/60 level of £17·16 million. Revenues fell to £15·30 million in 1962/3 and only rose to £16·27 million in 1965/6, despite a substantial increase in exports.

This instability of export taxes as a source of revenue has affected each region differently, owing to the concentration of the production of most of the major crops in a particular region, and the fact that changes in the world prices have been more unstable with some commodities than with others (see Table 7.5). Cocoa, the mainstay of the economy of Western Region, has been the most adversely affected, and consequently the finances of the Western Region government have been the most severely affected.

Another feature of federal-regional finance in the field of export

direction. Present evidence suggests that the elasticities of supply are positive, in the long run at least, and perhaps even in the short run for such crops as palm produce, cotton, and groundnuts, but not for cocoa. See P. T. Bauer, 'The Economic Development of Nigeria', *Journal of Political Economy*, 1955; and J. M. Adler, 'The Economic Development of Nigeria', *Journal of Political Economy*, October 1956.

[1] P. T. Bauer and B. S. Yamey, op. cit., pp. 29–31.

taxation is the regionalisation of the marketing boards. The Nigerian marketing boards have become a permanent instrument of taxation. Their role as trustees of the producers (see chapter 5) has been subordinated to their role as an additional means of taxing export crops. Each regional government expects its marketing board to generate surpluses and pass a large part of them to the regional treasury. In the 1962–8 development plans of the regional governments, projections of surpluses from the boards form part of the total projection of resources during the planning period, especially for capital programmes. This has meant that producer prices are fixed not only in relation to world prices, but also in relation to government revenue needs. In some cases, when surpluses generated in a particular year have been less than the contribution expected from the boards, the boards have been required to cover the gaps from accumulated reserves.

Table 7·5 compares world prices with producer prices for three of the major Nigerian export crops since 1955. The differentials between world prices and producer prices are much more than could be justified on the basis of administrative expenses and the need to accumulate reserves for stabilisation purposes.

Table 7.6 shows the income and expenditure of each of the marketing boards for the years 1961/2 to 1964/5, the surplus generated, and their contribution to the capital funds of the regional governments. It will be seen from this table that the marketing boards of the West and the East have made very substantial contributions to the revenue of their respective regional governments over and above current revenues from export taxation.

It was rightly suggested by Prest that if the marketing boards are to have powers of taxation, they should be fully integrated with the tax system, and if they are not to be so integrated, they must not 'act as to be a permanent instrument of taxation of the producer groups [they are] supposed to represent'.[1] However, the regional governments, for political reasons, have found it convenient to maintain the myth that these boards still operate as trustees for the benefit of the producers.

[1] A. R. Prest, op. cit., p. 71.

TABLE 7.5 *World and producer prices of Nigeria's major export crops, 1955-65*

(£)

Year	Cocoa		Palm Oil		Palm Kernels	
	WP	PP	WP	PP	WP	PP
1955	360	193·0	82	46·7	52	29·7
1956	215	192·3	93	43·9	53	28·6
1957	182	143·0	92	44·4	51	28·3
1958	291	142·6	83	49·9	56	26·7
1959	283	142·4	77	40·6	70	27·2
1960	220	153·0	81	41·9	61	26·8
1961	169	141·5	66	46·8	43	30·0
1962	162	92·5	59	36·0	43	26·0
1963	176	97·5	63	36·0	49	26·0
1964	180	110·0	65	28·0	41	28·0
1965	144	112·5	76	28·0	51	28·0

NOTES: WP world price; PP producer price. WP for cocoa is Lagos (f.o.b.); for palm oil and palm kernels, European Ports (c.i.f.). Both WP and PP are £ per ton. Prices are for crop years.

SOURCES: Western Region Marketing Board and Eastern Nigeria Marketing Board, *Annual Reports*, 1955-65; and Ayo Ogunseye, 'Marketing Boards and the Stabilisation of Producer Prices and Incomes in Nigeria', *Nigerian Journal of Economic and Social Studies*, vol. 7, No. 2, July 1965, pp. 131-43.

It will be seen from the above evidence that the taxation of exports is *de facto* a regional jurisdiction in Nigeria, although export duties are a federal tax. Any regional government, through the manipulation of produce sales taxes, producer prices, and the allocation of the boards' surpluses, can obtain substantial revenues from export crops. The only limitation is a fluctuation in world prices. (The impact of changes in producer prices on money incomes and the monetary system in Nigeria is discussed in chapter 9.)

Another problem which the regionalisation of export taxes poses is in the field of industrial development. All the governments in

TABLE 7.6 *Financial operations of the marketing boards, 1961–5*

(£ million)

Year	Income	Expenditure*	Surplus (+) or Deficiency (−)	Contribution to Regional Government Capital Funds
WESTERN REGION MARKETING BOARD				
1961/2	33·63	29·90	+3·73	4·83
1962/3	33·39	28·04	+5·35	8·36
1963/4	46·42	39·42	+7·00	—
1964/5	42·52	39·12	+3.40	—
EASTERN REGION MARKETING BOARD				
1961/2	18·77	18·75	+ ·02	4·00
1962/3	14·59	12·89	+1·70	2·00
1963/4	17·16	13·98	+3·18	3·00
1964/5	17·15	14·69	+2·46	2·00
NORTHERN REGION MARKETING BOARD				
1961/2	43·40	44·66	−1·26	—
1962/3	50·83	50·40	+0·43	—
1963/4	45·00	45·00	—	—
1964/5	44·00	44·00	—	—

* Including reimbursements made for all services provided by the regional governments, but excluding contributions to the regional governments' capital funds.

SOURCES: Marketing boards' *Annual Reports*; regional governments' *Estimates*, various years.

the federation are committed to a policy of promoting the rapid industrialisation of the country; however, the use of export crops as raw materials by industries results in serious repercussions on the finances of the regional governments. Thus a chocolate factory using cocoa produced in the West will reduce the revenues of Western Nigeria, because export duties will not be payable on the cocoa used for manufacturing the chocolate. Although the income generated by these manufacturing industries in the long run will possibly more than compensate for the loss of the export revenue, the regional governments have found it difficult to accept these short-term fiscal losses, particularly as company and excise taxes are federal and the revenues therefrom accrue to the federal government. The marketing boards also lose the differential between the world price and the producer price, since local manufacturers will purchase the raw materials at domestic producer prices.

The problem is further complicated if the manufacturing industry is being established in a region other than the one producing the export product. In such a case, the loss of revenue from the export tax and the profits from the differential between the world price and producer price has proved too much of a sacrifice for the region producing the crop. The regional government has accordingly insisted that the local manufacturer should buy the produce at the world price less the cost of transportation.

For example, a textile mill was recently established in the West on the basis that it would use cotton produced in the North. The Northern Region Marketing Board refused to sell cotton to the mill at a price less than the world price (f.o.b.). The result was that the mill lost its competitive advantage over foreign-produced textile goods. If, as in the case of the textile mill, the region producing the export product succeeds in attracting the industry to its territory by selling the crop at the local producer price to manufacturing firms within its territory only, it could be argued that the regionalisation of the taxation of export products would not have any adverse effect on the over-all industrial development of the country. However, it would still affect the location of industry, and this more often than not makes a significant difference in the viability of industrial projects. Thus, the regional control over export produce has probably restricted the pace of industrial development in the country by affecting the location of industry and the allocation of resources.

Import and excise taxes

Table 7·1 has indicated the overwhelming importance of import duties as a revenue producer and the steadily growing importance of excise taxes in the revenue structure of the country. Like exports, the taxation of imported and locally manufactured goods falls within the federal sphere. But unlike export taxes, most of the revenues derived from import duties are shared by the federal and regional governments. All the revenue from the import duties on tobacco and motor vehicle fuels (motor spirits and diesel oil) is shared among the regions on the basis of regional consumption. Revenue from the import duties on beer, wine, and potable spirit is retained exclusively for federal use. Revenue from all other imports is shared between the federal and regional governments in the proportion of seventy and thirty per cent respectively.[1] With regard to excise duties, the constitution provides that the whole of the revenue from the excise duty on tobacco is to be distributed among the regions on the basis of proportionate regional consumption. And with effect from 1 April 1965, revenue from excise duties on motor spirit and diesel oil is allocated among the regions on the same basis as revenue from the excise duty on tobacco.[2]

The above rather complicated formulae for allocating revenue from import and excise duties have inevitably posed several fiscal and economic problems. As may be seen from Table 7.7, revenues from import duties on tobacco, motor spirits, and diesel oil accounted for about nineteen per cent of total revenues from import duties, while revenue from beer, wine, and potable spirits accounted for only seven per cent in 1961/2 and 2·9 per cent in 1964/5. Revenues from other imports (general import revenue) accounted for about three quarters of total revenue from import taxes. Since the federal government retains seventy per cent of this revenue for its own use, the proportionate revenue share of the federal and regional governments from import taxes is about sixty and forty per cent respectively.

Table 7.8 shows the increasing importance of revenue from excise duties. Between 1961/2 and 1965/6, revenues more than trebled, which compensates for the fall in revenues from import

[1] Since 1 April 1966, the proportionate federal and regional shares of revenue from general imports are sixty-five and thirty-five per cent respectively. See chapter 10.
[2] *Allocation of Revenue (Constitutional Amendment) Act*, No. 18 of 1965.

duties on beer, wine, and potable spirit in 1964/5 and 1965/6. Nigeria now brews most of the beer it consumes and it has started to distil some of its potable spirit. Excise duties have been imposed on other commodities which were not being produced in the country at the time of the Raisman Fiscal Commission.

TABLE 7.7 *Structure of revenues from import duties, 1961/2, 1964/5 and 1965/6*

Imported Products	1961/2 £m.	1964/5 £m.	1965/6 £m.
(1) Tobacco	3·72	3·35	2·92
(2) Motor spirit and diesel oil	7·19	12·69	10·24
(3) Beer, wine and potable spirits	3·90	2·08	1·68
(4) Other imports	42·22	65·30	60·06
(5) Total revenues from import duties	57·03	83·42	74·90
(1) and (2) as a percentage of (5)	19·0	19·2	17·5
(3) as a percentage of (5)	7·0	2·6	2·2
(4) as a percentage of (5)	74·0	78·2	80·3

SOURCES: Federal government *Estimates* and *Official Gazettes*, various years.

TABLE 7.8 *Derivation of revenues from excise duties, 1961/2 and 1965/6*

Products	1961/2		1965/6	
	£m.	Percentage	£m.	Percentage
Tobacco	4·69	73·3	7·5	33·8
Beer, wine and potable spirits	1·39	21·8	4·6	21·3
Petroleum products	—		4·0	18·5
General excise revenues	0·30	4·7	5·7	26·4
Total revenues from excise duties	6·38	100·0*	21·8	100·0

* Figures do not add up to 100 because of rounding.

SOURCES: Federal government *Estimates* and *Official Gazettes*, various years.

Tariff structure and trade policy have affected federal finance and economic policy. Since 1958, the federal government increasingly has used tariff policy to achieve three main objectives: to provide additional revenues, to reduce the balance-of-payments disequilibrium, and to encourage and protect local industry. Traditionally, revenue considerations have played a major role in the tariff policy of the federal government, since import taxes are its main source of revenue. But with increasing external deficits on trade account, the government has had to depend on increases in tariff rates for dampening the demand for imports.

A reduction in imports may be achieved in one of four ways: (1) by restrictive credit policy; (2) by imposing quota restrictions on imports; (3) by devaluation; and (4) by the imposition of additional import duties. The first method, which can only be effective where there is a highly developed financial and monetary system, is hardly appropriate for Nigeria at the present stage of her development. Quota restriction on imports cannot be discriminatory against imports from selected countries without impinging on GATT. If it is to be used, therefore, it must apply to all imports of the commodities in question. This would necessitate a considerable and rather unproductive increase in the country's administrative machinery and would, as the Federal Minister of Finance acknowledged in his budget speech in 1959, 'open innumerable avenues for fraud and evasion, to say nothing of illicit markets'.[1] Devaluation has been ruled out as a practical proposition because the federal government (1) is determined to protect the value of the Nigerian £ at all costs, and (2) does not believe that such devaluation would result in any appreciable increase in the demand for Nigerian primary products.

The government has accordingly followed the fourth course of action—imposition of additional import duties. As the external trade deficit increased, the tariff rates were progressively increased, luxury and semi-luxury goods being particularly taxed. Between 1959 and 1965 there have been no less than fifteen changes in tariff rates. And in 1965, a more comprehensive Custom Tariff Act re-

[1] Hon. Festus Sam. Okotie-Eboh, *The Responsibility Budget*, 1959 Budget Speech (Lagos: Government Printer, 1959).

placed the one of 1958 (Table 7.9). Most of the commodities formerly imported free of duty now bear a relatively high duty. Whereas the 1958 Act listed only thirty-two dutiable goods, the

TABLE 7.9 *Tariff rates for selected products, 1958 and 1965*

Item	Unit of Measurement	1958	1965
Meat and edible offals	—	f.d.	$66\frac{2}{3}\%$
Fish, fresh, chilled or frozen	—	f.d.	50%
Stockfish	pound	f.d.	1d
Butter	pound	4d	1s 6d
Cereals—rye, barley, oats, maize and rice	—	f.d.	40%
Sugar, beet and cane	—	f.d.	40%
Tobacco, imported for manufacture	pound	15s 3d	15s 3d
Cigars and cigarettes	pound	£1 17s 6d	£2 15s
Cement	ton	£1 8s	£5 or 75%
Cement clinker	ton	£1 2s 3d	£1
Cotton	—	20%	33%
Clocks and watches	—	20%	100%
Motor vehicles not exceeding 1,750 cc	—	15%	$33\frac{1}{3}\%$
between 1,750 and 2,750 cc	—	15%	50%
between 2,750 and 3,500 cc	—	15%	75%
above 3,500 cc	—	15%	100%
Beer, ale, porter and stout	gallon	4s	15s
Spirits (brandy, gin, whisky, rum, bitters and liquors)	gallon	£5	£10 10s or 100%
Motor spirit	gallon	10d	1s 9d
Kerosene	gallon	1s	1d
Gas or diesel oil	gallon	2d	4d

NOTE: f.d. free of duty.

SOURCES: *Customs Tariff Act*, 1958 (Act No. 60 of 1958); *Customs Tariff Act*, 1965 (Act No. 3 of 1965).

G

1965 Act has over a thousand items on its list, consolidating all the amendments previous to 1958.

In addition to increasing the number of taxable imports, the rates on most of these imports have increased. In the list shown in Table 7.9, only two—tobacco imported for local manufacture and kerosene—out of the eighteen items still bear the same tax. And the reasons for this are obvious. Imported tobacco is required for blending with locally produced tobacco; kerosene is an essential household good in most parts of the country.

Although total revenues from import duties continued to rise until 1964, the annual rates of increase between 1961 and 1964 were relatively low. Taking 1958/9 as a base year, import tax revenue rose by seventeen per cent between that year and 1959/60 and thirty-nine per cent between 1959/60 and 1960/1. On the other hand, the rates of increase in 1961/2, 1962/3 and 1963/4 are six, eleven, and seven per cent respectively. It increased very steeply in 1964/5 but fell by fifteen per cent in 1965/6 (see Figure 5). Major tariff increases were made in 1960, 1962, and 1964.

This tariff policy has achieved a measure of success in dampening the demand for imports and thereby reducing the imbalance in the country's terms of trade. Table 7.10 shows the trend in the imports of major commodities between 1961 and 1965. The values of imported sugar, flour, beer, cotton and rayon piece goods, household enamelware, cement, passenger cars, footwear, and clothing have showed a marked downward trend. Some of the commodities whose tariff rates have been increased most steeply within recent years are also shown. The favourable effect of this on the country's balance of trade is already manifest. As is shown in Table 7.11, the trade deficit has, in every year but 1964, become increasingly smaller, and in 1966 the country had a surplus on trade account. This surplus was, however, made possible more by the very rapid increase in the production of petroleum than by a reduction in imports. As can be seen in Figure 5, the index of imports by value follows very closely the index of average tariff rates, i.e., imports taxes divided by total value of imports.

The infant-industry argument for a protective tariff is clear from a study of Tables 7.9 and 7.10. The products whose import

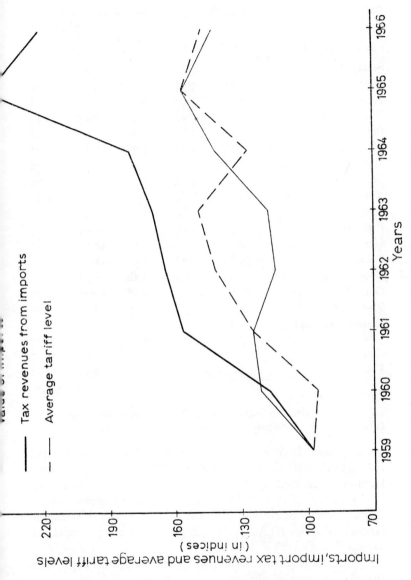

FIGURE 5 *Indices of value of imports, import tax revenues and average tariff levels, 1959–66 (1959=100)*

TABLE 7.10 *Nigerian imports of major commodities, 1961–5*

(£ million)

COMMODITY	1961	1962	1963	1964	1965
Stockfish	7·56	7·22	6·43	6·25	6·67
Sugar	3·11	3·39	3·48	3·05	2·62
Flour	3·23	2·97	0·13	0·17	0·08
Wheat	*	1·54	3·44	2·24	3·43
Beer (including stout)	3·92	2·83	0·89	0·79	0·23
Motor spirit	4·10	3·56	4·66	6·06	4·91
Gas, oil and diesel oil	1·52	2·93	5·53	5·52	4·40
Medicine	5·13	4·64	5·08	5·10	5·67
Cotton piece goods	26·43	18·65	20·46	21·95	21·42
Rayon piece goods	7·36	3·84	2·53	3·51	3·70
Paper products	4·78	4·15	5·28	6·09	6·69
Household enamelware	2·70	2·03	2·15	1·06	0·93
Cement	3·66	2·36	1·98	1·22	1·32
Roofing sheets	2·69	2·04	2·18	1·10	0·22
General machinery	18·14	15·37	15·58	23·62	32·99
Passenger cars	6·53	6·33	6·27	8·22	9·66
Commercial road vehicles	9·39	3·27	4·62	8·75	7·94
Clothing	2·32	5·50	5·49	6·22	4·37
Footwear	3·29	2·84	2·69	2·50	1·54

* £218 only.

SOURCE: *Economic Indicators*, vol. 2, No. 11, November, 1966 (Federal Office of Statistics, Lagos).

tax rates have been increased the most, and whose total imports also have been diminishing, are those which are now being manufactured in the country. However, for the tariff policy to be effective in encouraging local industry, it was supplemented with two major pieces of incentive legislation—the Industrial Development (Income Tax Relief) Act and the Industrial Development (Import Duties Relief) Act.

Under the latter legislation, the government may repay either the whole or part of any imported duty paid on imports employed

TABLE 7.11 *Nigeria's external trade, 1961–6*

(£ million)

Period	Imports (c.i.f.)	Exports (f.o.b.)	Re-Exports (f.o.b.)	Deficit (−) or Surplus (+)
1961	222·52	170·07	3.56	−48·89
1962	203·22	164·01	4.61	−34·60
1963	207·56	184·86	4·83	−17·87
1964	253·79	210·23	4.18	−39·38
1965	275·32	263·34	5·02	−6·96
1966	256·37	278·70	5·38	+27·71

SOURCE: *Economic Indicators*, vol. 2, No. 11 (Federal Office of Statistics, Lagos).

in the manufacture or processing of goods or in the provision of services, provided that the government 'is satisfied that the assistance rendered by such repayment would be to the overall economic advantage of Nigeria having regard amongst other matters to the amount of such repayment and the nature of such manufacture'.[1] The Act also provides for repayment of import duties on goods introduced for the purpose of manufacture processing. Finally, the Act provides that the federal government should bear in full the loss of revenue which results from the repayments. It is officially estimated that this loss amounted to about £200,000 in 1963/4.

Undoubtedly, the high tariff rates and the concessions provided under the Industrial Development (Import Duties Relief) Act have contributed to the increase in industrialisation in the country. And with this, the number of goods subject to excise duties has increased. More important, revenue from these duties has also increased substantially. Revenue from excises increased by an average of 11·5 per cent per annum between 1959/60 and 1962/3, by an average of 38·5 per cent per annum in 1963/4 and 1964/5, and by about 160 per cent from 1964/5 to 1965/6. In relative importance, excises are now the second most important single source of revenue, following import duties.

The coverage of excise duties has also increased considerably.

[1] Section 3 of the Act.

The Excise Tariff Act of 1958 had only four goods listed as dutiable: cigarettes, whose duty varied from thirty to fifty per cent of the selling price; cigars and tobacco at 2s 6d per lb; and beer at 2s 9d per gallon. The Excise Tariff Act of 1965, which repealed the 1958 Act, listed twenty-five commodities as being dutiable. These goods included beer, biscuits, blankets, cigarettes, enamelware, matches, motor spirits, and cotton piece goods.

Although the policy of the federal government is to impose excise duties on domestic products when duties can be borne, these duties are in most cases levied at substantially lower rates than the equivalent import duties. Most commodities bear a tax of only five to ten per cent. Substituting domestic manufactures for imports naturally reduces the revenue from import and excise taxes and it is the federal government that suffers most. It can, however, recoup its loss of revenue from these taxes by an increase in revenue from company taxation, since an increase in industrial activity will be accompanied by a growth of companies. As may be seen in Table 7.1, revenue from the company tax has indeed increased substantially since 1961/2.

But in the long run, it is not sufficient for the government simply to maintain through the imposition of excises the level of import tax revenues lost by import-substitution. It will need to convert excises into an income-elastic tax revenue if it is to increase the ratio of government revenue to the GDP to a level that is consistent with the needs for more resources to finance recurrent expenditures and the capital requirements of the development plan. This means that the levels of excise taxes will have to be raised and the bases widened to cover existing import-substitutes that are now free of excise tax. Moreover, the government, in developing its future tax policy, needs to establish rational relationships between tariff levels and excise tax levels in order to satisfy the need both to protect growing industries and yet provide pressure for efficient low-cost production. Such consideration may lead to both higher tariff and excise tax levels, a reconsideration of the generous tax incentives currently granted to companies (see chapter 8 below), and a possible shift to a system of internal indirect taxation that is more efficient and economically neutral.

The present system of collecting individual excises makes the administration of excise taxation relatively easy. The officials are able to collect many excises on a simple 'physical count' basis. This is convenient for manufacturers who do not maintain adequate records or who may be reluctant to reveal gross revenues and/or value-added. In addition, the system of excises enables the government to establish specific rates for each industry on the basis of the particular conditions facing such industry. Individual excise tax rates can also be fixed at a lower level than the individual tariff rates in order to provide adequate protection for infant industries and to discriminate in favour of those industries which are considered more important for development purposes.

However, the system of individual excise tax rates has several disadvantages. It sacrifices economic 'neutrality' among industrial cost structures, and thereby makes inter-industry comparisons of real cost, efficiency, and profit difficult. The rates, once established, are also difficult to increase, as producers resist any changes. Too much effort tends to be devoted by producers to securing higher profits through pressure to reduce excise tax rates rather than in increasing industrial efficiency.

The experience in other countries suggests that it would appear advisable to consider substituting a broad-based indirect tax for the series of individual excises now used in Nigeria. Such a broad-based indirect tax could either be a general sales tax or a value-added tax. It would be superior to the present system not only on the grounds of economic neutrality and efficiency, but also in equity and certainty. For administrative reasons it would probably be preferable to confine a broad-based indirect tax to the manufacturing level.

Taxation of extractive industry

Since Nigeria became a federation in 1954, the federal government has been responsible under the Constitution for all matters concerning mines and minerals, including oil-fields, oil mining and geological surveys. It also has exclusive jurisdiction over mining royalties and rents. Until 1958, the chief minerals were coal, tin and columbite, but since then mineral oil has been produced in commercial quantities. From a daily production of 6,000 barrels in 1958, oil production has risen sharply to 200,000 and 560,000 barrels per day in 1965 and 1967 respectively (Table 7.12). This phenomenal increase in the production of petroleum (and gas) has resulted in these commodities becoming Nigeria's most important foreign exchange earner, accounting for 33·1 per cent of the total export earnings of the country in 1966 (Table 7.4). Nigeria

TABLE 7.12 *Production of oil and gas, 1959–66*

Year	Oil Production (in Million Tons)	Gas Production (in Million Cubic Feet)
1959	0·538	4·939
1960	0·847	5·095
1961	2·219	10·943
1962	3·274	17·179
1963	3·712	22·105
1964	5·859	36·332
1965	13·324	94·287
1966	20·668	101·582

SOURCES: *Annual Reports*, Petroleum Division of the Ministry of Mines and Power, 1958 to 1965; *Digest of Statistics*, vol. 16, No. 2, April 1967 (Federal Office of Statistics, Lagos); *Economic Indicators*, vol. 3, No. 12, December 1967 (Federal Office of Statistics, Lagos).

has thus emerged as an important oil-producing country, second in importance in the Commonwealth and third in Africa.

Table 7.13 shows the value of the major minerals and mineral oil exported from Nigeria for selected years since 1956. Tin has yielded first place to oil, the latter accounting for eighty-five per cent of the total value of minerals and mineral oil exported from the country in 1966.

Oil production will assume even greater importance in the future. The taxation of the extractive industry is therefore of great importance to Nigeria, and the basis of the allocation of tax proceeds is already dominating inter-governmental fiscal relations.

TABLE 7.13 *Value of major minerals and mineral oil exported, selected years, 1956–66*

	1956	1958	1960	1962	1964	1966
					(£ million)	
Tin	7·3	3·4	6·0	7·0	12·3	14·8
Columbite	1·8	0·5	2·1	1·1	1·3	1·2
Petroleum	—	1·0	4·4	16·7	32·1	92·0
Total value of exports of minerals and mineral oil	9·1	4·9	12·5	24·8	45·7	108·0
					(In percentages)	
Tin	80	70	48	28	27	14
Columbite	20	10	17	5	3	1
Petroleum	—	20	35	67	70	85

SOURCE: Federal Office of Statistics, Lagos.

Table 7.14 compares the total revenues which have accrued to the governments from minerals and mineral oil in 1961/2 with 1965/6. Rents from oil and gas increased 2·6 times. By comparison, royalties from oil and gas increased 6·5 times in the same period. Royalties from tin increased only 2·5 times during the period.

As it has been indicated in the preceding section, the tax on oil companies is fifty per cent of their chargeable profit in accordance with the provisions of the Petroleum Profits Tax Act of 1959. However, the companies are allowed to deduct from their assessable tax all royalties paid by them during the tax period, and any other tax, duty rate, or fee imposed on them by any government— regional or local. In other words, the total tax liability (including royalties and rents) of an oil company cannot be greater than fifty per cent of its profit.

Because of the considerable build-up of depreciation allowances due to the heavy back-log of investment during the two decades of exploration, the share of government in profits is less than fifty per cent. The full fifty-fifty share is unlikely to become fully effective until after 1968 or 1969. When it does, the annual contribution of the oil industry to Nigerian revenue will be considerable.

TABLE 7.14 *Mining revenues, 1961/2 and 1965/6*

	(£'000s)	
	1961/2	1965/6
ROYALTIES		
Oil and gas	1,186	7,767
Columbite	88	88
Tin	1,222	3,108
Other minerals	8	123
Sub-total	2,504	11,086
RENTS		
Mineral oil licences and leases	1,691	4,413
Mining leases	50	68
Other rents	7	18
Premiums on mineral oil licences and leases	6	42
Sub-total	1,754	4,541
NON-RECURRING RECEIPTS*	5,657	—
TOTAL	9,915	15,627

* Lump-sum payments by new oil companies for prospecting rights.

SOURCES: *Estimates of the Federal Government*, 1963/4 and 1967/8.

Like the main export crops of Nigeria, the production of minerals and mineral oil is localised by regions. Tin and columbite are produced in the North, while mineral oil and gas are found in the East and Mid-West. The West is the only region where neither minerals nor mineral oil have been discovered in commercial quantities. The sharing of revenues from the extractive industry between the government of the region in which the mineral or mineral oil is produced and the other governments of the federation has been severely criticised by the regions producing the minerals and mineral oil, particularly the East.

It will be recalled that prior to 1959, revenues from the extractive industries were received in full by the regions in which the minerals were produced. This was changed on the recommendation of the Raisman Fiscal Commission, which had argued that because of the uncertainty which then surrounded the production of oil in commercial quantity, the dependence on it by any regional government for revenue should be minimised. 'There is nothing so uncertain as an oil prospect right up to the time commercial production is, or is not finally achieved,' the Commission observed. And should oil be discovered in commercial quantity, it was argued further, it would be a source of income too sizeable to ignore. The Commission accordingly recommended a tripartite division of the revenues from oil and minerals, with the government of the region producing the oil or mineral receiving the largest percentage.[1]

It is the view of the government of the Eastern Region that revenues from the extractive industries should be allocated on the same basis as revenues from export duties on agricultural products, i.e., on the basis of derivation. Unlike the other regions, the agricultural exports of the East are relatively small—a large proportion of its main export crops, palm produce, is consumed domestically. Hence the revenues derived by the government of the East from export duties are much smaller than those of the North and the West. For example, in 1965/6, the Eastern government received only £2·90 million from export duties as compared to £6·07 and £5·03 million received by the North and West. Since the production of mineral products is as regionalised as the production of agricultural products, and since it is also a primary product, it is argued that the lack of complete parity in the treatment of mining revenues and revenues from export duties is unfair and inequitable to the oil-producing regions.[2]

An acceptance of this view would lead to a drastic change in the relative financial strength of the regions. The fact that the East already receives most of the revenue from oil has strengthened its financial position relative to the other regions. Transferring the

<hr/>

[1] *Raisman Report*, pp. 24–5.
[2] This case was most strongly made in a memorandum submitted by the government of the East to the 1964 Fiscal Review Commission. See K. J. Binns, *Report of the Fiscal Review Commission* (Federal Ministry of Information, Lagos, 1965), pp. 13–14.

whole of the proceeds of rents and royalties from oil would give the East such financial strength that with the present trend of oil production, regional disparity would be accentuated.[1] On the other hand, the financial problems of the North and the West would be aggravated. Although the government of the Mid-West would benefit, it would do so to a lesser extent than the government of the East, since at present the Mid-West produces only one third of Nigeria's oil output. In view of the increasing importance of revenue from oil in the revenue structure, its allocation will remain one of the principal areas of contention in Nigeria.

Another contentious fiscal problem posed by the oil industry is the treatment of oil from the continental shelf. The Constitution of the Federation of Nigeria[2] defines the continental shelf of a region as part of that region for the purposes of mining royalties and rents. But the Raisman Fiscal Commission had assumed that oil resources found within the area of the continental shelf should be within federal jurisdiction. However, the Commission did not make specific recommendations as to the share of revenue from oil within the continental shelf, and the Nigerian leaders, under pressure from the East, agreed to the inclusion of the continental shelf in the area of a region for the purpose of mineral and mineral oil exploitation.

The non-oil-producing regions have been very critical of this arrangement. They have pressed that the continental shelf should cease to be regarded as part of a region on the grounds that it may be technically possible for oil to be drawn from far-off places within the continental shelf which extended beyond the borders of the oil-producing regions. They cite that it is the accepted international practice for a country's continental shelf to be regarded as belonging to the whole of the nation, and for any resources discovered therein to benefit the federal government primarily and all the regional governments to a secondary degree. This issue remains unresolved. It will be one of the most critical issues to be

---

[1] This view, of course, assumes that oil may not be found in commercial quantities in the North and West, where prospecting is at present going on.

[2] Act No. 20 of 1963, section 140, sub-section 6.

determined by the framers of the country's future constitution. Now that the country has been divided into twelve states, a large number of which are land-locked, the pressure to regard the continental shelf as belonging to the whole of the nation for mineral and mineral oil production will be considerable.

8 Federal finance and taxation: direct taxes

Personal income taxation

Personal income taxation in Nigeria is bedevilled by an historical legacy. As soon as the Protectorate of Northern Nigeria was founded in 1906, Lord Lugard introduced direct taxation together with the system of indirect rule. Long before British rule came to Northern Nigeria there had existed an elaborate system of taxation. The purpose of introducing the direct tax in the protectorate was therefore to consolidate and cleanse the pre-colonial tax system of its imperfections, as well as to provide a source of revenue for both the government and the native authorities. The direct tax soon became the financial foundation on which the native authority system was built.

The essential features of the tax may be summarised as follows. First, the tax took the form of a rough income tax on each person. Second, since the North was predominantly an agricultural economy, the income in question was usually derived from the land. Third, the basis of assessment for the tax was communal rather than personal. Fourth, native authorities played an important role in the assessment of the tax and were responsible for its collection. And finally, although the tax was essentially a government tax, its revenue was subject to a division at source between the government and the native authorities.

When Nigeria came into existence in 1914, and the system of indirect rule was extended to the South, direct taxation inevitably came with it.[1] But because the southern provinces did not have a tradition of communal assessment nor the institutions (large emirates with strong native authorities) upon which the northern tax was assessed and collected, the direct tax in the South had a simpler form. It was both a poll tax (for adults whose income was not more than a certain assumed minimum) and a slightly progressive income tax (for persons whose incomes were more than the assumed minimum). But it was neither an equitable nor a popular tax. The Hicks-Phillipson Fiscal Commission commented as follows on the tax:

'Southern tax is a worse tax, both in principle and in practice, than the Northern one; many of the [tax] troubles of Nigeria . . . spring from its defects. . . . The poll tax part of the Southern direct tax . . . like all poll taxes . . . falls with proportionately heavier weight upon the poorer than upon the wealthier of those people who are liable to it; and in consequence of this it is a highly unpopular tax, so unpopular as to be a bad source of revenue.'[2]

Apart from the difference in the direct tax system of the North and the South, there were also differences between the tax liabilities of Africans living outside the Colony of Lagos and of those resident in the Colony, and of all expatriates living in Nigeria. Only Africans living in the protectorate (i.e., throughout the country except Lagos) were subject to the direct tax. Africans resident in Lagos and expatriates in Nigeria were subject to the income tax under the Income Tax Ordinance.

In 1940, an attempt was made by the government to integrate the income tax with the direct tax. It was proposed that persons with incomes above £200 should pay an income tax which would be administered by the Department of Inland Revenue, irrespective of where they lived, while those with income below £200 would pay the direct tax.[3] This attempt, and similar ones made

[1] It was introduced over the greater part of what is now Western and Mid-Western Nigeria in 1916, and in the greater part of Eastern Nigeria in 1928. Its introduction in the East sparked off a number of disturbances of which the Aba Women's Riot of 1929 is the best known.
[2] *Hicks-Phillipson Report*, op. cit., p. 122.
[3] This proposal would eliminate the discrimination between Africans resident in Lagos and those resident in the rest of the country, on the one

between 1940 and 1954, failed. Thus at the time that Nigeria became a federation in 1954, direct taxation was still the main source of revenue for the native authorities and the government (now the regional governments); the poll tax element still existed, particularly in the South; the assessment and collection of the tax was still the primary responsibility of native administration; and the discrimination remained between Africans resident in Lagos and those resident elsewhere in Nigeria, and between expatriates and Africans.

These were the historical and practical factors which weighed heavily in favour of regionalising the income tax jurisdiction when federalism came into being. They are also the factors which have rendered income taxation relatively unimportant both as a source of revenue and as an instrument of economic control. Today there are four income tax systems in the country. The Eastern Region introduced income taxation in 1956,[1] and was followed by the West in 1957.[2] It was not until 1962 that the North introduced its own income tax system.[3] In 1961, the federal government introduced the Income Tax (Lagos) Act, and the Income Tax Management Act. The multiple income tax systems prevailing in the country have resulted in many problems. The systems are neither modern nor progressive. For most people the taxes are also not a tax on income *per se*. Moreover, there are wide differences in the rate structures of the four tax systems.

Table 8.1 relates the average rates of taxes paid to total income, and compares the rates of the four tax systems for incomes between £50 and £700. All the governments, except that of the East, have regressive tax structures within this income range, yet about ninety-nine per cent of Nigerian taxpayers are within the range.

hand, and the discrimination between Africans and expatriates on the other hand. Thus the only cause of discrimination in taxation would be on account of income and not of race or residence.

[1] The Finance Law, 1956 (E.N. Law No. 1 of 1956), which was repealed by the Finance Law, 1962 (Law No. 5 of 1962).

[2] The Income Tax Law, 1957 (W.N. Law No. 16 of 1957), and subsequent amending laws. The Mid-Western Region still operates under the Western Nigeria tax laws.

[3] The Personal Tax Law, 1962 (Northern Nigeria Law No. 6 of 1962).

TABLE 8.1 *Comparative average personal income tax rates on incomes between £50 and £700*

(In Percentages)

Gross Income (£)	50	100	200	300	400	500	600	700
Single Person								
Federal (Lagos)	1·0	0·5	0·5	1·0	2·0	2·6	3·0	3·2
West and Mid-West	6·0	6·0	6·0	6·0	6·0	6·0	6·5	6·5
North	2·5	2·5	2·5	2·5	2·5	3·2	3·7	4·0
East	1·0	3·0	4·0	5·0	5·2	5·6	6·0	6·0
Family (Married Couple with Four Children) Receiving Maximum Allowances								
Federal (Lagos)	1·0	0·5	0·5	1·0	0·7	0·6	0·5	0·4
West and Mid-West	6·0	6·0	6·0	6·0	4·5	3·6	3·0	2·5
North	2·5	2·5	2·5	2·5	2·5	2·5	2·5	2·5
East	1·0	2·0	2·5	3·3	3·7	4·0	4·2	4·2

SOURCES: Federal and Regional Income Tax Laws (as amended).

Figures 6 and 7 compare the average tax rates of the four tax systems between the incomes range of £700 and £10,000: Figure 6 shows the average tax rates for a single person and Figure 7 shows those for a married couple with four children receiving maximum allowances (the maximum number of dependants under the tax law is four). Again, the tax systems show a marked degree of regressivity up to £2,000 income, the only exception being in the East.

This regressivity of the tax systems is further heightened by a number of other factors. First, certain forms of income (e.g., rental income, dividends, capital gains, expense allowances, foreign income) are excluded from the income tax base. Secondly, evasion and tax avoidance is more characteristic of middle and upper income groups.[1] Thirdly, in the assessment process, there is a strong tendency for taxpayers with incomes above the 'assumed minimum income' level (of £50 in the West and Mid-West and £60 in the East) to be taxed at this minimum level. Finally, there are addi-

[1] G. Oka Orewa, *Taxation in Western Nigeria* (Oxford University Press, 1962), chapter 2.

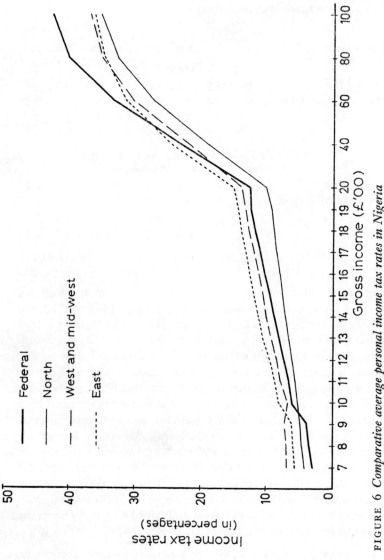

FIGURE 6 *Comparative average personal income tax rates in Nigeria on incomes between £700 and £10,000 (for single persons)*

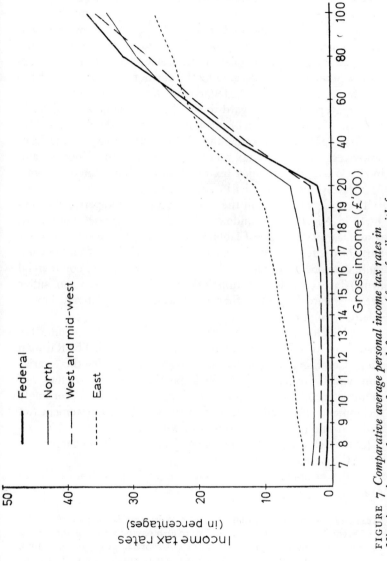

FIGURE 7 *Comparative average personal income tax rates in Nigeria on incomes between £700 and £10,000 (for a family with four children and receiving maximum allowances payable)*

tional flat-rate local income and special (e.g., educational) rates levied on a per capita basis in the West, Mid-West, and East.

Table 8.2 shows the divergences in personal allowances and deductions. With the exception of the Eastern Nigeria government, all the governments have been overly generous. This divergence is perhaps best illustrated by the taxation of women under the four tax systems. Under the federal and Northern Region tax laws, all taxpayers, without regard to sex, have the same tax reliefs: in the case of the first £300 of income under the federal law, and on the first £240 of the income under the Northern law. In the East, employed women have tax relief on the first £100 of income, and in the West, women enjoy tax relief on the first £100 of income. Men receive no such relief in either region.[1]

The wide variations in the rates of taxation and personal allowances in Nigeria have undoubtedly reduced the free mobility of resources, particularly of labour and capital, between the various parts of the federation. Employers whose activities extend beyond more than one state (such as the federal government or commercial firms) face considerable difficulties; their employees too suffer personal hardship when they are posted from relatively low to relatively high tax areas.

The likelihood of wide variations arising in the income tax systems of the regional governments was anticipated. The Raisman Fiscal Commission suggested measures for minimising these variations and for overcoming, as far as possible, the disadvantages of multiple income tax jurisdictions. The Commission accordingly recommended[2] the enactment of an Income Tax Management Act which would ensure uniformity of treatment in:

(a) the definition of taxable income and the basis of charge;

(b) the period of assessment;

(c) the taxation of income remitted to Nigeria from overseas sources;

---

[1] It should be pointed out that women in Western Nigeria paid tax under the Direct Taxation Ordinance and were also paying tax until 1960,when an amending law exempted income of not more than £300 per annum from tax. This amount was reduced to £100 with effect from 1 April 1968.

[2] *Raisman Report*, paragraphs 87–94, pp. 19–21.

TABLE 8.2 *Personal income tax allowances in Nigeria (as at 1 April 1966)*

	FEDERAL	WEST AND MID-WEST	EAST	NORTH
(a) Single Person (Male)	£300	None	None	£240
(b) Single Person (Female)	£300	£300	£100 provided income is less than £400	£240
(c) Married Man	£100 (in addition to the personal allowance)	£200 (in addition to the personal allowance)	No allowance if income exceeds £100 but tax rates are low	No special allowance
(d) Children	£60 basic for each unmarried child (up to a maximum of four children maintained and either under sixteen years of age or undergoing full-time instruction as a student or an apprentice)	£40 for each child. Conditions same as for Federal Income Tax	£40 for each child up to a maximum of three	£60 for each child. The stipulations are the same as those in the Federal Income Tax Act

	FEDERAL	WEST AND MID-WEST	EAST	NORTH
(e) Children's education	Cost of school bills to the extent that they exceed £60, subject to a limit of £190. This brings total allowance (d & e) to a maximum of £250 per child	Cost of maintenance and education if it exceeds the basic allowance of £40 up to a maximum of £210. This brings the total allowance (d & e) to £250 per child. The extra allowance allowable to any individual is subject to a limit of £240	None	Same as in the Federal Law but subject to a maximum of £500 for any number of children
(f) Dependent relatives	Actual amount spent subject to a maximum of £100	Actual amount spent up to a maximum of £50	None	Same as in the Federal Law
(g) Life assurance	Actual premium paid on the life of the taxpayer or his spouse subject to a maximum of one fifth of the taxpayer's total income or £1,000 including contributions to pension or provident funds	Actual premium paid subject to a maximum of one fifth of total income or £500, whichever is less	Actual premium paid subject to a maximum of one fifth of total income or £1,000, whichever is less	Actual premium paid subject to a maximum of one fifth of total taxpayer's income or £300, whichever is less

	FEDERAL	WEST AND MID-WEST	EAST	NORTH
(h) Passage allowance	None	None	None	Expenditure incurred in the previous year by the taxpayer on himself or his dependants on transport to and from any place outside Nigeria in pursuance of the terms of his employment in Nigeria, subject to a maximum of £100 for one person and overall maximum of £600

SOURCES: Federal and Regional Income Tax Laws as amended; Income Tax Management Act, 1961.

(d) the taxation of income accruing in Nigeria to residents overseas;

(e) the approval of pensions and provident funds for tax purposes;

(f) the treatment of dividends;

(g) the taxation of partnerships; and,

(h) the type of information to be exchanged among tax authorities.

In accordance with these recommendations, the Constitution[1] provides that Parliament may make laws for Nigeria or any part thereof with respect to taxes on income and profits other than the income and profits for companies for the purpose of:

(a) implementing any treaty convention or agreement between the Federation and any other country or any arrangement with or decision of an international organisation of which the Federation is a member with respect to taxes on income and profits;

(b) securing uniform principles for the taxation of income and profits accruing to persons in Nigeria from countries other than Nigeria, and of income and profits derived from Nigeria by persons outside Nigeria;

(c) securing uniform principles for the computation of income and profits of all persons including members of partnerships and profits of all persons (including members of partnerships) for purposes of assessments of tax and for the treatment of losses, depreciation of assets and contributions to pension or provident funds or schemes;

(d) regulating the liability to tax of persons within Nigeria by reference to their place of residence or otherwise for the purpose of ensuring that any income or profit does not bear tax under the Laws of more than one territory;

(e) providing, in pursuance of any arrangement in that behalf subsisting between the Governments of a Region, for the exemption from liability to tax in respect of all or part of the income or profits of any person or class of persons;

(f) obtaining information with respect to income or profits from

[1] Section 76 of the 1963 Constitution of the Republic of Nigeria, formerly Section 70 of the 1960 Constitution.

any source and providing for the exchange of information between different tax authorities; and,

(g) providing, in pursuance of any arrangement in that behalf subsisting between the Government of the Federation and the Government of a Region, for the establishment and regulation of authorities empowered to promote uniformity of taxation and to discharge such other functions relating to the taxation of income and profits as may be conferred upon them in pursuance of any such agreement.'

The Income Tax Management Act took effect in 1961.[1] Much of this Act is devoted to a detailed exposition of the income which may be the subject of regional taxation, the deductions which may be allowed by the regions and those which must be allowed against gross taxable income before computing the tax due.[2] The regional governments are, however, free to allow others, such as the number and rates of personal allowances. The Act also makes necessary provisions against double taxation.[3]

The Income Tax Management Act, although it was the first serious attempt at harmonising the income tax laws of the various governments, has merely mitigated the evils of complete regional autonomy in the income tax field. Since the Constitution did not empower the federal government to enact a uniform tax code throughout the country, the rates of taxes and personal allowances are, as already pointed out, quite divergent. Had the Constitution given the federal government income tax jurisdiction, the administrative, economic, and fiscal defects of regional income taxation would have been avoided. And the courts would have had to construe only one tax law and not five.

Another attempt which has been made to mitigate the defects of regional jurisdiction of personal income taxation is the establishment of a Joint Tax Board,[4] which is called upon to 'use its best endeavours to promote uniformity in the incidence of tax on individuals throughout Nigeria'. Each income tax authority has a

---

[1] It became operative with effect from 1 April 1961.
[2] Sections 4, 17, 18 and 26.
[3] Sections 21–26 of the Act.
[4] Set up under Section 27 (1) of the Act.

representative on the Board. But since its powers are advisory, it acts primarily as a clearing house for tax disputes, and its recommendations are subject to the concurrence of all the governments.

Another major problem which faces personal income taxation in Nigeria is how to cut it loose from the long-established tradition of indirect rule and direct taxation. Although all the regional income tax laws repealed the Direct Taxation Ordinance, the main features of the tax system established under that law are still to be found in current income tax legislation. Three of these features which are relevant to this discussion are the poll tax element of the income tax, the dependence of local (or native) authorities on it as their main source of revenue, and the administration of the tax through local councils.[1] The Eastern Nigeria government has succeeded to a large extent in overcoming this problem by assuming the administration of the income tax and by denying local authorities a share in the revenue from the tax. But in the other regions income tax revenue is still the main source of local revenue and local authorities still participate in the assessment and collection of the tax.

In the income tax laws, there is an assumed minimum income for every male person who is sixteen years of age and above and is not pursuing full-time studies or apprenticeship.[2] Such a person, whether gainfully employed or not, pays a poll tax of £3 in the West and Mid-West; £1 7s 6d in the East; £1 5s in the North and 10s in Lagos. This is a legacy of direct taxation. In fact the community tax introduced by Lord Lugard early in the century still forms part of the Northern Nigeria income tax law.[3]

Except in the East the proceeds of the poll or flat-rate tax are received by the local authorities. In addition, local authorities in Western and Mid-Western Nigeria assess, collect, and retain taxes on income in the range of £51 to £300 from self-employed persons. In the case of wage and salary earners who come under the

[1] cf., Adebayo Adedeji, 'The Future of Personal Income Taxation in Nigeria', *Nigerian Journal of Economic and Social Studies*, vol. 7, No. 2, July 1963, p. 163.

[2] The assumed minimum income is £60 in the East and £50 in the West and Mid-West.

[3] Personal Income Tax Law, 1962 (Northern Nigeria Law No. 6, of 1962), Part III, Sections 49–53.

PAYE scheme, the tax received from incomes up to £300 is also received by the local authorities. In the North, 87·5 per cent of the revenue from the community tax and twenty per cent of the proceeds of the assessed income tax are received by the native authorities.

The involvement of local (and native) authorities in personal income taxation is one of the major defects in the Nigerian income tax system. The administration of the income tax is inhibited by inefficiency and political considerations. The great majority of taxpayers have incomes below the assumed minimum income. Not less than eighty per cent of the taxpayers come under this category in each of the regions. For example, the number of males who were sixteen years of age and above in the West in 1963/4 was estimated at 2·25 million. Only 250,000 of these were either wage or salary earners who were under the PAYE scheme or were self-employed individuals earning over £300. In other words, ninety per cent of the taxable population fell within the jurisdiction of the local authorities. Of these, less than half paid any tax, and most were grossly under-assessed. Almost invariably, only a fraction of the people assessed pay tax, as Table 8.3 shows:

TABLE 8.3 *Tax assessment and collection in Western Nigeria on incomes up to £300, 1962/3 and 1963/4*

		(£)
	1962/3	1963/4
(a) Amount assessed for collection	2,327,367	2,050,201
(b) Arrears of tax brought forward from past years	229,871	713,601
(c) Total tax due	2,557,238	2,763,802
(d) Actual collection	1,625,836	1,593,798
(e) Actual collection as a percentage of total amount due	63·6	57·9

SOURCE: Regional Tax Board, Western Nigeria Ministry of Finance.

It will be seen from Table 8.3 that only about three fifths of the taxes assessed are actually collected. The defective assessment and collection machinery at the local level is one of the principal causes of under-assessment and poor collection performance. There can be no doubt that a regional tax organisation would be more effective than the local organisations. Regional administration would have more authority, have access to wider information, and would ensure that taxpayers did not avoid liability by moving from one district to another. *A fortiori*, a national tax authority would be even more effective than a regional organisation.

Another principal cause of the inefficient administration of the tax system is partisan political interference. In another context, the writer has observed:

'The regionalisation of income tax jurisdiction has also resulted in some undesirable political consequences. Opposition parties, in their desire, no doubt legitimate, to defeat the governing parties at the poll, have criticised regional governments' income tax measures and have alleged discrimination and nepotism in their administrations. And the governments themselves have not been entirely free from narrow party political considerations in their tax measures and administration. In this regard, it is significant that those taxes, which are levied and administered by the federal government but which, as sources of revenue, are considerably more important than income taxes, have never figured prominently in partisan politics. Had such taxes been regional, it is not unlikely that they might have become issues of partisan and regional politics. The reality of the Nigerian political situation is that party politics tend to be more intense (if not more bitter and unwholesome) at regional than at federal level for the simple reason that the federal government has always been a coalition of two or more parties which may not see eye to eye at regional level but which find cooperation at federal level at best a desirable thing or at worst a necessary evil.'[1]

Personal income taxation in Nigeria therefore suffers from a number of problems. Some of these are legacies of the past, while others are political and administrative. Many of these problems have arisen, however, because the income tax is a regional and not a federal tax, and also because the regions, with the exception of

[1] Adebayo Adedeji, loc. cit., p. 171.

the East,[1] have remained content to administer the income tax in conjunction with local authorities. Thus, if the personal income taxation is to become an important and growing source of revenue in Nigeria, the governments will have to break completely from the tradition of direct taxation, separate it from local government taxation, reduce the number and scale of personal allowances and reliefs, increase the tax rates, and improve the administrative machinery. In other words, a uniform tax system is clearly to be preferred.

Ideally, the federal government should assume jurisdiction over income taxation. The revenue which accrues from the tax could be shared among the various governments in accordance with an agreed formula. But it is very difficult to foresee what the attitude of the state governments will be to a proposal that they should hand over their jurisdiction over personal income tax to the federal government. However, it should be possible for Nigeria to achieve at least the same degree of personal income tax harmonisation as has been achieved in East Africa. The governments of Kenya, Zambia, and Tanzania have operated a uniform income tax system since 1939, when they were all British dependencies. Although the allowances and rates are enacted separately by each of the three governments, they are agreed upon in advance and announced simultaneously.[2]

While harmonisation will simplify the Nigerian tax system, it will not automatically solve the other problems discussed above. For reasons both of equity and revenue yield, immediate steps are required to eliminate the regressivity of the income tax systems. This will necessitate a reconsideration of the rate structure and of

[1] It is not without significance that only the Eastern Nigeria government has applied income taxation vigorously and efficiently. This is because until petroleum was discovered in commercial quantities in the region, it was the poorest of all the regions.

[2] A detailed analysis of the income tax systems of these countries is to be found in the *Report of the East African Commission of Inquiry on Income Tax, 1956–57* (Nairobi: East Africa High Commission, 1957). See also John F. Due and Peter Robson, 'Tax Harmonization in East Africa', in Carl S. Shoup (Ed.), *Fiscal Harmonization in Common Markets* (New York: Columbia University Press, 1967), vol. II, pp. 553–605.

the personal allowances and exemptions. It will also require the widening of the concept of 'taxable income' to include such elements of income as rental income, income in kind, capital gains, dividends, interest, and gifts. It is only by undertaking these reforms that income tax revenues can become income-elastic and the income tax systems can achieve such other desirable fiscal goals as equity and allocative efficiency.

Company income taxation

The organisation and control of public companies is one of the subjects on the exclusive federal legislative list. It is therefore logical that the taxation of companies should be an exclusive federal subject. There are many compelling reasons in the over-all national interest why this should be so. The encouragement of industrial and commercial investment, whether from overseas or domestic sources, makes it particularly desirable that a single jurisdiction should apply over the company tax throughout the country.

This jurisdiction over companies and company taxation has given the federal government an important instrument of economic control. The Companies Income Tax Act[1] and the Industrial Development (Income Tax Relief) Act[2] have been used as instruments for promoting industrial, agricultural, and commercial development, and for channelling the activities of these companies to productive and risky investment. The Companies Income Tax Act provides liberal depreciation allowances for capital expenditures, such as for machinery and fixtures, the construction of buildings, and the development of mines and plantations.

Initial allowances are provided at the following rates for qualifying capital expenditures:

Machinery and Equipment	40 per cent
Mines	25 per cent
Industrial buildings	20 per cent
Plantations	25 per cent
Buildings other than industrial buildings	Nil

[1] Act No. 22 of 1961.
[2] Chapter 87 of the Laws of the Federation of Nigeria, Lagos, 1958.

In addition to these initial allowances, annual allowances are given at a reducing balance basis at the following rates:

Plant varying rates depending on the life of the particular asset in question.
Mines fifteen per cent or such higher rate as may be appropriate in view of the rate of exhaustion of the mineral deposits.
Buildings (whether industrial or not) ten per cent
Plantations according to the productive life of the plantings.

The Act also provides special relief for small private companies incorporated and controlled in Nigeria during the first six years of their commencement.[1] Such companies are entitled to a remission of the full rate of the company tax for the first two years, two thirds of the full rate for the third and fourth years, and one third of the full rate for the fifth and sixth years, provided assessable profits do not exceed £1,000. The Act also discriminates in favour of public limited liability companies incorporated and controlled in Nigeria.

The Industrial Development (Income Tax Relief) Act empowers the federal government to grant pioneer status to any industry which is not being carried on in Nigeria 'on a scale suitable to the economic requirements' of the country, or where it is expedient in the public interest to encourage the development or establishment of the industry in Nigeria.[2] Pioneer certificates may be granted to any company operating in a pioneer industry or producing a pioneer product for a period varying from two to five years depending on the amount of qualifying capital invested;[3] the company is exempted from paying the company tax during that period.

The cumulative effect of both the generous depreciation allowances and the tax holidays granted under the Industrial Development (Income Tax Relief) Act is that revenues from company income taxation represent a small proportion of total tax revenue,

[1] The relief is limited to private companies established not earlier than 1 April 1944.
[2] Section 3 (i) of the Act.
[3] There is a basic period of two years. Thereafter, the pioneer certificate can be extended by another year if the qualifying expenditure is up to £15,000, by two years if it is increased by £50,000, and by three years if it is £100,000.

even though the tax rate is relatively high. Revenue from the company income tax has stagnated over the two years. It was seven per cent of total tax revenue in 1961/2, but decreased to 3·7 per cent in 1962/3, to five per cent in 1963/4 and 1964/5, and to 5·4 per cent in 1965/6. Yet the number of companies, both private and public, has increased very substantially over those same years.[1]

Although it is difficult to estimate the potential revenue which has been lost as a result of the generous treatment of companies, it seems not unlikely that the revenue sacrifice is out of proportion to the gains in increased investment induced by the provisions of both Acts. There is a growing body of opinion among economists which is sceptical of the effectiveness of this fiscal device in bringing about higher levels of private investment.[2]

While generous relief provided by the legislation has led to a substantial loss of revenue, the separation of jurisdiction over both personal and corporate income taxation has accentuated the problem. Since the regional governments have jurisdiction over partnerships, trusts, and other unincorporated associations, there is a tendency on the part of many of these institutions, such as individual traders and partnerships, to become private or public

---

[1] An industrial survey of Nigeria undertaken in 1963 by the Federal Office of Statistics shows an increase of 200 per cent in the number of companies, both private and public, between 1958 and 1963. See *Industrial Survey of Nigeria, 1963* (Federal Office of Statistics, Lagos), p. 4.

[2] See, for example, Jack Heller and Kenneth M. Kauffman, *Tax Incentives for Industry in Less Developed Countries*, International Programme in Taxation, Harvard University Law School, Cambridge, Massachusetts, 1963, S. A. Aluko, *Fiscal Incentives for Industrial Development in Nigeria* (mimeographed), May 1967; and A. O. Phillips, 'Nigerian Industrial Tax Incentives: Import Duties Relief and the Approved User Scheme', *The Nigerian Journal of Economic and Social Studies*, vol. 9, No. 3, November 1967, pp. 315–27. It should be pointed out that the Central Bank of Nigeria, in its *Economic and Financial Review* (June 1964), estimated that while manufacturing and processing constituted only 22·1 per cent of foreign investment in fixed assets at the end of 1952, this sector received 50·9 per cent of the net inflow of foreign capital in 1961 and 1962. The presumption is that the tax incentive programme induced a greater shift of new investment to this sector than would otherwise have occurred.

companies in order to avoid the relatively high rates of regional income taxation and to benefit from the more generous allowances provided by the federal government.

Given the present regional jurisdiction over personal income taxation, the possibility of evasion would have been reduced if company taxation had been two-tiered—tax on profits and a tax on incorporation, with the profits tax being a regional tax. But this would have adversely affected the development of companies in Nigeria, and the location and growth of industries. A superior solution, from the point of view of fiscal incentives, revenue, and equity, would be to give the federal government jurisdiction over both the personal and company income taxes.

In addition, there is need to reform the company income tax without jeopardising the objectives of increasing capital formation and of inducing a shift in investment to manufacturing. This can be achieved in a number of ways, the most important of which are a reduction in the rate of capital allowances and a more selective use of the pioneer industry programme under the Industrial Development (Income Tax Relief) Act. The criteria which would qualify an industry for a pioneer status should be rigorously defined, and the list of pioneer industries should be reviewed periodically. It is also necessary to discriminate in favour of re-invested profits in order to encourage re-investment.

Both the Companies Income Tax and the Industrial Development (Income Tax Relief) Act apply to all companies, except those in the petroleum industry, which are taxed under the Petroleum Profits Tax Act of 1959. The main difference between these taxes is that instead of applying a fixed rate of tax in the £ to the assessable income of the ordinary company, the tax on oil companies is assessed by halving their statutory 'profits' in such a way that the government's share includes all payments made by the company to government in respect of rents, royalties, and other taxes. This is the usual 'fifty-fifty' agreement in the oil industry. Since the profits tax does not become payable until there is a profit, and since profit does not develop until all depreciation provisions are covered as well as operating costs, the Act provides that some profits tax should be paid when the surplus, after operating costs

H

have been covered, represents more than the payment of rents and royalties.

Profits tax was accordingly paid for the first time in the 1964/5 fiscal year—six years after commercial production of oil began in Nigeria. The amount was only £375,000, but it increased to £1·3 million in 1965/6. In view of the rate of growth of the oil industry, the tax on the profits of the oil companies is likely to become a rapidly expanding source of revenue. The rate at which revenue expands will depend, however, not only on the rate of expansion of the production of oil and gas, but also on the rates of royalties. Since royalties are a major source of revenue to the regions, particularly the region in which the oil is produced, there will no doubt be a growing pressure for rates to be increased as the revenue from the petroleum profits tax increases. Already the major oil-producing region in the country, Eastern Nigeria, has pressed for the profits tax on petroleum to be declared a regional tax. This pressure has been resisted by the other regional governments and the federal government.

Conclusions

The problems which face each of the major taxes in Nigeria have been discussed at some length in this and the preceding chapter because of the overwhelming importance of tax revenues in the revenue structure of the country. Each of the major taxes has been examined. The problems which have tended to limit their revenue productivity have been identified and examined. In addition, their effective uses for purposes other than raising revenue have been considered. In particular, their utilisation for achieving a more efficient allocation of resources and for achieving inter-governmental, inter-regional, and inter-personal equity has been discussed. The peculiar problems of each tax, and of the formula for allocating the revenue derived from it within the framework of Nigeria's federal fiscal system, have also been dealt with.

One over-all conclusion which has emerged is that a fundamental change is taking place in the revenue structure of the country. Revenues from export and import taxes, which used to dominate the finances of the governments, have yielded to mining revenue, excise duties, and company taxation, including the petroleum profits tax. During the next five years, oil revenue is likely to dominate the government finances. The reforms which have been suggested in these chapters are designed to make the taxes, particularly those with high income elasticities, more productive of revenue, as well as more effective instruments of economic, social, and political control. The question as to how their revenues should be allocated in the future will be taken up in chapter 11, where the prospects and future development of federal finance in Nigeria are discussed.

9 Federal finance, loans and public debt policy in Nigeria

Internal and external borrowing constitutes the principal alternative to tax revenue as a source of governmental receipts. Whenever internal borrowing is from the banking system rather than from the public, it results in the creation of new money, and this could have an effect on the stability of the price level. It is therefore necessary to examine the role which internal and external borrowing has played in the country's fiscal system in particular and in the economy in general. It is also appropriate to consider the impact of the monetary system on public finance in Nigeria. But first it is necessary to present a description of the constitutional position with regard to currency and banking, foreign exchange, and the raising of internal and external loans.

In the older federations, federal powers over these matters are today both extensive and highly centralised. Yet, when the majority of these federations were established, they did not have many of these powers. This was because money at that time consisted mainly of coin, and the issuance of banknotes was in some countries a private business. Moreover, central banks as they are known today did not exist and the role of government in the economy was limited and circumscribed.[1]

In modern times the granting of these powers as the exclusive jurisdiction of the federal government is now generally regarded as one of the minimum requirements of federalism. Accordingly, the

[1] See R. R. Bowie and C. J. Fredrick (Ed.), *Studies in Federalism* (Little, Brown and Company, 1954), pp. 413–42.

Nigerian constitution gives to the federal government powers over the issuance of bills of exchange and promissory notes, the borrowing of money outside Nigeria for its own as well as the regional governments' use, and the borrowing of money within Nigeria for its own use. It is also given the constitutional power to control capital issues, foreign exchange, currency, coinage, and legal tender. The public debt of the federation is also a liability of the federal government.

On the other hand, the regions have jurisdiction over internal borrowing for their own purposes. And they can borrow outside Nigeria for a period not exceeding twelve months on the security of any of their funds or assets held outside Nigeria. Thus, except for these qualifications, the country's monetary system as well as its internal financial affairs are vested in the federal government.

The advantages of a single monetary system to the economy of Nigeria cannot be over-emphasised. It facilitates inter-regional trade and the use of external reserves. The centralisation of the monetary system also enables an effective monetary policy to be pursued, which can be used in stabilising the price level. It is also a means of achieving forced savings through the creation of credit, i.e., deficit financing. It is the last of these objectives that has been pursued to a considerable degree by the Nigerian federal government during recent years. The temptation to substitute deficit finance for increased tax revenue has proved irresistible, as it has also in many other developing nations. Thus, a study of federal finance in Nigeria should take into account the monetary system and its policies.

Until a Central Bank was established in 1958, the currency board system operated in Nigeria.[1] The country's currency was backed one hundred per cent by sterling reserve, and the monetary system was neutral; that is, it did not exercise discretionary control over the economy nor on the availability of foreign exchange. The regional governments and their statutory corporations, as well as the federal government and its statutory corporations, held separ-

[1] This was the West African Currency Board, whose activities extended to all the then British West African colonies: Nigeria, the Gold Coast (Ghana), Sierra Leone and the Gambia.

ate overseas assets. Even though the Central Bank was equipped with the necessary tools of credit control from the start, it played a limited role during its first four years of existence in regulating money and credit or balance-of-payments disequilibria. Instead, it concentrated its efforts on establishing new financial institutions, such as a clearing system, a short-term money market, a stock exchange, and within the past two years a development bank. Apart from the issuance of treasury bills, it has provided the federal government with advances which have averaged £71·8 million per annum since 1962.[1]

The Central Bank was expected to contribute £40 million toward the financing of the country's first National Development Plan which extends from 1962 to 1968. But during the first two years of the plan, it had contributed £19·36 million by the issuance of long-term government securities (development stock), and by 31 March 1966 these securities had increased to £82·96 million. The Central Bank has therefore played an important role in credit creation since 1962.[2]

This development poses vital issues for federal finance. The federal government now possesses powers for mobilising additional resources which were non-existent before the Bank was created, and since there are no constitutional means of regulating these powers, and no institutional means of securing an equitable distribution of the additional resources created, the regional governments are at a new disadvantage vis-à-vis the federal government. This is deeply resented by them.

Monetary role of the marketing boards

One of the fiscal implications of the regionalisation of the marketing boards (considered in chapter 5) was the imposition by the regional governments of an additional tax on export produce through the

---

[1] See the *Annual Reports of the Central Bank of Nigeria* and O. Olakanpo, 'Monetary and Banking Problems in Nigeria', *The Bankers' Magazine*, March 1966.
[2] Although some of these securities are sold to the public, most of them are held by the Central Bank.

manipulation of producer prices. These governments also in-
herited, through the regional boards, large sums of money which
the former commodity boards had accumulated before 1954.

In addition to the fiscal impact of the regional marketing boards
arising from their authority to vary the rates of producer prices,
there are monetary consequences. A change in the producer prices
for export produce affects the money incomes of the farmers, and
therefore the demand for money. And such a change cannot but
have an effect on the price level. A substantial increase in the
producer prices of the major export crops tends to increase the
price level and to create inflationary pressure, or to intensify the
pressure on the price level when it already exists. Since a large proportion of the additional money income given to farmers by increases in the producer prices is expended on imported goods,
producer price policy also has repercussions on the country's
balance of payments. Variations in the producer prices therefore
have considerable impact on the supply of money and the balance
of payments.

Yet the regulation of producer prices is entirely in the hands of
the regional marketing boards and their respective governments,
and the machinery for coordination among the regions is very
rudimentary. The marketing board whose region produces the
bulk of the export crop usually fixes the producer price for that
commodity, and other marketing boards follow its lead. The
Central Bank and the federal government are seldom consulted.

As an illustration, in 1961/2 the Western Nigeria Marketing
Board reduced the producer price for cocoa from £141 10s to
£92 10s per ton. In that year, the Western Region exported
186,000 tons of cocoa. The consequent reduction in the money
income of the producers was £9·11 million. This was about one
twelfth of the total money supply in that year. Changes in the world
prices for export crops, however, are not the only reason for a
change in producer prices. Revenue needs and political considerations also play important and sometimes decisive roles. In the
example just quoted, the world price of cocoa fell by only £5 per
ton, whereas the producer price was reduced by £49 per ton.

The federal government has, from time to time, expressed concern over the regional control of producer prices. In his 1962 budget speech, the Federal Minister of Finance expressed the concern of the federal government as follows:

'. . . there must be effective coordination and consultation between the various authorities whose major activities have a major bearing upon the supply of money and credit in the economy. Paramount in this field are the Regional Marketing Boards, whose producer price policies have a major and direct bearing upon the supply of money within the economy—indeed their impact upon the overall economy is probably the greatest of all monetary factors operating in Nigeria today. Without wishing to derogate from the ultimate responsibility of the regional authorities to determine producer prices, it is clearly in the national interest that these prices should be fixed only after consultation with the national monetary authorities and in the light of the overall monetary situation prevailing. A steep increase in the producer prices for a major crop in only one region could, in unfavourable circumstances, add overwhelming weight to pressures in the economy. The converse is, of course, equally true.'[1]

A recent development in financing the purchase of the export produce by the marketing boards is, however, likely to give the Central Bank more influence in the determination of producer price policies. Because they have all depleted their reserves, the boards have to resort to short-term loans from the banking system for the purchasing and marketing of their export produce. These loans are retired as soon as the produce has been sold in the world market. Since 1962, the Central Bank has accepted a responsibility to provide the short-term credit required by the boards. In that year it financed the crops of the Northern Nigerian Marketing Board to the extent of £13 million. Since then it has continued to be actively involved with the financial problems of the boards. By the beginning of the 1966 marketing season, the Bank had increased its credit to £30 million.

In addition, the Bank undertook direct lending to the Western Nigeria Marketing Board in 1965 to finance cocoa purchases when,

[1] *The Mobilisation Budget*, Budget Speech by the Federal Minister of Finance, 29 March 1962, p. 11.

on the instruction of the Cocoa Producers' Alliance, that Board together with other producers withdrew supplies from the market following the Alliance's failure to obtain agreement for a minimum price of £190 per ton from the consumers. For three months Nigeria stopped selling cocoa. Since the Board is required by law to purchase all cocoa offered for sale, it would have been unable to do so but for the substantial credit which the Bank made available: £14·4 million. Sums of £6 million and £5·3 million were also borrowed from the federal government and the commercial banks respectively.

The provision of credit facilities for financing the purchase of export crops gives the Central Bank some influence in the determination of producer prices. With this influence, it could become one of the most powerful means of controlling the amount of money in circulation. And since the Bank is most likely to use its influence in favour of stabilising the economy as a whole, it would generally be opposed to the wide fluctuations in producer prices which have occurred in the past. Thus the producer is likely to fare better as the Bank's influence increases. The regional authorities, on the other hand, would in turn have to delimit or de-emphasise revenue and political considerations in the fixing of these prices. In any case the new state structure makes a complete review of the marketing board system inevitable. Should Nigeria have twelve marketing boards, each with the power to fix producer prices, or should the country revert to the pre-1955 marketing arrangements whereby a board was set up for each of the major export crops on a countrywide basis? Then there were four Nigerian commodity boards—for cocoa, oil palm produce, groundnuts, and cotton. In addition, another board could be established for the marketing of rubber. The establishment of four or five commodity marketing boards, each operating on a nationwide basis in respect of each commodity, is likely to cause less problems administratively, economically, and even politically than the setting up of twelve all-produce state marketing boards would do. Each commodity board would share its profits on an agreed basis among the state governments in accordance with proportionate production of each state. Coordination of producer price policies of the different commodity boards would be easier to achieve; political considerations and the rather unwholesome inter-state rivalry of producer price-fixing would also be de-emphasised. The country's monetary authority would be in a stronger position to influence producer price policies and harmonise such policies with its general monetary policy.

Internal borrowing

As was indicated earlier, internal borrowing for the purposes of the federation is on the exclusive federal legislative list. Borrowing internally for the purposes of any region is, however, residual. Partly because of their appreciation that internal borrowing is intimately concerned with the general control over monetary policy, and partly because the local loan market is limited and must be heavily supported by the Central Bank, the regions agreed at the first meeting of the Loans Advisory Board, held in January 1958, that for the period from 1958 to 1960 only the federal government should raise loans internally. It was also agreed that such loans should be made available to the regions on the terms at which they had been raised. This arrangement has continued since its inception. Thus, in spite of their constitutional jurisdiction over internal borrowing for their own use, the regions have been content to allow the federal government to borrow on their behalf.

At the time of independence in 1960, Nigeria's internal debt was relatively small. Funded debt was £12·84 million and the floating debt was only £2·00 million. But since 1960, as Table 9.1 shows, the Nigerian internal public debt has increased tremendously: between 1962 and 1966 by about 270 per cent.

This growth in the volume of loans raised internally has been made possible by credit creation from the Central Bank, since a substantial part of the amount realised from internal borrowing represents the Bank's financing of public investment. For instance the Bank had to buy 36·9 per cent of the Second Development Loan of 1961 and 34·8 per cent of the Third Loan of 1962. Nearly two thirds of the Fourth Development Loan of 1963 and eighty-five per cent of the Federal Republic First Development Loan of

TABLE 9.1 *Internal public debt of Nigeria 1962-6 (as of 31 March)*

(£ million)

	1962	1963	1964	1965	1966
Funded	19·36	34·36	54·36	68·96	82·96
Unfunded	11·84	11·56	11·76	12·22	11·61
Floating debt	18·23	21·45	30·00	35·00	37·00
Total internal debt	49·43	67·37	96·12	116·18	131·57

NOTE: Funded debt has a sinking fund, while there is no such fund in the case of unfunded debt. Floating debt consists mainly of ninety-one-day treasury bills and other short-term credit.

SOURCE: Federal Government of Nigeria *Estimates*, various years.

1964 came at least initially from the Bank.[1] A much larger proportion of the floating debt is financed by the Bank.

The proceeds of these loans have not been shared between the governments on the basis of any objective criteria. The Loans Advisory Board and its successor, the annual Conference of Finance Ministers, have allocated the proceeds of loans entirely on the basis of negotiation—negotiation which is invariably one-sided since the federal government decides some time before the Conference is held the proportion of any loan it will retain for its own use. It is only the allocation of the balance among the regional governments that is negotiable. It is therefore not surprising that the federal government has received 65·7 per cent of the total loans raised internally, as Table 9.2 shows. Next to the federal government is the Northern Nigeria regional government, which has received 12·9 per cent; the Western, Eastern, and Mid-Western regional governments have received nine, 8·8, and 3·6 per cent of the loans.

[1] The following are the amounts raised under each loan:

First Development Loan, 1959	..	..	..	..	£2·3 million
Second Development Loan, 1961		..	..	..	£10·0 million
Third Development Loan, 1962	..	..	..	..	£7·0 million
Fourth Development Loan 1963		..	..	..	£15·0 million
Federal Republic First Development Loan, 1964			..		£20·0 million

TABLE 9.2 *Distribution of the internal borrowing of Nigeria (as of 31 March 1966)*

(£ million)

	Federal	Western Region	Eastern Region	Northern Region	Mid-West	Total
Funded	42·89	8·86	10·56	17·05	3·60	82·96
Unfunded	9·61	1·00	1·00	—	—	11·61
Floating debt	34·00	2·00	—	—	1·00	37·00
Total	86·50	11·86	11·56	17·05	4·60	131·57

SOURCE: Federal Government of Nigeria *Estimates*, 1967/8.

The lack of an objective basis for allocating the proceeds of internal loans and the tendency on the part of the federal government to take the largest share, have caused much resentment and criticism by the regional governments. In the inter-regional allocations political consideration would appear to have had undue weight. While it is desirable that the present arrangement of centralising internal loans in the hands of the federal government should be continued, it is essential that a system be devised which would ensure an equitable allocation of the proceeds. A Finance Commission should be established to devise a formula for the allocation of the proceeds of internal loans with respect to the needs and other financial resources available to the various governments. This would be part of a process of biennial fiscal adjustment. (See chapter 11 for a more detailed projection of this proposal.)

External borrowing

Nigeria's public and publicly-guaranteed external debt has also increased significantly since independence. From £42 million at the end of 1961, it grew to £226·5 million by 1 April 1965. External financing has therefore become a most important source of public capital in Nigeria. Under the National Development Plan 1962–8, half the total projected capital expenditure of all the governments was expected to come from foreign aid, i.e., £327·1 million out of a total projected expenditure of £653·8 million.[1] Over one third of Nigeria's public debt is, however, in the form of suppliers' credit and contractor finance.

The federal government has received an even greater share of the proceeds of external loans than it has of internal loans. For example, between 1962 and 1964 the federal government received eighty-six per cent of the total external loans, while the shares of the regional governments were as follows: the North 5·4 per cent, the West 5·5 per cent, and the East 3·2 per cent. Almost all the external loans have been received for specific projects; in the final analysis, the choice has been that of the lending country or institution. The proportion of the off-shore cost element of each project is a big consideration: the higher this proportion the more attractive such projects seem to the aid-giving country or institution. Since the federal projects are mainly in the field of social overhead capital (transport, communications, and electricity) where the heavy capital requirements have a high foreign exchange component, they are preferred by the lenders. On the other hand, primary production and social services, which are the main concern of the regional governments, have relatively small off-shore cost components and are therefore not so attractive. It is primarily for this reason that the federal government has received a high proportion of the total external aid which has been extended to Nigeria.

Because the federal government has exclusive control over foreign loans, any region wishing to raise foreign capital must do so through federal authorities. So far no case has arisen in which the federal government has refused a regional request. This is due partly to the informal consultation which takes place between the ministries of finance[2] and also to the favourable attitude of the

[1] Federal Ministry of Economic Development, *National Development Plan, 1962–68*, pp. 32–3.
[2] A great deal of consultation takes place at official level between the federal and the regional ministries of finance. The regional officials are informed at an early stage of any aid proposal that is not likely to receive the federal government's approval, and of the reasons for disapproval.

federal government toward external aid. The problem which the country faces in this regard is the dearth of aid.

Under the present arrangement it is left to each regional government to select the project for which external financing is required, to encourage the interest of a lending country or institution in the project, and to undertake all the preliminary negotiations with the

TABLE 9.3 *Estimates of debt servicing capacity of Nigeria, 1964-71*

(£ million)

	1964/5	1965/6	1966/7	1967/8	1968/9	1969/70	1970/1
Ten Per Cent of Export Earnings	19·2	20·5	21·6	22·5	23·6	24·5	25·4
External Public Debt Service Charges	6·9	9·5	18·1	12·5	13·0	13·1	12·1

SOURCE: *National Development Plan Progress Report, 1962-64* (Federal Ministry of Economic Development), p. 19.

would-be lender or donor. As yet, there is no inter-governmental machinery for coordinating external aid, but this need to exercise more effective control over foreign aid will become increasingly urgent as the gap between the country's debt-servicing capacity and its external public debt charges diminishes.[1] Lenders and donors have until now supported individual projects rather than the whole of the development plan, but a centralised guide and clearing-house is now necessary. Table 9.3 presents an estimate of the country's debt service capacity from 1964/5 to 1970/1. This shows that there is still a considerable gap between capacity and estimated liabilities. These projections shown in Table 9.3 are,

Rather than submit a formal request which is liable to be rejected, a proposal is either withdrawn or modified in such a way as to make it acceptable to the federal government.
[1] In 1962, a Ministerial Coordinating Committee on External Aid was formed. Unfortunately, it has never functioned.

however, not entirely realistic, because anticipated borrowings and private debt charges have not been included. When account is taken of both of these, the gap will be much narrower. And as the burden of servicing the debt rises, it will be more difficult for Nigeria to raise loans externally. This consideration alone would appear to necessitate a more strict control over external loans than has been the case in the past.

In addition to the limitation imposed by the country's export earnings in meeting its external liability, there is also the limitation imposed on each government by revenue considerations. If the rate of growth in debt service charges for internal and external loans increases faster than the rate of growth in revenue, these charges will absorb an increasing proportion of government finance. A state government might conceivably reach a position where, given the total claims on its recurrent revenue, it would be unable to meet all of its liabilities. There are provisions in the country's constitution[1] for the federal government to deduct from its statutory payments to a region or state any sum for the payment of loans due in case of default, but this is a situation which, if it ever arises, is bound to cause a great deal of conflict and strain on federal-regional relationships. It is therefore in the interest of both the federal government and the regional or state governments to prevent such a situation. This could be achieved by instituting a coordinating mechanism for external loans.

[1] Section 143.

In chapter 1 we discovered that no single comprehensive theory as yet exists which encompasses all the different goals of fiscal adjustment. Fiscal adjustment in a federation is necessitated by a number of factors. First, there is the problem of resolving the imbalance of resources and needs between the federal and regional governments. Second, there is the problem of harmonising income with needs in the different regions. Third, there is the need to ensure that 'economic equilibrium' is achieved for the federation as a whole. And finally, there is the need to 'level up' so that the poorer regions are raised and the level of services provided in the different regions is equalised.

Even long before Nigeria became a federation, resources were being transferred from one part of the country to develop another part. Immediately after the amalgamation in 1914, and for several years thereafter, resources were transferred from the relatively developed South to the less developed North. And in the thirties, forties, and early fifties, resources were transferred from the West and the North to the East to raise the level of social services in that region. In fact, the emphasis which was placed on the principle of derivation as the basis of allocating revenue amongst the regions at the time of federation was due to a reaction by officials and politicians against the use of resources from the North and the West for the development of the East.

That the regions of Nigeria differ in size, population, level of development, resource-endowment, and therefore revenue capacity, has been shown in the preceding chapters of this study. The North,

accounting for more than half the country's population and about
three quarters of its land area, was the poorest of the regions. The
East, which in the fifties was considered comparatively poor, became potentially the richest region through the discovery and
production of petroleum in commercial quantities. The well-being
of the West has changed with the vagaries in the world demand for
cocoa, its principal export crop. These variations in sizes, populations, level of development, resource endowment, and fiscal
capacity exist today among Nigeria's twelve states. The only
significant difference between the regions and the states is that
none of the states is in so dominant a position by area and population as the Northern region had been.

The Raisman Commission did recognise the need for a periodic
review and adjustment of the fiscal system—both as between the
federal government and the regional governments and among the
regions. Accordingly, it recommended that provision should be
made in the Nigerian Constitution for a periodic review of the
distribution of revenue so that 'the balanced development of the
federation could be maintained'[1]—this was the 1964 Fiscal Review
Commission.

Fiscal adjustment in Australia and India: the lessons of experience

Of all federations, the Commonwealth of Australia has the longest
experience in making fiscal adjustments on a regular, rational, and
institutionalised basis between and among the state and federal
governments. By studying the Australian experience, which is the
most logical, cooperative, and enlightened, Nigeria can gain
important knowledge about fiscal adjustment.

After experimenting with a series of financial agreements
designed to solve federal-provincial financial problems on an *ad
hoc* basis, the Commonwealth Grants Commission was established
by an Act of Parliament in 1933 and was charged with the function
of inquiring and reporting upon:

(i) applications made by any State to the Commonwealth for the

[1] *Raisman Report*, p. 39.

grant by the Parliament of financial assistance in pursuance of Section 96 of the Constitution;[1]

(ii) any matter relating to grants of financial assistance made in pursuance of that section by the Parliament to any State which are referred to the Commission by the Governor-General; and,

(iii) any matter relating to the making of any grant of financial assistance by the Parliament to any State in pursuance of that section, which is referred to the Commission by the Governor-General.[2]

In addition to receiving evidence, the Commission conducts its own research into the problems involved in its work. As the Commission aptly stated it in its first report, '. . . it is obvious that a scientific measurement of the disabilities of the States cannot be achieved without an exhaustive and convincing assessment of the effects of a number of fundamental and very complex factors which more or less govern the economic and financial life of the nation'.[3]

During the initial period of its operation, the Commission was asked by the claimant states of South Australia, Western Australia, and Tasmania to consider disabilities arising from federation as a basis for compensation. However, the Commission rejected this on the ground that it is 'impracticable to assess grants on the basis of disabilities arising from federation and from the operation of federal policy'.[4] It chose, instead, the principle of financial need as the basis for making fiscal adjustments. It enunciated this principle most clearly in its Third Report (1936) in the following terms:

[1] Section 96 of the Australian Constitution reads as follows: 'During a period of ten years after the establishment of the Commonwealth and thereafter until the Parliament otherwise provides, the Parliament may grant financial assistance to any state on such terms and conditions as the Parliament thinks fit.'

[2] Commonwealth Grants Commission, *First Report* (1934), and subsequent reports. The membership of the Commission is composed of a chairman and two members, and the tenure of office of each is three years. The Commission exercises advisory rather than judicial powers, but takes evidence on oath.

[3] Commonwealth Grants Commission, *First Report* (1934), p. 12.

[4] Commonwealth Grants Commission, *Sixth Report* (1939), p. 88.

'Special grants are justified when a State through financial stress from any cause is unable efficiently to discharge its functions as a member of the federation and should be determined by the amount of help found necessary to make it possible by reasonable effort to function at a standard not appreciably below that of other States.'[1]

Since then, this principle has remained unaltered as the basis on which the Commission's recommendations have been made, even though the methods of applying it have had to be adapted to changing circumstances. The Commission has devised a formula for assessing the fiscal need of the claimant states. This formula is generally regarded as providing an objective measurement of need, particularly by the claimant states.

Since 1949, the grant recommended for payment to a claimant has been set out in two parts, which are called respectively the *first part* and the *second part*. The first part is a fiscal adjustment of the grant paid two years earlier as a result of the Commission's examination of the audited budget figures for all states. The second part is in the nature of an advance, and is based on a forecast of the total financial assistance which is likely to be justified as a payment. In calculating the grants payable, the Commission not only corrects the audited accounts of both the claimant and the non-claimant states, but to ensure comparability it also adjusts the accounts 'for differences between the claimant state and the standard states in efforts to raise revenue and in levels of expenditure in providing certain services'.[2] Thus, in calculating fiscal need, the Commission takes full cognisance of revenue effort and the level of public services in the claimant states.

By basing the fiscal adjustment on need, and by recommending block grants, the Australian Commonwealth Grants Commission has repudiated the notion that the authority which spends money should also have the responsibility of raising it. The Australian experience has proved that the authority which is best fitted to administer a public service is not necessarily the one which can obtain the revenue to finance services of national importance.

On the whole the Commission has earned the confidence of the

[1] Commonwealth Grants Commission, *Third Report*, para. 164.
[2] Commonwealth Grants Commission, *Twenty-ninth Report* (1962), p. 43.

states and has thus become a fiscal court of conciliation and arbitration. Among the older federations of the world, Australia is the only one which has approached the problem of the poorer states and has tried to achieve fiscal equity and equalisation among them. This has, of course, not been without its disadvantages, the principal one being that the states have lost a great deal of fiscal autonomy. On the other hand, the grievances of the poorer states have faded into the background since the Commission was established.[1]

The Australian experience in fiscal adjustment no doubt exercised great influence on those who drafted the Indian Constitution. Not only did that Constitution provide for a sharing of revenue and for grants-in-aid from the Union government to those states in need of assistance, with power to fix different sums for different states, but it also provided for the appointment by the President of India of a Finance Commission. This Commission, consisting of a chairman and four other members, was to be appointed within two years from the commencement of the Constitution and thereafter at the expiration of every fifth year or earlier if necessary. Accordingly, the first Finance Commmission was appointed in November 1951, and subsequent ones have been appointed in 1956, 1960, and 1965.

The duty of the Finance Commission is to make recommendations to the President for:

(a) the distribution between the Union and the States of the net proceeds of taxes which are to be, or may be, divided between them . . . and the allocation between the states of the respective shares of such proceeds;

(b) the principles which should govern the grants-in-aid of the revenues of the States and of the Consolidated Fund of India;

(c) any other matter referred to the Commission by the President in the interest of sound finance.[2]

This constitutional provision for an independent commission to

---

[1] In 1933, the year the Commission was established, Western Australia voted in a referendum by a 2:1 vote in favour of secession from the federation because of the strong feelings against federation and federal policy.

[2] See Clause 3 of Article 280 of the Constitution of India.

advise on the allocation of grants and the distribution of revenue from shared taxes is indeed novel and unique. Because the Commonwealth Grants Commission in Australia was constituted by an Act of Parliament, there is no constitutional barrier to its termination. On the other hand, it would require a constitutional amendment to abolish the Indian Finance Commission or even to modify its duties or its composition. Moreover, while the Commonwealth Grants Commission is a permanent body, the Indian Finance Commission is an *ad hoc* body set up once every five years. On the other hand, the Finance Commission has wider powers than the Commonwealth Grants Commission. It does not merely advise on grants-in-aid, but also on the sharing of divisible taxes and the principles on which allocations are to be made. Given these wide powers, there is no gainsaying the fact that the Commission would have been most effective had it been a permanent rather than a quinquennial body.

Successive Indian Finance Commissions have felt the limitations which the *ad hoc* nature of their existence imposes. To overcome these limitations they have recommended the introduction of an element of permanency. The First Finance Commission recommended the establishment of a small organisation for studying the finances of the state governments, the rates of taxes in operation, the effects of proposed taxes, and other relevant matters. Such an organisation would have obtained data from the state governments in regard to the progress of various social services, analysed and tabulated them, and made available the results of these studies to successive Finance Commissions. Although this recommendation was accepted by the government, only a small unit was established, initially in the President's Secretariat and subsequently in the Ministry of Finance. The Second, Third, and Fourth Finance Commission made further suggestions, especially for the reorganisation and strengthening of this unit, and also noted the necessity of making reliable statistical data available to the Commission. As K. V. S. Sastri has pointed out, such '. . . continuity of work is capable of ensuring the most economical utilisation of federal fiscal transfers by the recipients and the closest possible alignment of transfer to States' needs. Under the present quinquennial system, . . . both these advantages are missing.'[1] A permanent Commission would overcome these difficulties, with a consequent substantial gain in efficiency and effectiveness.

The Indian Finance Commission has faced an even more serious but related problem. This is the overlap in its functions with those of the Planning Commission. The government of India constituted the Planning Commission as an independent body for formulating its own and the state governments' quinquennial national plans. To formulate each five-year plan, the Commission makes an assessment of all available resources, and determines the size and priorities of the national plans from this assessment. This planning exercise involves the examination and acceptance of the revenue and expenditure forecasts of the Union and the state governments. The additional tax efforts to be made are similarly determined as part of the planning exercise.

Thus the emergence of the Planning Commission as the supreme economic authority has largely defeated the intention of the constitution, and created an overlap of functions with the Finance Commissions. At the time of the first Finance Commission, the Planning Commission had not begun to play a prominent role. The second Finance Commission, after noting the overlap of functions, urged effective coordination of both Commissions, but it was left to the third Finance Commission to advance two suggestions to alleviate the problems.

The first suggestion was that the functions of the Finance Commission should be enlarged to 'embrace total finance to be afforded to the States, whether by way of loans or devolution of revenues, to enable them both to balance their normal budgets and to fulfil the prescribed targets of the Plan'.[2] The enlargement of the functions of the Commission in this comprehensive manner would solve the problem of multiplicity of agencies involved in fiscal adjustment, for in addition to both Commissions' responsibilities in this field, the Indian government is also empowered to make specific purpose grants entirely on its own. As the third

[1] K. V. S. Sastri, *Federal-State Relations in India* (Oxford University Press, 1966), p. 7.
[2] *Report of the Finance Commission* (1961), pp. 35–6.

Finance Commission rightly pointed out, these grants tend to be 'discretionary in character, not necessarily on the principle of uniform application'.[1] The second suggestion was that the Finance Commission should be abolished, and the Planning Commission be transformed into a Finance Commission at the appropriate time.

The Indian Finance Commissions have emphasised the fiscal needs of the states as the basis for making fiscal adjustments. However, the definition of fiscal needs and the determination of these needs have varied from time to time. The first Commission formulated certain principles which should regulate the assessment of fiscal needs and, in doing so, also defined their scope. The principles which it laid down were the budgetary needs of the states, the tax effort made by each state, economy in state expenditure, the level of social services reached in each state, special obligations, and broad purposes of national importance.

These principles are unexceptionable, but the difficulty lies in applying them. As the third Finance Commission admits:

'The comparative administration of tax efforts of the States cannot be in absolute terms. It has to be related to their tax potential, and this calls for a special study. Similarly, the assessment of the measure of economy effected or the degree of efficiency reached in a states' administration is a complicated exercise which, in any event, we [the Finance Commission] could hardly undertake with the organisation and time at our disposal. Yet, without reliable and comparative information on these essential ingredients of grants-in-aid, it is difficult to determine the quantum of assistance that would be necessary and justified.'[2]

The result is that all the Commissions have attempted to cover the annual budgetary gaps of the states rather than meet their fiscal needs, having taken into account those principles enumerated by the first Commission. Some states have accordingly relaxed their tax efforts and are not making maximum effort in effecting economies in expenditure. 'Secure in the knowledge that the annual budgetary gap would be fully covered by devolution of

[1] ibid., p. 34.
[2] ibid. (1961), p. 29.

Union resources and grants-in-aid,' wrote the third Commission, 'the States are tending to develop . . . an allergy to tap resources.'[1]

Constitutional provision for fiscal adjustment in Nigeria

The Nigerian Constitution provides that the federal government 'acting after consultation with the governments of the regions, shall from time to time appoint a Commission to review and make recommendations' with respect to the allocation of the proceeds of mining rents and royalties and the distribution of funds in the Distributable Pool Account among the regions.[2] The Constitution has thus excluded from review a number of important sources of revenue, such as export taxes, import duties, excise duties, and the company tax. Therefore, whenever fiscal adjustment is to take place, it will be accomplished only through changes in the allocation of revenue from mining rents and royalties and the Distributable Pool Account.

It will be readily seen that the fiscal adjustment process in Nigeria is more circumscribed than it is in India and Australia. While the Indian Constitution authorises the Finance Commission to review the distribution of the proceeds of taxes shared by the Union and the states, no such provision is in the Nigerian Constitution. Although the Nigerian Constitution empowers the federal government to make grants to the regions,[3] it does not stipulate, like the Indian Constitution, that the fiscal review Commission should advise on the principles which should govern grants-in-aid to the states out of the federal government consolidated fund. It might be added, however, that the Nigerian Constitution does not exclude the consideration of such a matter, should the federal government decide to refer it to the Commission. On this issue of whether any other matter besides those stipulated in Section 164

[1] ibid., p. 38.
[2] *The Constitution of the Federation (Act No. 20 of 1963)*, Section 164. This was the constitution promulgated when Nigeria became a republic. The same provision was contained in the *Nigeria (Constitution) Order in Council No. 1652 of 1960*, i.e., the Independence Constitution.
[3] *Nigerian Constitution*, Section 73.

of the Constitution may be referred to the Commission, there is no guide. Judging from the terms of reference of the 1964 Commission, however, it would appear that there is no limitation as to what may be referred to the Commission, provided, apparently, that there is a consensus among the governments.

This discussion raises another problem. If the federal government can only appoint a Fiscal Review Commission 'after consultation' with the regional governments, does this mean that each of the regional governments must agree to the need for a Commission and on its terms of reference? One gathers (but there is no incontrovertible evidence) that there was agreement on both of these before the 1964 Commission was appointed. Moreover, the Constitution is vague about the periodicity of the review. It simply states that a commission should be appointed 'from time to time'. The Finance Commission of India meets every five years, while the Commonwealth Grants Commission of Australia is a Standing Commission. This vagueness with respect to the frequency of the Nigerian fiscal review could be a source of chronic inter-governmental conflict. For example, the state governments may press for a review at a time when the federal government does not think that one is required.[1] Or the federal government could exploit a review to the detriment of the regions. Thus, although the vagueness is conducive to flexibility, it may also be the source of inter-governmental friction.

In the preceding section, the limitation which the *ad hoc* nature of its existence imposes on the effectiveness of the Indian Finance Commission was noted. This limitation applies *mutatis mutandis* to the Nigerian Fiscal Review Commission. There is no doubt that a permanent commission would be the most effective method of assessing the need for fiscal adjustment. It can be argued, however, that whereas the scope of the Indian Finance Commis-

---

[1] One gathers that the 1964 Fiscal Review Commission was set up after considerable pressure from the regions, particularly the East. The federal government was indifferent about the need for a review. The suggestion by the Raisman Commission that the first review should take place within three to five years of the coming of the inception of the 1959 changes in the fiscal system was used most effectively by the regions.

sion is wide enough to justify a permanent commission, the scope of responsibility of the Nigeria Fiscal Review Commission is too narrow to justify permanent deliberations and study. But if the terms of reference of the 1964 review commission are to be taken as setting a precedent, its scope is already wider than is provided in the Constitution. It is not clear why the Raisman Fiscal Commission rejected the establishment of a standing review commission.[1]

The Nigerian Constitution, unlike the Indian, is silent on the composition of the Commission. The Raisman Fiscal Commission, which gave the matter some thought, decided that the composition should be left for the decision at the time of establishing the Commission. This appears to be a rather cavalier way of dealing with such an important matter. Here again the Indian Constitution is more concrete, for it provides that the Finance Commission shall consist of a chairman and four other members.

The Indian Finance Commission (Miscellaneous Provisions) Act of 1951 even went further than the country's Constitution. This law prescribes that the chairman of the Commission should be selected from among those persons who have experience in public affairs, and that the four other members should be selected from among the persons who: (1) are or have been qualified to be appointed as judges of the High Court; or (2) have special knowledge of the finances and accounts of the government; or (3) have had wide experience in financial matters and in administration; or (4) have special knowledge of economics. The Act of Parliament which set up the Commonwealth Grants Commission of Australia also stipulated that the Commission should consist of a chairman and two members, and that each should be appointed for a period of three years.

Thus, compared with the system in both India and Australia, the fiscal adjustment system in Nigeria leaves much to be desired. First, the functions constitutionally stipulated for the Fiscal Review Commission are too narrow. Second, the Constitution is silent as to how frequently the fiscal review should be undertaken,

---

[1] *Raisman Report*, p. 39, para. 172, merely states: 'We do not support one suggestion made to us that a Standing Review Committee . . . should be set up . . .'

and on the composition of the commission. If the machinery for fiscal adjustment in India needs to be reformed, that of Nigeria needs complete overhauling.

Nigerian experience in fiscal adjustment:
the 1964 Fiscal Review Commission

In June 1964, six years after the implementation of the recommendations of the Raisman Fiscal Commission, the federal government appointed Mr K. J. Binns, C.M.G., as the Sole Commissioner.[1] His terms of reference were:[2]

(a) to review and make recommendations with respect to the provisions of sections 140 and 141 of the Constitution of the Federation;

(b) to examine the appropriateness, in the prevailing circumstances of Nigeria, of—

(i) the formula for the allocation of the proceeds of mining rents and royalties laid down in section 140 of the Constitution of the Federation;

(ii) the formula for the distribution of funds in the Distributable Pool Account laid down in section 141 of the Constitution of the Federation;

(c) to take into account for the purpose of such examination—

(i) the experience of the various Governments of the Federation in the working of revenue allocation now in force;

(ii) the creation of the new Mid-Western Region and the proportion of the percentage of quarterly allocation payable to it under section 141 of the Constitution;

(iii) all sources of revenue and other receipts available or potentially available to each of the five Governments in the Federation; and,

(iv) the legitimate requirements and responsibilities of each of the five Governments in the Federation;

---

[1] Under-Treasurer and State Commissioner of Taxes in the State of Tasmania, Australia.

[2] *Official Gazette of the Federal Republic of Nigeria*, vol. 51, p. 911, Government Notice No. 1072.

(d) to consider the financial implications of the non-availability of promised foreign aid for university education and other unfulfilled pledges for financial assistance to Nigeria; and,

(e) to make recommendations to the Federal Government on the above matters.

Section 164 of the Constitution had provided for a more limited, but similar review of fiscal problems.[1] Judging from the evidence submitted by some of the regional governments, their influence in broadening the scope of the Commission's task is readily discernible. They interpreted the terms of reference 'as though they embraced a complete review of all aspects of federal/regional financial relationships'.[2] On the other hand, the federal government held the view that the Commission 'was virtually limited to making recommendations regarding the size of the Distributable Pool Account and its distribution amongst the regions'.[3]

Because of differences in interpretation as to the scope of the Commission's job, the submissions of the various governments covered a wide variety of matters.[4] For instance, the Mid-Western government submitted recommendations on such matters as the companies income tax, export duties, radio and television licences, and the payment of a block grant 'to assist with the establishment of the new region'.[5] Although the Commissioner refused to be 'rigidly tied to and restricted by any literal construction of the matters',[6] he refrained from commenting or making recommendations on those issues which he considered irrelevant and outside his terms of reference.

In its submission to the Commission, the federal government

---

[1] Section 136 is concerned with the proportion of the proceeds of duties payable in respect of the import into Nigeria of certain goods.

[2] K. J. Binns, *Report of the Fiscal Review Commission*, Federal Ministry of Information, Printing Division (Lagos, 1964), p. 6.

[3] ibid., p. 16.

[4] Each government in the federation submitted a written memorandum. In addition, the Eastern Region submitted a supplementary memorandum. The submissions by the five governments are summarised at pp. 11–16 of the Commission's report.

[5] K. J. Binns, op. cit., p. 16.

[6] ibid., p. 13.

expressed opposition to any further allocation of federal revenue to the regions, but argued strongly in favour of increasing its own shares of mining rents and royalties (at the expense of the regional governments). The federal government offered no suggestion as to the formula which should govern the allocation of the Distributable Pool Account among the four regions, although it expressed general support for the four principles which had been adopted by the Raisman Commission—continuity, minimum responsibilities, population, and balanced national development.

The regions for their part were unanimous in asking for an additional share of federal revenue—partly on the grounds of growing regional need, but also on the grounds, as the Northern Region government expressed in its memorandum to the Commission, that a reduction in federal revenue would limit the spending capacity of the federal government for low-priority projects.[1] The memorandum of the Eastern Region went even further than that of the North. It suggested that most federal revenues should be allocated to the regions in full on the basis of derivation, and that the federal government should recoup for the lost revenue by levying a capitation tax of £1 or more on every adult in Nigeria.

All three regions which were in existence at the time of the 1959 Raisman Commission argued that they had suffered vis-à-vis the other regions under that Commission. The North claimed that it had been unable to narrow the gap in its services and investment expenditure as compared to the other regions because the revenues of the other regions, particularly the East, had been more buoyant than its own. The East claimed that the existing system of revenue allocation had proved 'extremely unreasonable, unfair and inequitable'. The West criticised the 'check' which was imposed on its rate of economic growth by the Raisman Commission. It claimed that 'what was intended as a temporary check had turned out to be a perpetual victimisation and penalisation'.[2]

Before considering the claims and counter-claims of the federal and regional governments, the Fiscal Review Commission examined the principles which, in its view, should govern 'the periodi-

[1] ibid., p. 13.
[2] ibid., p. 14.

cal adjustments to the basic financial arrangements'.[1] It rejected the suggestion that Nigeria was a loose federation and that greater financial autonomy should therefore be given to the regions. This claim, the Commission maintained, is not borne out by the country's Constitution, which gives wide powers and vital functions to the federal government: 'any doubt concerning the interest primacy of the Federal Government is immediately dispelled by considering the importance of its responsibilities which are set out in the Exclusive Legislative List of the Federal Parliament, and also . . . the concurrent Legislative List of the federal Constitution'.[2]

Given this primacy of the federal government, the Commission reiterated the Raisman Commission's assertion that 'the financial stability of the federal centre must be the main guarantee of the financial stability of Nigeria as a whole'.[3] However, the Commission felt obliged to reject the federal government's position that there should be no further allocation of federal revenues to the regions. The government 'is in a stronger financial position than might at first appear and . . . its revenue prospects are more favourable than submitted',[4] the Commission stated.

If federal funds are to be transferred to the regions, how is the level of the distributable funds to be determined, and by what means should the transfer to the regions be effected? The Commission's approach to the first part of this question was a pragmatic one—first, a determination of the extent to which federal revenue is likely to be more buoyant over the next four years than perhaps conservatively estimated by the federal government; second, the extent to which certain federal expenditures might be deferred; and third, the extent to which the additional funds might, without threatening the over-all strength of the federation as a whole, be made available to the regions.[5]

With regard to the second part of the question—the means of affecting further transfers of federal funds to the regions—the

[1] ibid., p. 16.
[2] ibid., p. 17.
[3] ibid., p. 17.
[4] ibid., p. 18.
[5] ibid., p. 19.

Commission did not favour the use of the distributable pool formula for the allocation of funds. This is because the pool consists of two elements which are of paramount concern to the federal government, namely, shares of import revenue and of mining rents and royalties.[1] The fact that the regions share the revenues from these two taxes with the federal government means that any change in federal policy affects the position of the regions. 'This in itself,' concluded the Commission, 'places the regional governments in a situation of uncertainty, and where they may seek unduly to influence federal policy by reason of their own financial problems.'[2] Thus, the sharing of these revenues places the federal government in a situation in which it cannot refer the appropriate policy solely to the needs of the nation as a whole, but must have some regard to the impact of its policies on the finances of particular regions.[3]

In view of these limitations on the use of the distributable pool, the Commission recommended that further federal funds for the regions should be distributed on the basis of a stated amount of revenue and not on the basis of a formula. The Commission realised, however, that the governments might prefer that any increased payments to the regions should be made through the distributable pool, and accordingly allowed for this possibility in its recommendations.

On the issue of how the additional federal funds should be allocated among the regions, the Commission rejected the principle of derivation. It also rejected the principle of financial need—the basis upon which the Commonwealth Grants Commission in Australia recommended the award of grants to the states. 'Need' is a relative concept, the Commission felt, and in the uneven development of Nigeria's regions, its application raises particular problems. The Eastern Region was also opposed to this criterion of need on the grounds that it would tend to impede national economic development by restraining the free flow of factors of production into those areas of greatest potential economic growth.[4]

[1] ibid., p. 18.
[2] ibid., p. 19.
[3] ibid., p. 19.
[4] ibid., p. 20.

The Commission alternatively suggested placing each regional government in an approximately comparable financial position. In applying this suggestion, consideration was given to the over-all cash position of each regional government and the extent of its efforts to provide for its own fiscal needs and services. These bases involved an examination of not only the budgetary position of the regional governments, but also of their statutory corporations.

Having stated the principles and methods of the fiscal adjustment which it favoured, the Commission proceeded to make its recommendations. Since the Commission favoured further fiscal adjustments in the form of specific amounts of revenue payable from federal revenue to the regions, and not through the use of the Distributable Pool Account, it recommended no change in the existing allocation of thirty per cent of revenue from import duties on certain commodities and mining rents and royalties payable to the Account under Sections 136 (1) and 140 (2) respectively of the Constitution. The Commission proposed, however, the conversion of the regional shares of the Pool from ninety-fifth fractions to percentages as follows:

	Ninety-fifth fractions	Percentages recommended
Northern Nigeria	40	40
Eastern Nigeria	31	31
Western Nigeria	18	21
Mid-Western Nigeria	6	8

The increased shares of the West and the Mid-West under the percentage system were justified by the Commission on the grounds that the West, by the creation of the Mid-Western Region, lost practically the whole of its former revenue from mining rents and royalties. The larger share to the Mid-Western Region was justified by the relatively high costs of administration in the new area.

An additional annual payment of £3·75 million was recommended to be paid by the federal government to the regions. It further recommended that this amount should be shared among the regions as follows:

	£ million
Northern Nigeria	2·00
Eastern Nigeria	0·80
Western Nigeria	0·60
Mid-Western Nigeria	0·35
Total	3·75

This allocation was advanced on the basis of the Commission's principle of placing each region on a comparable financial position. The additional payment to the regions was to be made annually for four years, from 1965/6 to 1968/9.

The Commission further recommended the discontinuation of the sharing with the regions of part of the revenue from general excises. If this recommendation proved unacceptable to the governments, and if the sharing of excise revenues were continued, the Commission recommended that the annual payment should be reduced from £3·75 to £3·00 million, and should be shared among the regions as follows:

	£ million
Northern Nigeria	1·70
Eastern Nigeria	0·60
Western Nigeria	0·40
Mid-Western Nigeria	0·30
Total	3·00

The Commission also anticipated a preference on the part of the governments for further federal-regional fiscal adjustments to be affected through the Distributable Pool Account rather than on the basis of annual lump sum payments. It accordingly made the alternative recommendation that the percentage of the general import duties (Section 136 (1) of the Constitution) payable to the Distributable Pool Account could be increased from thirty to thirty-five per cent. It also recommended that the percentage of revenue from mining rents and royalties credited to the Account could be increased from thirty to thirty-five per cent, and the federal government's share could be reduced by a corresponding percentage. This would necessitate a change in the formula for

I

allocating the pool among the regions to place each one in a comparable financial position. Under these recommendations, the following percentage shares of the total pool were suggested:

	Percentages
Northern Nigeria	42
Eastern Nigeria	30
Western Nigeria	20
Mid-Western Nigeria	8
Total	100

The Commissioner was correct in anticipating that the regions would prefer that further allocations of federal revenue to them should be channelled through the Distributable Pool rather than by payment of an annual block grant. At a meeting of the National Economic Council held in 1965 to consider the report of the Commission,[1] all the governments accepted this alternative system of fiscal adjustment. They also accepted a recommendation to discontinue the sharing of revenue from general excise taxes. All of these recommendations were given constitutional effect by the amendment of the appropriate section of the Constitution and the resulting modified fiscal system came into operation on 1 April 1966.

As the first fiscal review commission to be appointed under Section 164 of the Nigerian Constitution, the Binns Commission occupied a unique position in the fiscal history of Nigeria. Unlike

---

[1] The National Economic Council was the highest inter-governmental body in Nigeria. Presided over by the Prime Minister, it consisted of representatives of each of the five governments. Each regional government was represented by its Premier and three to four of its ministers, including the Minister of Finance. The federal government delegation was led by the Federal Minister of Finance, and also consisted of three to four other ministers. The Council was set up in 1955 on the recommendation of the 1954 World Bank (I.B.R.D.) Mission to Nigeria. (See I.B.R.D., *The Economic Development of Nigeria* published by Johns Hopkins, 1954, p. 48.) Although the Council is an advisory body and its decisions are only in the form of recommendations to the governments, it has over the years acquired such a standing that these decisions are invariably ratified by the governments.

the pre-independence fiscal commissions which formed part of the process of constitutional development in Nigeria and of the country's evolution toward a federal structure of government, the Binns Commission was only a means of making periodic financial adjustment between and among the federal and the regional governments. Any future fiscal adjustment is therefore most likely to take account of the 1964 Commission and look to its report for guidance. It is by following precedents (or at least acknowledging them) that countries such as India and Australia have been able to evolve a set of principles on the basis of which financial adjustments have been made from time to time.

The guiding principles used by the Binns Commission in making its recommendations for financial adjustment, the method of its analysis, and the procedure it followed need therefore to be examined carefully. The likely effects of its recommendations on federal-regional fiscal relationships and on inter-regional fiscal equity also deserve close scrutiny.

The first criticism which may be made of the Commission is that it carried out its work in secrecy. Only the governments were asked to submit memoranda. All the hearings were held in private, and all the persons who appeared as witnesses before the Commission did so as representatives of their respective governments and, with the exception of two consultants to two of the regional governments, all were officials of the government and statutory corporations.[1] This procedure differs markedly from that of the Finance Commission of India and the Commonwealth Grants Commission of Australia. For example, the Indian Finance Commissions receive both oral and written evidence from non-governmental organisations, universities, and individuals, as well as from the federal and state governments.[2] In addition, the commissions gave

[1] See Appendix 1 of the Report of the Commission—*Proceedings of the Commission*—for the list of witnesses. Lady Ursula Hicks acted as an advisor to the Eastern Nigeria government, while the author served as adviser to the government of Western Nigeria.

[2] See, for example, Appendix V, pp. 159–61, of the *Report of the Finance Commission, 1965*, for a list of organisations and individuals which submitted written and/or oral evidence to that Commission, and Appendix VI, pp. 91–8, of the *Report of the 1961 Finance Commission* for a similar list.

the widest possible publicity to their assignments. It is not clear why the Nigerian Fiscal Review Commissioner did not adopt a similar procedure. Had he done so he would have had the benefit of other views besides those of the governments. Certainly, fiscal adjustment in a federation is of concern and interest not only to the governments but also to organisations and individuals.[1]

The Commission rejected the Australian Commonwealth Grant Commission's concept of financial need[2] on the grounds that (1) its application raises particular problems in a federation like Nigeria where development among the regions is uneven and (2) 'relative position of the several regions may be expected to change quite significantly in the foreseeable future'.[3] Both arguments are of doubtful validity. If per capita national income is used to measure the relative level of development of the regions, the gaps between the regions are not as wide as it is often supposed, and there has been a substantial reduction of this gap in the past decade and a half, as the following indices of per capita income by regions for the years 1950/1 and 1964/5 show:

Region	1950/1	1964/5
North	100	100
East	122	105
West	177	131

[1] In fairness to the Commissioner, it is not unlikely that this procedure was suggested to him by the federal government. In Nigeria, there is a tendency to secrecy in matters of public interest, even those in which the public at large should be encouraged to express views. The National Development Plan of 1962 to 1968 also was prepared in secrecy, and was not published until several months after the planning period had commenced!

[2] 'Special grants are justified when a State through financial stress from any cause is unable efficiently to discharge its functions as a member of the federation, and should be determined by the amount of help found necessary to make it possible for that State by reasonable effort to function at a standard not appreciably below that of other States.' Commonwealth Grants Commission, *Third Report* (1936).

[3] K. J. Binns, *Report of the Fiscal Review Commission*, Federal Ministry of Information, Printing Division (Lagos, 1964), p. 20.

The very likelihood of future changes in the relative position of the regions is precisely the reason for periodic fiscal reviews. By suggesting biennial reviews the Commission could have helped erase this problem of regional inequality; rather, it suggested that the next review should be undertaken four years after the adoption of its recommendations.

Although the principle of financial need as the basis on which the Commonwealth Grants Commission's recommendations have been made has remained unchanged since 1936, the methods of applying the principle have been adjusted to changing circumstances from time to time. The Fiscal Review Commission could have accepted this equitable system of fiscal adjustment and then devised its own methods of applying it, leaving it to succeeding commissions to accept these methods or devise new ones.

It may be argued with some degree of validity, of course, that the way the so-called principle of financial comparability was interpreted and applied by the Binns Commission makes it appear like merely another name for the principle of need. In the opinion of the Commission it was 'important that the Northern Region be enabled to provide essential social services to a greater number of its population and to a standard now generally accepted as proper in the three southern regions'. This is entirely in accord with the principle of need.

In applying the so-called principle of placing each regional government in a comparable financial position, the Commission used certain criteria in its assessment. These included the cash position of each region, recurrent budget prospects, the relationship of regional to local government finance, and the effects on the region's finances of their statutory corporations. Each of these criteria had certain limitations, as the Commission admitted in the following paragraph:

'It is inherently difficult to forecast the budgetary position of each Region for the next financial year, and such difficulties increase greatly the longer the period of time for which projections must be made. In examining recurrent budget prospects, the Commission has endeavoured to make appropriate allowances for the effort being made by a government to improve its financial position, particularly the relative severity of regional taxation and also the standard of services being provided, especially in the fields of education, health and agriculture. Such detailed comparisons are so much the more difficult because in some Regions many of these services are in part provided by Local Government authorities. There are significant differences in the extent to which Local Authorities in the several Regions finance such services from their own revenue collections or rely on grants-in-aid from their Regional Governments. A comparison of the financial position of the Regions is further complicated because of the different relations with their Marketing Board. In some Regions, the Marketing Board is expected from its trading to achieve a substantial annual surplus, to be made available to the Regional Government either by way of grant or loan. In this way the Marketing Boards are in a sense used as taxing agencies. The ability of a Marketing Board to make a contribution to the finances of its Regional Government partly depends on factors outside its control, particularly seasonal conditions and world prices. At the same time, in so far as they fix the prices paid to producers, after due allowance for Regional Produce Sales taxes and Export taxes, the Boards are to some extent in a position to determine the extent of their ability to assist their Governments.'[1]

In spite of the limitations of these various criteria, the Commission depended on them in recommending the additional payments which should be made to the regions and how these should be shared among them. In addition to the difficulties of making inter-regional comparisons, the Commission also admitted that it was not possible to quantify them, and that only limited statistical data were available. Because of all these difficulties, the Commission necessarily was forced to rely in large measure on its own judgement. In other words, the recommendations as to the volume of payments and their distribution lacked a firm quantitative foundation.

The Commission decided, after careful consideration, that it would be 'reasonable and appropriate' for the federal government to pay the regions an additional amount of £3·0 million per annum for four years. This, in its view, was the maximum amount

[1] ibid., pp. 21–2.

that the federal government could be expected to pay. If the regions relinquished their claims to part of the general excise revenue (other than the revenues from excise duties on motor spirit and diesel oil), the Commission recommended that the annual grant should be increased by £0·75 million.

In 1964/5, the regional share of general excise revenue amounted to £0·69 million. It was expected to increase to £1·71 million in 1965/6 and to £2·43 million in 1967/8, as revenue from excise duties has become an expanding source of finance because of the increasing tempo of industrial development in Nigeria.[1] The regions were asked, therefore, to surrender an elastic source of revenue in exchange for a fixed grant of £0·75 million. Furthermore, Nigeria's manufacturing firms are primarily import-substituting. To the extent that these industries use primary products as raw materials that would otherwise have been exported, the regional governments suffer a loss of revenue. As locally manufactured goods replace imports, the total import revenue is also likely to diminish, and the regional share of revenues from general import duties would be correspondingly reduced. Thus, the fixed grant of £0·75 million per annum for four years recommended by the Commission was grossly inadequate to compensate for these losses.[2]

The additional payment of £3·00 million annually is less than three per cent of the total revenue of the federal government in 1964/5.[3] On the other hand, the surplus of revenue over expenditure generated by the federal government in that year was over thirteen per cent of total revenue. Having regard to the increased financial need of the regional governments due to increased responsibilities—a fact which the Commission admitted—the additional payments recommended by the Commission were obviously minimal.

[1] The contribution of manufacturing activities to the GDP has increased by over seventeen times between 1950 and 1963 at current prices, and by about thirteen times at 1957 prices. This is several times more than the increase of any other activity in the economy.

[2] A rough estimate is that these two revenue losses would amount to about £4·5 million between 1965/6 and 1968/9.

[3] That is, total federal revenue less statutory appropriations to the regions.

One of the most criticised recommendations of the Raisman Commission was the formula it proposed for allocating the funds in the Distributable Pool, considering immediate needs, minimum responsibilities, population as an indicator of need, and balanced development. But the Raisman Commission failed to face the immense practical difficulties of quantifying each of these factors. Of these four criteria, only population was quantifiable, and there was even some uncertainty about this criterion. No wonder that after the Raisman Commission had discussed these factors in broad general terms, it proceeded to produce an entirely subjective formula.

One would have expected the Fiscal Review Commission to have devised a new formula based on objective and quantifiable data rather than on the vague and subjective criteria of the past commission.[1] Unfortunately, this did not happen. Although the Commission increased the allocated shares of the North, West and Mid-West from the Distributable Pool by two per cent, one per cent and two per cent respectively, and reduced that of the East by a little over one per cent, it did not desire to bring about any significant changes in the relative regional positions. The North continued to receive the largest share, a situation which the other regions, particularly the East, resented as unjustifiable.

Fiscal and financial problems of creating new states in Nigeria

The creation of more regions or states was one of the unsettled political issues before independence. Apart from the imbalance which existed among the regions, both in size and population,

---

[1] The Commission was pressed by some of the regions to use measurable criteria. For example, the Western Region submitted that the allocation should be based on three factors: population, the gap between planned capital expenditure and resources, and certain objective indicators of minimum responsibility. The indicators suggested were urban population, primary and secondary school population, and the mileage of tarred regional roads. The West also suggested that each of the three factors should be weighted, each receiving equal weight in the allocation of the Distributable Pool. See K. J. Binns, op. cit., p. 15.

each of them had minority ethnic groups which were outnumbered by one preponderant ethnic group. These minority groups have persisted in asking for the creation of more states in the country in spite of the fact that the commission appointed in 1958 to enquire into the fears of the minority groups and the means of allaying them did not recommend the creation of new regions/ states. Instead, that commission recommended the creation of special area boards so that minority groups could better foster their 'well-being, cultural advancement and economic and social development . . . and to exercise such powers as might be delegated to (them) by the regional government'.[1] As this solution did not satisfy the population of these minority areas the clamour for the creation of more regions continued unabated after independence. However, the Nigerian constitution provides for the creation of new regions/states from the existing regions.[2] The creation of the Mid-Western Region in August 1963, and the division by decree of the four regions and federal territory of Lagos into twelve states in May 1967, are in accord with the country's Constitution although the political crisis prevailing in 1967 and the suspension of parliamentary democracy since January 1966 made the observance of the procedure laid down in the Constitution for the creation of new states impossible.

However, the Constitution makes no specific provision for the financing of these new states, once created, particularly during their transitional period. Under the Constitution, the new states have all the powers and functions of the regions. The system of revenue allocation which applies to the regions automatically applies to the states. They assume jurisdiction over regional taxes and share federal revenue on the same basis as the regions. But the creation of new states raises a host of fiscal and financial problems the most important of which are (1) how to share the Distributable Pool Account; (2) how the new state governments are to meet the substantial and immediate capital requirements of creating their administrative and political machinery; and (3) what claims, if any,

[1] *Report of the Commission Appointed to Enquire into the Fears of Minorities and the Means of Allaying Them*, 1958, Cmd. 505, p. 41.
[2] *Constitution of the Federation of Nigeria*, Section 4.

the new states may have to the assets of the regions from which they have been created.

Unfortunately, the Constitution provides no guide to the solution of these problems. Even the obvious need for revising the formula for allocating the Distributable Pool which the creation of new states automatically necessitates was not provided for by the Constitution. With no specific constitutional provisions which take cognisance of the special needs of a new state, such a state is left entirely to its own devices and to the discretion of the federal government. Such a situation can cause considerable conflict between the government of the new state and that of the state from which it has been created (as in the case of the Mid-West vis-à-vis the West) as well as between it and the federal government.

When the Mid-West was created in 1963, the problem of devising a new formula for the sharing of the Distributable Pool Account was solved by dividing the share of the West into four parts and giving the new region one part thereof. This ratio of 3 : 1 was based on the ratio of the populations of the two regions. Thus, of all the four criteria used by the Raisman Commission in devising its formula, only one was used in dividing the West's share between it and the Mid-West. In the absence of a complete review, this was probably the only rational solution possible. On the other hand, the division distorts the very purpose which the pool was meant to serve. The solution fails to recognise the high costs of administration in a new region. It also fails to recognise the fact that the costs of administration in the region from which the new area has been carved were not likely to fall in the same proportion as the reduction in the population. In fact, the recurrent expenditure of the West was not reduced by one quarter simply because one quarter of its population had been transferred to the new region. In reality it fell by only eleven per cent between 1962/3 (the last full fiscal year before the creation of the Mid-West) and 1964/5 (the first full fiscal year after the creation of the new region), i.e., from £24·9 million to £21·0 million. By 1965/6 recurrent expenditure in the West had risen to £24·2 million, and was only 2·8 per cent lower than the 1962/3 level.

Yet on the creation of twelve states, the Federal Military

Government simply followed the 1963 precedent by dividing each region's share in the Distributable Pool Account among the states into which each region had been divided. Each of the six Northern states is given one sixth—seven per cent—of the Northern Region's share of the pool, while the share of the former Eastern Region is divided among the new states—Central-Eastern, South-Eastern, and Rivers—in the following respective ratios 7 : 3 : 2. One tenth of the share of the Western Region has been allocated to the Lagos State. The percentage distribution of the pool among the twelve states is now as follows:[1]

States	Percentages
North-Western	7·0
North-Central	7·0
Kano	7·0
Benue-Plateau	7·0
Central-West	7·0
Kwara	7·0
Lagos	2·0
Western	18·0
Mid-Western	8·0
Central-Eastern	17·5
South-Eastern	7·5
Rivers	5·0
Total	100·0

It is not clear why population has been used as the basis for dividing the shares of the Eastern and Western Regions among the states created from them while the shares of the Northern Region have been divided equally among the six Northern states. While population need not be the only criterion to be used, nor even one of the criteria, the lack of any discernible objective criteria for the allocation of the Northern Region's share among the six states of the North is likely to arouse considerable resentment in the larger states and might cause inter-state misunderstanding in the North.

[1] The Constitution (Financial Provisions) Decree, 1967, Decree No. 15 of 1967, *Official Gazette Extraordinary*, No. 37, vol. 54 of 27 May 1967.

The second major problem posed by the creation of new states is the provision of additional financial resources for setting up the administration of each state. A newly-created state needs to be put on a firm footing. And the responsibility for doing so unquestionably falls on the federal government. There are precedents in at least some other federations. In India, for example, the federal government has provided special grants and loans to new states for the construction of their new headquarters and for meeting their initial administrative requirements.

That the government of the Mid-West expected similar assistance from the federal government in 1963 cannot be gainsaid. In its memorandum to the Fiscal Review Commission it proposed a capital grant of £2 million and an annual loan of £1 million for a period of three years 'to enable it to overcome the teething troubles associated with the setting up literally from scratch a new government and to enable it to make a very modest start'.[1] If the new states structure is to survive, there is no doubt that the Federal Military Government will have to come to the assistance of most of the new states, particularly the smaller ones. Otherwise they will be unable to establish even the nucleus of state administration. The federal government appears to have realised its responsibility in this regard and has already made available a small initial grant to each of the new states for capital expenditure in setting up state administration.

The last and perhaps the most intractable of the three problems of statehood is the claim, if any, which a new state can legitimately have on the assets of the region out of which it has been created. In 1963 the government of Western Nigeria apportioned to the government of the Mid-West all its physical assets located in the areas which now constitute the region. It also apportioned the assets of its statutory corporations located in the Mid-West to the government of that region, and shared the accumulated assets of the marketing board on the basis of derivation.

The Mid-West government has claimed, however, that in addition to these receipts, all the assets of the government of Western

[1] *1964 Fiscal Review Commission: Memorandum by the Mid-Western Nigeria Government* (Ministry of Internal Affairs, Benin City), p. 9.

Nigeria at the time the new region was created (e.g., investments, loans, advances, cash balances, etc.) should be shared between the two governments. The Western Region rejected this claim on the grounds that the West was continuing its organic existence even after the new region had been created; that is, a company was not dissolving, and no assets and liabilities would have to be distributed amongst the share-holders or partners. There can be no just basis, the West continued, for sharing such assets, even if the principle of sharing is accepted, since it would be a most difficult exercise to determine the contribution of the areas which now constitute the Mid-West Region to the accumulation of these assets.

Most of the assets which the Mid-West government had in mind were the physical and financial assets. It contended that these assets had been acquired primarily with grants and loans from the region's marketing board, and to a lesser extent with budgetary surpluses transferred to the development fund. Since about ninety per cent of the marketing board's surpluses arose from the sale of cocoa, and since the Mid-West had produced only three per cent of the total Western Region's output of cocoa, should the assets be shared on the basis of a 97 : 3 ratio between the West and the Mid-West? The West further argued that from 1952 to the creation of the Mid-West in 1963 more was spent in the Mid-West area in the provision of public services and infra-structure than was received by way of revenue from this area.

The distribution of assets between the West and the Mid-West was still an unresolved issue when the twelve states were created in May 1966. Because of the civil war it has not been possible to tackle the distribution of assets and liabilities among the Eastern states. But in the North where six states have been created out of the Northern Region, this problem has been solved rather successfully and in a way which is not dissimilar from the solution proposed in 1963 by the government of the West.

The task of sharing the assets and liabilities of the Northern Region government has been facilitated by an Administrative Council set up under the Administrative Councils Decree (No. 18

of 1967) which was promulgated by the Federal Military Government.[1] Three criteria have been used to divide the assets and liabilities. The first is a constitutional one, necessitating the division of the assets and liabilities in such a way that each of the new states is able to discharge its functions under the Constitution. The second criterion is based on geographical consideration: immovable assets which are located in a particular state are allocated to the government of that state. The third divides movable assets among the six states on the basis of population.

There are however certain assets which cannot readily be divided among the states, partly because there are considerable financial and administrative advantages in having a centralised control of them and partly because the technical problems of division are immense. Most of the assets which come under this category are training institutions and services such as the Air Communication Flight, the Audit Department, the Sokoto Irrigation School, the Schools of Agriculture at Samaru and Kabba, and tsetse and trypanosomiasis control. For the maintenance of such services a Common Services Agency in which all the states will participate has been established. This agency, which is an administrative body with no legislative power, is to exist for five years in the first instance. It will coordinate the common services of the participating states.

The financial assets of the Northern Region government primarily consists of (1) Native Authority Surplus Funds; (2) Revenue Equalisation Fund; (3) loans and investment; and (4) cash balance. The first of these can be easily identified with particular states and therefore presents no problem in apportionment, the basis being the amounts contributed by the native authorities in each state. The other three cannot be so easily identified with individual states and so are divided on population basis. With regard to loans received by the Northern Region government, those for specific projects become the liabilities of the states in which the projects are situated or which benefit from the projects. With respect to general loans, the capital expenditures incurred by the Northern Region government during the two plan periods, 1956–62 and

[1] *Official Gazette Extraordinary*, No. 40, vol. 54, of 31 May 1967.

1962–8 have been used as the basis for apportioning liabilities among the states.

The division of assets and liabilities of the Northern Region government among the six northern states has been undertaken in a most comprehensive way and in a manner which is likely to cause very little inter-state conflict. The fact that the Northern Region ceased completely to exist after the creation of six states in the North and the setting up of an Administrative Council to ensure an orderly dissolution of the region has made this possible. In 1963, when the Mid-West was created, Western Nigeria continued to exist—the only difference which the creation of the new region made to the West being that its territory and population became smaller.

Conclusions

Compared with the older federations of Australia and India, the process of fiscal adjustment in Nigeria leaves much to be desired. Since independence in October 1960, only one fiscal review commission has been appointed to make financial adjustment in spite of the great changes which have taken place in the relative financial strengths of the governments. The new twelve-state structure of the country has introduced new dimensions to the fiscal system. The states are smaller in size, population, and fiscal resources than the regions. Therefore, more than ever before, a continuous review of the financial arrangements will now be necessary in order to ensure a smooth process of fiscal adjustment. Nigeria therefore needs a standing Finance Commission to look after fiscal adjustment on a continuing basis. In setting up such a commission, the country should learn from the experiences of India and Australia. The Nigerian Finance Commission should be composed like that of India but it also should be a permanent body like the Australian Grants Commission with a secretariat of its own. It should submit reports annually and make adjustments on a biennial basis. Its function should be as comprehensive as possible, covering not only fiscal adjustment but such matters as the division of shared revenues and the allocation of non-tax receipts.

Summary of conclusions

The development of federal finance in Nigeria has gone through four main phases. During the first phase, which began in 1946 and ended in 1952, the then newly-created regions of the North, West, and East were given limited fiscal powers vis-à-vis the central government. Each region had its own budget out of which was borne the cost of government services in that region. Regional revenues came from two sources—regional taxes and block grants from excesses of central government revenues. These grants were to be allocated among the regions entirely on the basis of the principle of derivation; that is, each region receiving grants in strict proportion to the contribution which it made to the central revenues. Perhaps the most enduring contribution made to the evolution of federal finance during this period was the introduction of this derivation principle—a principle which has been the main cause of inter-regional rivalry and conflict.

The second phase, which lasted for two fiscal years from 1952, was the period when the first move towards a truly federal financial arrangement was made. The regions were given independent tax jurisdictions and statutory shares of central revenues. Partly because the derivation principle had proved unworkable in practice and partly because it had strained inter-regional fiscal and political relationship, two new principles of federal finance—need and national interest—were added to the derivation principle as the basis of revenue allocation among the regions. But inter-regional rivalry and antagonism had become so deep-rooted that the Northern and Western Regions believed that they were contributing more to the central treasury than they were receiving, and disliked this new fiscal arrangement. Only the East favoured revenue allocation on the basis of need and national interest. But then the East was the most needy at that time.

In 1954, the champions of the derivation principle succeeded in getting it reinstated virtually to the exclusion of other principles. It was also used as the basis for sharing the accumulated reserves of the powerful commodity marketing boards which were put under regional control. These arrangements completely altered the relative financial strengths of the governments of the federation. The federal government lost a high proportion of its revenues to the regions. Moreover, regional imbalance was accentuated; the West becoming the strongest region financially and the East becoming the weakest. This phase lasted for four fiscal years, 1954-9. During this period also, the revenues from export taxes statutorily became regional and the dependence of the regions on this most unstable source of finance was thereby greatly increased.

The fourth and final phase in the development of federal finance was from 1959 to 1966. The period began with an attempt to reduce the weight given to the derivation principle and the reintroduction of other principles of revenue allocation with a view to redressing the fiscal imbalance among the regions in the interest of national unity and balanced national development. The financial power of the federal government was also strengthened. During the period, a fundamental change took place in the relative economic position of the regions. The East became an important producer of petroleum products while the economy of the West was no longer as buoyant as it was in the early fifties due to the slump in the world prices for cocoa. The North was still overly dependent on its exports for revenue. The East accordingly emerged the strongest, generating substantial surpluses on current account, while both the North and the West found it increasingly difficult to balance their budgets. Because of its new-found wealth, the East has become an advocate of the full application of the derivation principle in the allocation of revenues—particularly oil revenue—a demand which is now opposed by both the North and the West. Another development during this period was that federal revenues became buoyant.

Thus the derivation principle bedevilled the development of a rational and equitable system of revenue allocation in Nigeria. It has poisoned inter-governmental relationships and has exacerbated inter-regional rivalry and conflict. Perhaps more than any other single factor it has hampered the development of a sense of national unity and common citizenship in Nigeria. Moreover, its application has been arbitrary and lacking in consistency: in some tax revenues it is applied in full, in others only partially, and in others not at all. Nigeria must move away from the straitjacket in which she has placed herself. The change which has taken place in the relative economic and financial position of the regions between 1946 and 1966 has showed how myopic it is for anyone to assume that one region or area is certain to be the richer and another the poorer in perpetuity. The past twenty years have underscored the importance of developing a national long-term approach to the economic and fiscal problems of Nigeria.

The whole financial arrangements have inhibited the development of an effective, development-oriented national fiscal policy. Where tax powers are federal and the revenues accruing from such taxes are either fully or partially regional it has not been easy for the federal government to use such taxes as an effective instrument of fiscal policy without bringing about federal/regional conflicts. Important fiscal powers (e.g., income tax, and producer price policy) essential to the formulation of a dynamic national fiscal policy are given to the regions. The demands of efficiency in tax administration have been ignored. The country's leaders who mapped out the constitution and its fiscal system drew up a charter for regional obscurantism rather than a fiscal system designed for economy, efficiency, and equity.

Inflexibility and instability have been built into the fiscal system. Fixed percentage distribution of revenue is enshrined in the country's constitution and any alteration of these percentages calls for an amendment to the country's fundamental law. The regional governments' dependence on revenues from exports has had considerable destabilising effects. There is no built-in flexible fiscal adjustment process to meet the changing needs of the governments. There is a lack of effective coordination of the producer price policies of the regions and their harmonisation with national monetary and fiscal policies. There is a lack of effective coordination of the public debt policy. The expenditure policies of the governments are also not effectively coordinated.

The remainder of this chapter is devoted to making proposals which are designed to remove these defects in the fiscal system. The objective is to maximise the three goals of public finance—allocation, efficiency and equity—within the framework of federalism in Nigeria, to enhance the utilisation of such other principles of federal finance as need, national interest, and equity, and to reduce considerably the importance of the derivation principle.

Future development of the fiscal system: allocation of the powers of taxation and tax revenues

One of the findings of this study is that although the federal government possesses wide jurisdiction over taxation, the exclusion of income taxation from its jurisdiction has rendered this tax ineffective both as a tool of fiscal control and as a source of revenue. The regionalisation of marketing boards and the unfettered regional control over producer price policy for export crops has considerably reduced federal government's power to use export tax as an instrument of policy.

The regions did not relinquish their jurisdiction over personal income taxation to the federal government, but under the state system, the twelve income tax administrations would be even more ineffective than the four previous regional tax systems. The states should be persuaded to give up their income tax jurisdiction. In any case, the potentiality of income taxation as a tool of national fiscal and economic control is so great that the federal government would sooner or later be unable to resist entering the field. In fact, what is surprising is that it has not used the civil war as an excuse for doing so.

A distinction should be made between progressive personal

income tax and personal (poll) tax. Jurisdiction over the latter should remain with the state governments, who should also retain the revenues from it or share such revenues with the local authorities. In our discussion of income taxation in chapter 8, we found that in all parts of the country except the East the poll tax is the main source of revenue for the local authorities. By allowing the state governments to retain jurisdiction over the personal (poll) tax element of the income tax system, the present system of apportioning income tax revenue between the local authorities and the state governments will not be disrupted. Such personal taxes will be limited to taxable people whose incomes are below £300. The federal government will then have jurisdiction over personal income tax which it will levy on incomes of £300 and above. The federal income tax will be progressive and the revenues from it will be divisible between the federal and the state governments. Alternatively, both levels of government could be given concurrent powers over personal income taxation. The federal government could then, like the Canadian federal government, enter into specific agreements with individual state governments. Under such agreements the participating state governments could, in return for compensation, refrain from levying personal income tax. Whatever arrangement is eventually agreed to, it is hoped that the federal government will be given entry into this vital field of taxation.

Another change which should be made in the fiscal system is the taxation of exports. Although only the federal government can impose export duties, the regional control over the marketing boards, the fixing of producer prices, and the complete freedom which the regions enjoyed in the use of the surpluses of these boards effectively limited its power over export taxation. As discussed in chapter 9, this regional control over marketing boards also makes the formulation of an effective monetary policy a most difficult task. The establishment of twelve marketing boards would definitely aggravate the situation, as an effective coordination of their price policies would be difficult to achieve. It has been proposed in chapter 9 that the country should revert to the pre-1955 arrangements whereby a commodity board was set up for each of the major export produce—cocoa, palm produce, cotton, groundnuts, and rubber. Each of these boards would be established by the federal government with country-wide responsibilities. The states where a particular crop is produced will have representation on the board of that commodity. For example, the majority of the membership of the Cocoa Marketing Board would come from the West, while most of the members of the Groundnut Marketing Board would be from the Northern states. The federal government and the Central Bank would also be represented on each board and the profits of each board would be shared among the state governments on the basis of the proportion of each year's total output of the particular commodity. The state governments should, however, retain jurisdiction over produce sales tax. Better still, they should be given general jurisdiction over agricultural production tax (including produce sales tax).

Finally, jurisdiction over general sales tax should become concurrent. At present it is now exclusively federal. Because of the rather buoyant revenue position of the federal government in the past, no use has been made of this tax. Had jurisdiction over it been concurrent, there is no doubt that some of the regions, particularly those whose revenue positions have deteriorated during the years, might have imposed a general sales tax to obtain additional revenue.

These changes in federal/state tax jurisdiction would substantially limit the tax power of the states. The changes are inevitable if the problems of overlapping tax jurisdiction, competitive exploitation of the same tax base, and duplication and inefficiency in the administration of the taxes are to be resolved. They would also give the federal government adequate tax powers to enable it to formulate and pursue a developmental fiscal policy. The states should be satisfied with this arrangement provided that the system of revenue allocation is such that the possibility of federal government arbitrariness is reduced to the minimum, and that equity, need, and tax effort by each state are given due weight in the allocation of revenue.

It is therefore in the sharing of tax revenue rather than in the allocation of tax jurisdiction that the most fundamental changes need to be made. The present formulae for revenue allocation are too complicated and rigid. For example, the formula for allocating revenues from import duties on tobacco and motor fuel is different from that for allocating revenues from duties on beer, wine, and potable spirit. The former are shared among the regions, while the latter are retained in full by the federal government for its own exclusive use. A third formula exists for allocation of revenues from duties on other imports. Specific percentages are laid down in the Constitution, and these can only be varied by constitutional amendments. The same inflexibility is to be found in the formula for allocating revenue from mining rents and royalties. The Constitution stipulates precise percentages.

The desire to allocate as much as possible of the tax revenue on the basis of derivation has also bedevilled the problem. Unfortunately the derivation principle is not applied consistently throughout the fiscal system, and this lack of consistency has caused more misunderstanding among the regions than anything else. The East is unhappy that royalties on exported mineral and mineral oil are not allocated on the same basis as revenues from export duties on agricultural products. On the other hand, the West, because it consumes a greater proportion of Nigeria's total imports than the other regions, wants the derivation principle to be applied to the whole of the revenues from all imports and not just to duties on tobacco and petrol.

The Distributable Pool Account was set up to redress the imbalance in revenues which the application of the derivation principle in allocating some of the tax revenues would cause among the regions. But the formula for allocating the proceeds of the account is laid down in the Constitution, even though the needs of the regions are constantly changing and their revenues are highly inelastic.

It is accordingly proposed that the taxes which are under the jurisdiction of the federal government be divided into four categories for the purpose of allocating their revenues. The first category would be taxes whose revenues the federal government would retain for its use. The second category would be taxes whose revenues are shared between the federal government and the states. The third category would be those taxes whose entire proceeds are shared among the states even though they are levied and collected by the federal government. Finally, the federal government could levy a tax but would allow the states to administer it and retain its revenue.

Under the present financial arrangement, the taxes whose revenues the federal government retains for its own use are company income tax, excise duties other than those on tobacco and petroleum and import duties on beer, wine, and potable spirit. The federal government should continue to retain the whole of the proceeds from company tax only.

In the second category come revenues from general import duties and mining rents and royalties. The formulae for allocating the revenues from these taxes are complicated and rigid. It would be enough for the new constitution simply to stipulate that their revenues are to be shared without laying down specific percentages. In addition, revenue from income tax and excise tax should be shared.

The third category of federal taxes are those whose revenues are shared entirely among the regions. The most important tax in this category is the export tax. The proceeds of the tax are shared entirely on the basis of derivation. If, as it has been argued before, premium should no longer be placed on the derivation principle, the revenue from export tax would have to be shared among the states on another basis. In any case, the derivation formula is now likely to be even less satisfactory and to cause more friction in the future with twelve states than in the past when the number of the regions was four. The allocation of the proceeds of the tax should be left entirely in the hands of the proposed Finance Commission.

The fourth category are taxes levied by the federal government but administered by the states and whose revenues are retained by them. At present, each state government is free to impose purchase tax on a limited number of commodities, the most important being motor vehicle fuel. But general sales tax is in the exclusive jurisdiction of the federal government. There is no reason why this tax could not become both federal and state, with the federal government imposing it while the state governments collect and spend it.

What will be the independent fiscal powers of the states? It is

most desirable that state taxes should satisfy the four basic conditions which the Hicks-Phillipson Fiscal Commission recommended in 1952: these taxes must be clearly localised within each
state; they must not hinder or endanger national interest and
national policy; they must not be difficult or expensive to administer; and they should have stable revenue yields. The taxes
which readily satisfy these criteria are agricultural production
tax or produce sales tax, property tax, and personal tax. The new
states, even though they are smaller in size and population than
the regions, should be able to administer these taxes satisfactorily.

Table 11.1 summarises the proposed fiscal system. It will be

TABLE 11.1 *Proposed allocation of tax jurisdiction and revenue*

Tax	Allocation of tax jurisdiction	Revenue allocation
Export tax	Federal	Shared among the states
Import tax	Federal	Shared between the federal government and the states
Excise tax	Federal	Shared between the federal government and the states
Company tax	Federal	Entire proceeds retained by the federal government
Personal income tax	Federal	Shared between the federal government and the states
Mining rents and royalties	Federal	Shared between the federal government and the states
Agricultural production (including produce sales) tax	State	Collected and retained by the states
Property tax	State	Collected and retained by the states
Personal tax	State	Collected and retained by the states or shared with local authorities
General sales tax	Concurrent	Collected and retained by the federal government or the state

seen from this table that the problems of overlapping tax jurisdiction, of competitive exploitation of the same tax base, and duplication of tax collection machinery have been eliminated. The fiscal power of the federal government has been increased by the transfer to it of personal income tax jurisdiction. This move would facilitate the formulation and pursuance of an effective fiscal policy. But the revenues from all the federal taxes other than those from company tax are to be shared between the federal government and the state governments on the one hand and among the states on the other hand. It has been proposed that in order to achieve flexibility in revenue allocation system, no specific formula should be laid down in the Constitution. Only the process by which the allocation is to be made should be stipulated. What this should be and how it should function is the subject of the next section.

Machinery and criteria for allocating shared revenue

The new Nigerian Constitution should, like the Indian Constitution, provide for the establishment of an independent Finance Commission; the composition of the commission, the tenure of office of its members, the method of its appointment, and its duties should all be clearly laid down. This commission, unlike the Indian Finance Commission, but like the Australian Commonwealth Grants Commission, should be a standing commission with a secretariat of its own. One of its main duties should be to recommend, on a biennial basis, the allocation of shared revenues between the federal and state governments and the allocation among the states of their shares of such revenues.

On what basis should the commission allocate the shared revenue between and among the federal and state governments? Two broad criteria seem most appropriate: (1) the fiscal needs of the federal government, having regard to its resources and functions; and (2) the need to ensure the financial integrity of Nigeria through the financial stability of the centre. The economic development of Nigeria will depend in a large measure upon the financial resources of the federal government. Its needs must therefore be viewed generously. Moreover, the financial strength of the government will continue to be a weighty factor in determining the amounts and terms of loans which Nigeria can raise (particularly external loans). However, the fact that some revenues which used to be exclusively regional would be shared between the federal and state governments should also be borne in mind. The primacy of the state governments in at least two of these taxes—export duty and mining rents and royalties—should be taken into account. At present, the federal government does not receive any part of the revenue from the former and only a small fraction of the revenue from the latter. Finally, while the revenues given to the federal government in any one year must be adequate for its needs and must be large enough to ensure that the financial strength of the country as a whole is not jeopardised, they must not be so large as to give the federal government budget surpluses while the state governments are having budget deficits.

The states' share of the divisible taxes—export, import, and personal income taxes, and mining rents and royalties—should be paid into the Distributable Pool Account. The Pool should be divided among the states on the basis of the following principles: budgetary needs, tax effort, economy in public expenditure, the level of development reached in each state, and broad purposes of national importance. The last of these criteria should take into account such factors as the preservation or continuity of government services and the provision of minimum services which a state government has to meet by virtue of its status as a government.

In this scheme, the principle of derivation has been thrown overboard, and with it, it is hoped, the incessant conflict among the regions and the inequity which results in its adoption due to lack of adequate and reliable data and the arbitrariness in the selection of the revenues to be allocated on this basis. It will indeed be extremely difficult to apply the principle now that the country has been divided into twelve states. But the new principles which have been proposed are not easy to apply either. They will require considerable study and research by the Finance Commission and its staff. For example, the determination of the relative tax efforts of the states cannot be undertaken in absolute terms. It has to be related to their tax potentials. Similarly, the assessment of the measure of economy in state expenditure is a complicated exercise which can only be undertaken on a continuous basis. Without reliable and comparative information on these criteria it would be difficult not only to determine the quantum of resources needed by the states but also how these resources could be most equitably and economically shared.

The suggestion that the Finance Commission should be a permanent body, with a secretariat and research staff of its own, will facilitate the compilation of the necessary data needed for making the allocations. The suggestion that the allocations should be made biennially will also facilitate necessary corrections being made in the intervening year between one award and another. In other words, the Commission will, on the basis of forecast of total financial resources which are likely to be available during the next two financial years and on the basis of application of the various criteria stipulated above, share divisible taxes between and among the federal government and the states by way of an advance. At the end of the first of the two financial years the Commission will make necessary adjustment in the allocations in the light of revenue outturn and actual budgetary performance of the governments. This adjustment will be reflected in the second year's allocations. If all the governments are to have full confidence in the Finance Commission it is most important that the Commission should establish itself as an impartial court of arbitration.

Future development of the fiscal system: allocation of non-tax receipts

These proposed financial arrangements will, it is hoped, solve most of the problems of fiscal adjustment in Nigeria. They will take care of the problems of fiscal equity, need, and national interest as far as tax revenues are concerned. It is essential that the scope of the proposed Finance Commission should be widened to cover non-tax receipts, principally internal and external loans and grants, if its allocations are not to be distorted.

Internal and external loans now constitute a very important source of governmental receipts in Nigeria. Although internal borrowing by any regional government is within the competence of that government, only the federal government has taken any loans since 1958. The way the federal government has distributed these loans, however, has left much to be desired. External loans and grants have not been equitably distributed either: the fact that most aid-giving countries and institutions tend to support individual projects rather than the country's development plan as a whole has made the problem of allocation easy, since the projects so supported are easily identifiable with a particular government or state.

Moreover, the loans, both internal and external, available to the governments have not been related to the country's other resources. Thus the federal and East Region governments which have had budget surpluses in the past have been more generously treated with regard to loans than the governments of the North and West. If this practice is allowed to continue in the future it will be difficult to relate total resources to needs—the aim of this proposed scheme. It is therefore essential that the Finance Commission should have responsibility for the allocation of external and internal loans among the governments. This will enable it to have a full picture of the total financial resources which will become available to each of the governments, and to relate these to their needs and the other factors mentioned above.

The centralisation of the marketing of the export produce as proposed in chapter 9 will minimise governmental interference in the fixing of producer prices, which has been the practice since 1954 when the boards were regionalised. It will also be possible to harmonise producer price policy with the monetary and fiscal policies of the federal government.

Future prospects for Nigerian federal finance

Nigeria needs peace and political stability in order to be able to concentrate its energies on the development effort. It is hoped that after the civil war the lessons of the first two decades will not be lost and that a fiscal system that will accommodate itself to growth and the minimisation of inter-regional and inter-state conflict, while at the same time ensuring equity, efficiency and the pursuance of an effective national fiscal policy can be worked out. There is no doubt that a fiscal commission of enquiry will be needed.* It is most essential that the terms of reference of such a commission should be wide enough to enable it to consider the whole of the fiscal arrangements in the light of the experience of the past twenty years.

While the proposals made in this study are far from being perfect, they should facilitate a more rational allocation of fiscal resources than in the past. But no matter what financial arrangements are eventually worked out, the calibre of the post-civil-war leaders, both at the federal and state governments levels, is most crucial to the successful operation of the system. It is to be hoped that a new leadership dedicated to the peaceful and rapid development of the nation will emerge. In the past, the political leadership has pursued regional and tribal interests to the detriment of national interest in fiscal as well as in other spheres. One hopes that the days of regional obscurantism are now past. The role of the Finance Commission is crucial to the successful operation of the fiscal system. The members of this Commission must be not only experts in all pertinent fields but also men of unalloyed integrity, who will discharge their duties with impartiality, honesty, and a high sense of responsibility.

* The Federal Military Government set up an Interim Revenue Allocation Committee, late in 1968, to advise on what interim fiscal arrangements should be made during the civil war and immediate post-civil-war periods. It was arranged that a Fiscal Review Commission will be constituted in due course to propose long-term solutions.

Appendix A

Area and population of the regions and states of Nigeria

TABLE A.1 *Area and population of the regions and the federal territory of Lagos*

Region	Area (square miles)	Per cent	Population [a] (in 000s)	Per cent
Northern	281,782	79·0	29,809	53·5
Eastern	29,484	8·3	12,395	22·3
Western	30,454	8·5	10,266	18·4
Mid-Western	14,922	4·2	2,536	4·6
Federal Territory of Lagos	27	...[b]	665	1·2
NIGERIA	356,669	100·0	55,671	100·0

NOTES: (a) Population figures are the official figures of the 1963 census. See footnote 2, page 36, about the problems of obtaining accurate population data for Nigeria.
(b) Negligible.

SOURCE: *Digest of Statistics*, vol. 15, 1966 (Federal Office of Statistics, Lagos).

TABLE A.2 *Area and population of the twelve states of Nigeria*

States	Provinces	1963 Population	Area (square miles)	Percentage of Nigeria population
North-Western		5,733,296	65,143	10·3
	Sokoto	4,334,769		
	Niger	1,398,527		
North-Central		4,098,305	27,108	7·3
	Katsina	2,545,005		
	Zaria	1,553,300		
Kano		5,774,842	16,630	10·4
	Kano	5,774,842		
North-Eastern		7,793,443	105,025	14·0
	Bornu	2,853,553		
	Adamawa	1,585,290		
	Sardauna	878,271		
	Bauchi	2,476,329		
Benue-Plateau		4,005,408	39,204	7·2
	Benue	2,641,960		
	Plateau	1,363,448		
Kwara		2,399,365	28,672	4·3
	Ilorin	1,119,222		
	Kabba	1,280,143		
Lagos		1,443,567	1,381	2·6
	Colony	778,321		
	Federal Territory	665,246		
Western		9,487,523	29,100	17·0
	Abeokuta	974,886		
	Ibadan	3,326,647		
	Ijebu	576,080		
	Ondo	2,727,673		
	Oyo	1,882,237		
Mid-Western		2,535,839	14,922	4·5
	Benin	1,354,986		
	Delta	1,180,853		
East-Central		6,223,831	8,746	11·2
	Onitsha	2,943,483		
	Owerri	3,280,348		

States	Provinces	1963 Population		Area (square miles)	Percentage of Nigeria population
South-Eastern		4,626,317		13,730	8·3
	Calabar		3,023,784		
	Ogoja		1,602,533		
Rivers		1,548,314		7,008	2·8
	Rivers		1,548,314		
NIGERIA		55,670,050		356,669	100·0*

* Figures do not add up to 100 because of rounding.

SOURCES: *Annual Abstract of Statistics*, 1966 (Federal Office of Statistics, Lagos); *Official Gazette of the Federal Government*, 27 May 1967.

K

Appendix B

Allocation of functions between federal and regional legislatures under the different Nigerian Constitutions since 1951

B.1 THE NIGERIA (CONSTITUTION) ORDER IN COUNCIL, 1951

1 *Matters with respect to which a Regional Legislature may make Laws*

1 Agriculture.
2 Animal Health.
3 Fisheries.
4 Forestry.
5 The development, regulation and supervision of local industries.
6 Cooperative Societies.
7 Social Welfare.
8 Education.
9 Acquisition of rights in land within the Region by persons other than Nigerians.
10 Compulsory acquisition of land.
11 Customary land tenures.
12 Lands and buildings vested in any Region.
13 Land settlement.
14 Rents and lands and buildings.
15 Conservation of soil and water resources.
16 Survey of land (but not including the profession of surveyor).
17 Regional Public Works.
18 Town and Country Planning.
19 The public service of the Region to such extent (if any) as the Governor, acting in his discretion, may by regulations prescribe.
20 Local government including constitution and powers (including the power to levy rates) of native authorities, township authorities, and other local authorities established for the purpose of local or village administration.

21 Public health and sanitation; hospitals and dispensaries; housing; the registration of births and deaths and marriages; burials and burial grounds.

22 Native courts (but not including appeals from native courts to authorities other than native courts).

23 Save as otherwise expressly provided in this Schedule, jurisdiction and powers of all courts with regard to any of the matters mentioned in this Schedule.

24 Taxation to such extent as may be prescribed by or under any Order of his Majesty in Council.

25 Borrowing of moneys within Nigeria upon the security of the revenues or assets of the Region for purposes relating to any matter mentioned in this Schedule or in the Fourth Schedule to this Order.

26 The appropriation from the revenues and funds of the Region for purposes relating to any matter mentioned in this Schedule or in the Fourth Schedule to this Order.

27 Loans and advances from the revenues and funds of the Region for purposes relating to any matter mentioned in this Schedule or in the Fourth Schedule to this Order.

28 Any matter declared to be within the competency of the legislature of the Region under Section 92 of this Order. (Section 92 provides that any matter, though not included in the Schedule, shall be within the competency of the Regional Legislature if it is so declared by any Central Law.)

29 Fees and other changes in respect of any of the matters mentioned in this Schedule.

30 Offences against laws in respect to any of the matters mentioned in this Schedule.

II *Matters (Additional to matters mentioned in the Third Schedule) in relation to which a Regional Legislature may make provision for the Appropriation, Lending or Borrowing of Moneys*

1 Administration including the Lieutenant-Governor's Office, the Regional Secretariat and the Provincial Administration.

2 The Accountant-General's Department.

3 The Nigeria Police.

4 Public Relations.

5 Expenditure reimbursable from funds of Marketing Boards.

6 The Regional Legislature (including, in the case of the Northern Region, the adviser on Moslem Law in the Northern House of Chiefs).
7 The Regional Executive.
8 Printing.
9 Charitable Grants.
10 Depreciation of Investments.

B.2 THE NIGERIA (CONSTITUTION) ORDER IN COUNCIL, 1954

1 *The Exclusive Federal Legislative List*

1 Accounts of the Government of the Federation, including audit of those accounts.
2 Aliens, including naturalisation of aliens.
3 Archives, other than the public records of the Governments of the former Northern Region, the former Western Region and the former Eastern Region relating to the period between the twenty-third day of January, 1952, and the thirtieth day of September, 1954, and the public records of the Governments of the Regions and the Southern Cameroons.
4 Aviation, including aerodromes, safety of aircraft and ancillary transport and other services.
5 Banks and banking.
6 Bills of exchange and promissory notes.
7 Borrowing of monies outside Nigeria for the purposes of the Federation or of any Region or of the Southern Cameroons or of Lagos.
8 Borrowing of monies within Nigeria for the purposes of the Federation or of Lagos.
9 Census.
10 Citizenship of Nigeria.
11 Companies, that is to say, general provision as to the incorporation, regulation and winding-up of bodies corporate, other than bodies incorporated directly by a law enacted by the Legislature of a Region or of the Southern Cameroons, and other than co-operative societies.
12 Copyright.
13 Currency, coinage and legal tender.
14 Customs and excise duties, including export duties.
15 Defence.

16 Deportation.
17 Exchange Control.
18 External affairs, that is to say, such external relations (not being relations between the United Kingdom and any Region) as may from time to time be entrusted to the Federation by Her Majesty's Government in the United Kingdom.
19 The following higher educational institutions, that is to say—
  The University College, Ibadan.
  The University College Teaching Hospital.
  The Nigerian College of Arts, Science and Technology.
  The West African Institute of Social and Economic Research.
  The Pharmacy School, Yaba.
  The Forestry School, Ibadan.
  The Veterinary School, Vom.
  The Man-o'-War Bay Training Centre.
20 Immigration into and emigration from Nigeria.
21 Legal proceedings between the Government of the Federation and any other person or authority or between the Governments of Regions or between the Government of a Region and the Government of the Southern Cameroons.
22 Maritime shipping and navigation, including—
  (a) shipping and navigation on tidal waters;
  (b) shipping and navigation on the River Niger and its affluents and on such other inland waterway as the Governor-General may by Order declare to be an international waterway or to be an inter-Regional waterway;
  (c) lighthouses, lightships, beacons and other provisions for the safety of shipping and navigation;
  (d) such ports as the Governor-General may by Order declare to be Federal Ports (including the constitution and powers of port authorities for Federal Ports).
23 Meteorology.
24 Mines and minerals, including oilfields and oil mining and geological surveys.
25 Museums of the Federation, that is to say—
  (a) the following existing museums, namely—
    The Jos Museum.
    The Oron Museum.
    The House of Images at Esie.
    The Nigeria Museum, Lagos.

(b) any museums established by the Government of the Federation.

26 Nuclear energy.

27 Passports and visas.

28 Patents, trade marks, designs and merchandise marks.

29 Pensions and gratuities payable out of the revenues of the Federation.

30 Police, including bureaux of intelligence and investigation.

31 Posts, telegraphs and telephones, including Post Office Savings Banks.

32 Public debt of the Federation.

33 Public relations of the Federation.

34 Public service of the Federation, including the settlement of disputes between the Federation and officers in the public service of the Federation.

35 Railways, including ancillary transport and other services.

36 Taxes on income and profits, except taxes on the incomes or profits accruing in or derived from, any Region or the Southern Cameroons of Africans resident in any Region or the Southern Cameroons and African communities in any Region or the Southern Cameroons.

37 Trade and commerce among the Regions, the Southern Cameroons and Lagos.

38 Trunk roads, that is to say, the construction, alteration and maintenance of roads declared by the Governor-General by Order to be Federal Trunk Roads.

39 Water from sources declared by the Governor-General, by Order, to be sources affecting more than one Region or a Region and the Southern Cameroons.

40 Weights and measures.

41 Wireless, broadcasting and television other than broadcasting and television provided by the Government of a Region or of the Southern Cameroons; allocation of times and wave lengths for wireless, broadcasting and television transmission.

42 Any matter, not mentioned elsewhere in this List, that is, incidental to the executive of any power conferred by or under this Order upon the Federal Legislature, not being a matter with respect to which power to make laws is also conferred upon the Legislature of a Region or the Southern Cameroons.

II *The Concurrent Legislative List*

1 Administration of estates.
2 Antiquities.
3 Bankruptcy and insolvency.
4 Chemical services, including analytical services.
5 Commercial and industrial monopolies, combines and trusts.
6 Commissions of inquiry.
7 Dangerous drugs.
8 Electricity.
9 Evidence.
10 Fingerprints, identification and criminal records.
11 Gas.
12 Higher education, that is to say, institutions and other bodies
    offering courses of a university, technological or of a professional
    character, other than the institutions referred to in item 19 of the
    Exclusive Legislative List.
13 Industrial development.
14 Insurance.
15 Labour, that is to say, conditions of labour, industrial relations,
    trade unions and welfare of labour.
16 Movement of persons between the Regions, the Southern
    Cameroons and Lagos.
17 National Monuments, that is to say—
    (a) monuments in a Region designated by the Governor-
        General by Order, with the consent of the Governor of
        that Region, as National Monuments;
    (b) monuments in the Southern Cameroons designated by the
        Governor-General by Order as National Monuments.
18 National Parks, that is to say—
    (a) the control of any area in a Region designated by the
        Governor-General by Order, with the consent of the
        Governor of that Region, as a National Park.
    (b) the control of any area in the South Cameroons designated
        by the Governor-General by Order as a National Park.
19 Prisons and other institutions for the treatment of offenders.
20 Professional qualifications in respect of such professions as, and
    to the extent that, the Governor-General may by Order designate;
    registration and disciplinary control of members of professions so
    designated.
21 Promotion of tourist traffic.

22 The maintaining and securing of public safety and public Order (but not including defence); the providing, maintaining and securing of such supplies and services as the Governor-General may by Order declare to be essential supplies and services.

23 Quarantine.

24 Registration of business names.

25 Sanctioning of cinematograph films for exhibition.

26 Scientific and industrial research.

27 Statistics.

28 Traffic on Federal Trunk Roads.

29 Trigonometrical, cadastral and topographical surveys.

30 Trustees, that is to say—
    (a) general and official trustees;
    (b) trustees of communities or of bodies or associations established for religious, educational, literary, social, scientific or charitable purposes.

31 Water-power.

32 Any matter, not mentioned elsewhere in this List, that is incidental to the executive of any power conferred by or under this Order upon the Legislature of a Region or of the Southern Cameroons, the Government of a Region or the Southern Cameroons or any department or officer of that Government.

33 Any matter with respect to which the Federal Legislature is authorised to make laws for a Region or the Southern Cameroons by the Legislature of that Region or the Southern Cameroons, as the case may be, to the extent of the authority conferred by that Legislature.

34 Any matter, not mentioned elsewhere in this List, with respect to which power to make laws is conferred by this Order upon both the Federal Legislature and the Legislature of a Region of the Southern Cameroons.

B.3 THE NIGERIA (CONSTITUTION) ORDER IN COUNCIL, 1960, AND THE CONSTITUTION OF THE FEDERATION (1963, NO. 20)

I *The Exclusive Legislative List*

1 Accounts of the Government of the Federation and officers, courts and authorities thereof, including audit of those accounts.

2 Archives, other than the public records of the Governments of the Regions since the twenty-third day of January, 1952.

3 Aviation, including airports, safety of aircraft and ancillary transport and other services.

4 Bills of exchange and promissory notes.

5 Borrowing of moneys outside Nigeria for the purposes of the Federation or of any Region, other than borrowing by the Government of a Region for a period not exceeding twelve months on the security of any funds or assets of that government held outside Nigeria.

6 Borrowing of moneys within Nigeria for the purposes of the Federation.

7 Control of capital issues.

8 Copyright.

9 Currency, coinage and legal tender.

10 Customs and excise duties, including export duties.

11 Defence.

12 Deportation; compulsory removal of persons from one territory to another.

13 Designation of securities in which trust funds may be invested.

14 Exchange control.

15 External affairs.

16 Extradition.

17 The following higher educational institutions, that is to say—
    The University of Ibadan.
    The University College Teaching Hospital at Ibadan.
    The University of Lagos.
    The Lagos University Teaching Hospital.
    The West African Institute of Social and Economic Research.
    The Pharmacy School at Yaba.
    The Forestry School at Ibadan.
    The Veterinary School at Vom.

18 Immigration into and emigration from Nigeria.

19 Incorporation, regulation and winding-up of bodies corporate, other than cooperative societies, native authorities, local-government authorities and bodies corporate established directly by any law enacted by the legislature of a Region.

20 Insurance other than insurance undertaken by the Government of a Region but including any insurance undertaken by the Govern-

L

ment of a Region that extends beyond the limits of that Region.

21 Legal proceedings between the Government of the Federation and any other person or authority or between the Governments of Regions.

22 Maritime shipping and navigation on tidal waters;
    (a) shipping and navigation on tidal waters;
    (b) shipping and navigation on the River Niger and its affluents and on any such other inland waterway as may be declared by Parliament to be an international waterway or to be an inter-Regional waterway;
    (c) lighthouses, lightships, beacons and other provisions for the safety of shipping and navigation;
    (d) such ports as may be declared by Parliament to be Federal ports (including the constitution and powers of port authorities for Federal ports).

23 Marriages other than marriages under Moslem law or other customary law; annulment and dissolution of, and other matrimonial causes relating to, marriages other than marriages under Moslem law or other customary law.

24 Meteorology.

25 Mines and minerals, including oilfields, oil mining, geological surveys and natural gas.

26 Museums of the Federation, that is to say—
    The Jos Museum.
    The Oron Museum.
    The House of Images at Esie.
    Any other museums established by the Government of the Federation.

27 Naval, military and air forces.

28 Nuclear energy.

29 Passports and visas.

30 Patents, trade marks, designs and merchandise marks.

31 Pensions, gratuities and other like benefits payable out of the Consolidated Revenue Fund or any other public fund of the Federation.

32 Posts, telegraphs and telephones, including post office savings banks.

33 Powers, privileges and immunities of each House of Parliament and its members.

34 The public debt of the Federation.

35 Public relations of the Federation.

36 The public service of the Federation, including the settlement of disputes between the Federation and officers in the public service of the Federation.

37 Railways, including ancillary transport and other services.

38 Taxes on amounts paid or payable on the sale or purchase of commodities except:
  (a) produce;
  (b) hides and skins;
  (c) motor spirit;
  (d) diesel oil sold or purchased for use in road vehicles;
  (e) diesel oil sold or purchased for other than industrial purposes.

39 Tribunals of inquiry with respect to all or any of the matters mentioned elsewhere in this List.

40 Trunk roads, that is to say, the construction, alteration and maintenance of such roads as may be declared by Parliament to be Federal trunk roads.

41 Water from such sources as may be declared by Parliament to be sources affecting more than one territory.

42 Weights and measures.

43 Wireless, broadcasting and television other than broadcasting and television provided by the Government of a Region; allocation of wavelengths for wireless, broadcasting and television transmission.

44 The matters with respect to which Parliament is empowered to make provision by sections 4, 8, 9, 13, 16, 32, 37, 38, 40, 42, 45, 49, 52, 68, 75, subsection (1) of section 76, sections 77, 78, 87, 96, subsections (2) and (5) of section 105, sections 111, 113, 114, 116, 118, 121, 128, 131, 132, 133, 139, 140, 145, 150, 159 and 165 of this Constitution.

45 Any matter that is incidental or supplementary—
  (a) to any matter mentioned elsewhere in this list; or
  (b) to the discharge by the Government of the Federation or any officer, court or authority of the Federation of any function conferred by this Constitution.

The Concurrent Legislative List

1 Antiquities.

2 Arms and ammunition.

3 Bankruptcy and insolvency.

4 Census.

5 Chemical services, including analytical services.

6 Commercial and industrial monopolies, combines and trusts.

7 Control of the voluntary movement of persons between territories.

8 Such drugs and poisons as may with the consent of the governments of the Regions be designated by the President by order.

9 Finger prints, identification and criminal records.

10 Higher education, that is to say, institutions and other bodies offering courses or conducting examinations of a university, technological or of a professional character, other than the institutions referred to in Item 17 of Part I of this Schedule.

11 Industrial development.

12 Labour, that is to say, conditions of labour, industrial relations, trade unions and welfare of labour.

13 The legal and medical professions and such other professional occupations as may with the consent of the governments of the Regions be designated by the President by order.

14 National parks, that is to say, the control of such areas in a Region as may with the consent of the Government of that Region be designated by the President by order as national parks.

15 National monuments, that is to say, such monuments in a Region as may with the consent of the Government of that Region be designated by the President by order as national monuments.

16 Prisons and other institutions for the treatment of offenders.

17 Promotion of tourist traffic.

18 The maintaining and securing of public safety and public order; the providing, maintaining and securing of such supplies and services as may be designated by the President by order as essential supplies and services.

19 Quarantine.

20 Registration of business names.

21 Scientific and industrial research.

22 Service and execution in a Region of the civil and criminal processes, judgments, decrees, orders and other decisions of any court of law outside Nigeria or any court of law in Nigeria other than the Supreme Court, the High Court of that Region or any court of law established by the legislature of that Region.

23 Statistics.
24 Traffic on Federal trunk roads.
25 Tribunals of inquiry with respect to all or any of the matters mentioned elsewhere in this list.
26 Trigonometrical, cadastral and topographical surveys.
27 Water-power.
28 The matters with respect to which Parliament is empowered to make provision by subsections (2) and (3) of section 76 and section 79 of this Constitution.
29 Any matter that is incidental or supplementary to any matter mentioned elsewhere in this list.

Appendix C

Evolution of federal finance in Nigeria: changes in tax jurisdiction and revenue allocation in the Nigeria fiscal system, 1914–66

Tax	Tax Jurisdiction and Formula for Allocating Revenue from Taxes					
	1914–26	1926–48	1948–52	1952–4	1954–9	1959–66
I IMPORT TAXES (a) Import duty on tobacco	Central government tax and revenue source	Central government tax and revenue source	Central government tax and revenue source	Central government tax; fifty per cent of the revenue from the tax distributed among the regions on the basis of proportionate regional consumption	Federal government tax; fifty per cent of the revenue from the tax distributed among the regions on the basis of proportionate regional consumption	Federal tax; one hundred per cent of the revenue from the tax distributed among the regions on the basis of proportionate regional consumption
(b) Import duty on motor vehicle fuel	Central government tax and revenue source	Central government tax and revenue source	Central government tax and revenue source	Central government tax; fifty per cent of the revenue from the tax distributed among the regions on the basis of proportionate regional consumption	Federal government tax; one hundred per cent of the revenue from the tax distributed among the regions on the basis of proportionate regional consumption	Federal tax; one hundred per cent of the revenue from the tax distributed among the regions on the basis of proportionate regional consumption

(c) Import duty on beer, wine and potable spirits	Central government tax and revenue source	Central government tax and revenue source	Central government tax and revenue source	Central government tax and revenue source	Central government tax and revenue source	Federal tax; proceeds of the tax formed part of the revenue from import duties (other) for purposes of revenue allocation	Federal tax; one hundred per cent of revenue from the source retained by the federal government
(d) General import duties or import duties (other)	Central government tax and revenue source	Central government tax and revenue source	Central government tax and revenue source	Central government tax and revenue source	Central government tax and revenue source	Federal tax; half of the revenue from the tax returned by the federal government and the other half distributed among the regions in the following proportion: North 15% West 20% East 14% Southern Cameroons 2%	Federal tax; seventy per cent of the revenue from the tax retained by the federal government and thirty per cent paid into the Distributable Pool Account, whose funds are allocated among the regions in the following proportion: North 40/95th West 18/95th East 31/95th Mid-West 6/95th

Tax	1914–26	1926–48	1948–52	1952–4	1954–9	1959–66
II EXPORT TAXES Export duties on all produce	Central government tax and revenue source	Central government tax and revenue source	Central government tax and revenue source	Central government tax and revenue source	Federal tax; fifty per cent of the proceeds of the tax distributed among the regions on the basis of proportionate regional production of each produce	Federal tax; one hundred per cent of the proceeds of the tax allocated to the regions on the basis of derivation, i.e., share of each region in the production of each produce
III EXCISE TAXES (a) Excise duties on tobacco			Central government tax and revenue source	Central government tax; fifty per cent of the revenue from the tax retained by the central government and the remaining fifty per cent distributed among the regions according to consumption	Federal tax; fifty per cent retained by the federal government; fifty per cent allocated to the regions according to consumption	Federal tax; one hundred per cent of revenue from the tax allocated to the regions according to consumption

Tax Jurisdiction and Formula for Allocating Revenue from Taxes

(b) Excise duty on beer	Central government tax and revenue source	Central government tax and revenue source	Federal tax and revenue; formed part of revenue from import duties (other) allocated as indicated above	Federal tax; one hundred per cent of revenue from the tax retained by the federal government
IV SALES TAX (a) Produce Sales Tax	Central government tax levied at the request of regional authorities; revenue from the tax collected and retained by the regions	Regional tax and revenue source	Regional tax and revenue source	Regional tax and revenue source
(b) Purchase/Sales Tax on motor vehicle fuel			Regional tax and revenue source	Regional tax and revenue source
(c) General Sales Tax				Federal tax and revenue source

Tax Jurisdiction and Formula for Allocating Revenue from Taxes

Tax	1914–26	1926–48	1948–52	1952–4	1954–9	1959–66
V DIRECT TAX (a) Personal Income (Direct) Tax on Africans outside Lagos	Central government tax; revenue shared between the governments of the North and South and their native authorities	Central government tax; revenue shared between the central government and the native authorities	Central government tax; revenue declared regional and apportioned between the regional governments and their native authorities	Central government tax; revenue apportioned between the regional governments and their native authorities	Regional tax; in the case of the East, revenue from the tax was retained in full by the regional government; in the other regions the revenue was shared between the governments and their local or native authorities	Regional tax; in the case of the East, revenue from the tax is retained for regional government use; in the other regions, it is shared between the governments and local or native authorities
(b) Personal Income (Direct) Tax on Africans residing in Lagos		Central government tax and revenue source; part of the proceeds allocated to the Lagos Town Council	Central government tax and revenue; part of the proceeds allocated to the Lagos Town Council	Western Region government tax and revenue; part of the proceeds allocated to the Lagos Town Council	Federal tax and revenue source; part of the proceeds allocated to the Lagos Town Council	Federal tax and revenue source; part of the proceeds allocated to the Lagos City Council

(c) Personal Income Tax and Non-Africans		Central government tax and revenue source	Central government tax and revenue source	Central government tax and revenue source	Federal tax; revenue from the tax paid to the regional governments on the basis of taxpayer's residence	Regional tax and revenue source
(d) Company Tax		Central government tax and revenue	Central government tax and revenue source	Central government tax and revenue source	Federal tax and revenue source	Federal tax and revenue source
VI MINING AND MINERAL TAX Mining Rents and Royalties	Central government tax; regional source of revenue	Central government tax and revenue source	Central government tax and revenue source	Central government tax and revenue source	Federal tax; revenue from the tax allocated in full to the regions (only the North during this period) from which the mineral was extracted	Federal tax; revenue from the tax shared as follows: fifty per cent to region of origin; twenty per cent to the federal government; thirty per cent to Distributable Pool

Tax Jurisdiction and Formula for Allocating Revenue from Taxes

Tax	1914–26	1926–48	1948–52	1952–4	1954–9	1959–66
VII MISCELLANEOUS TAXES Licences, fees, rent of government property, earnings of government property	Concurrent jurisdiction between the central government and the governments of the Northern Nigeria Protectorate and the Colony and Protectorate of Southern Nigeria	Central government jurisdiction and revenue source	Revenue declared regional; tariffs fixed by the central government	Regions granted legislative power over revenues declared regional	Concurrent jurisdiction and revenue source between the federal and regional governments	Concurrent jurisdiction and revenue source between the federal and regional governments
VIII STATUTORY ALLOCATIONS AND GRANTS			Grants to be made available to the regions where the balance remaining after the central government expenditure and budget surplus have	Regions received from the federal government: (a) capitation grants based on the number of adult male taxpayers; (b) education	Regions received from the federal government special grants of '£3 million, North; £2m., West; and £2m, East' to augment their	A Distributable Pool was created; thirty per cent of general imports revenue and thirty per cent of mining rents and royalties are credited to

been deducted from total 'non-declared' revenue. The available grants were then allocated among the regions on the basis of relative contribution made by each region to total non-declared revenue

and police grants based on regional expenditure—one hundred per cent in the case of education and regional police expenditure and fifty per cent in the case of native administration expenditure; (c) a special once-for-all capital grant of £2 million to the North

resources and as a contribution to their increased responsibilities. Special grants of £500,000 in 1954 and £250,000 in 1955 were paid to the East to help the regional government in its financial difficulties. Education, police and capitation grants abolished

the Pool. The Pool is then allocated among the regions as follows: From 1 April 1959 to 30 September 1960: North 40% West 24% East 31% Southern Cameroons 5% From 1 October 1960 to 8 August 1963: North 40/95th West 24/95th East 31/95th 9 August 1963 to 31 March 1966: North 40/95th West 18/95th East 31/95th Mid-West 6/95th

SOURCES: (a) *The Nigeria (Legislative Council) Order in Council, 1946*;
(b) *The Nigeria (Constitution) Order in Council, 1951*;
(c) *The Nigeria (Constitution) Order in Council, 1954*;
(d) *The Nigeria (Constitution) Order in Council, 1960*;
(e) *The Constitution of the Federation (1963, No. 20)*.

Appendix D

Distribution of Nigeria's gross domestic product by regions,
1958 to 1965

Although Nigeria is a federation, most of the official national income
estimates so far published relate to over-all national rather than regional
aggregates. Prest and Stewart provided a complete regional breakdown
of the national product for the year 1950/51—the only year covered by
their work on Nigerian national accounts. Okigbo, whose work covers
seven years, 1950–57, did not provide complete regional breakdown of
the national aggregate—the residual items of 'Distribution, etc.', were
left out unallocated among the regions. The regional breakdown
attempted in Tables D.1 and D.2 of this appendix is therefore unofficial.
It is a rough-and-ready exercise and is liable to a greater margin of
error than the calculation of the national aggregates. It is based on the
unpublished work of the Federal Office of Statistics, the Regional
Offices of Statistics particularly those of the West and the North and
Dr. R. O. Teriba.[1] Table D.1 shows the allocation of the total GDP
among the regions and the federal territory of Lagos between 1958/59
and 1964/65, while Table D.2 provides the detailed allocation of the
GDP among the regions by branch of activity for one year, 1962/63.

To the extent that three quarters to four fifths of the national GDP
figures were computed from regional sources, calculating regional
figures has presented little difficulty. Thus, as the total values added by
such activities as Agriculture, Livestock, Fishing, Forestry, Mining
(including Oil Exploration) and Manufacturing had been built up for
the over-all national GDP from regional data, regional breakdown has
been obtained by reference to region of origin. The value added by

[1] R. O. Teriba, *Western Nigeria: Public Sector and Economic Development,
1948–1962* (an unpublished Ph.D. thesis, University of Manchester, 1965),
Appendix A, pp. 410–17. None of these institutions or persons mentioned
is in any way responsible either for the accuracy or reliability of the
exercise.

TABLE D.I *Distribution of Nigeria's GDP at factor cost and 1957/58 constant prices among the regions, 1958–65*

| Year | Gross Domestic Product | | | | | (£ million) |
	North	East	West	Mid-West	Lagos	Nigeria
1958/59	447·5	184·7	218·7	—	49·1	900·0
1959/60	436·3	210·3	241·1	—	50·8	938·5
1960/61	464·4	192·7	270·7	—	53·5	981·3
1961/62	500·0	205·9	255·6	—	52·1	1014·0
1962/63	551·6	196·8	264·7	—	59·2	1072·3
1963/64	557·2	235·4	235·0	67·6	68·9	1163·9
1964/65	562·7	256·6	255·6	79·4	82·0	1236·3

Crafts has been allocated among the regions and Lagos in proportion to the number of craftsmen in them.

The Building and Civil Engineering figures have been allocated by reference to the proportion of gross fixed capital formation undertaken by the building and construction industrial sector of the federal, regional and local governments, and the firms and public corporations in each region. Electricity was allocated by reference to the units of electricity generated by electricity undertakings in each region.

Water Supply was allocated arbitrarily as follows: Lagos, 18 per cent; Western Region, 25 per cent; Eastern Region, 23 per cent; and Northern Region, 34 per cent. The figures for Communications (post and telegraphs) have been allocated by reference to revenue derived in each region from postal services, telephone calls and rentals, and telegrams.

The national figures for Government and Missions were built up from regional data, while the regional allocations of Banking, Insurance and the Professions were guesstimates. For Domestic Services the national figures have been derived from regional data.

The greatest difficulty lies in the allocation of Transport, Distribution and Miscellaneous activities which jointly constitute about 20 to 25 per cent of the GDP. Okigbo's attempt at a regional breakdown of the national accounts for 1950/51 and 1957/58 left out these items unallocated. In spite of the pioneering work of Messrs. A. M. Hay and

TABLE D.2 *Distribution of Nigeria's GDP among the regions by branch of activity at constant 1957/58 prices, 1962/63*

(£ million)

Activity	1962/63				
	North	East	West	Lagos	Nigeria
1 Agriculture	394·5	87·7	122·1	—	604·3
2 Livestock	37·4	7·3	12·8	3·6	61·1
3 Fishing	5·2	3·4	5·2	1·2	15·0
4 Forest Products	0·3	0·6	12·8	—	13·7
5 Mining (including Oil Exploration)	5·2	13·0	—	—	18·2
6 Manufacturing	9·6	8·3	12·7	6·4	37·0
7 Crafts	9·1	4·1	6·7	0·5	20·4
8 Building and Civil Engineering	6·2	10·2	11·3	1·5	29·2
9 Electricity	0·9	1·0	0·8	1·8	4·5
10 Water Supply	0·2	0·2	0·2	0·1	0·7
11 Transport	12·4	10·5	13·0	6·9	42·8
12 Communications	0·7	0·7	0·7	1·6	3·7
13 Government	8·0	5·1	6·0	13·3	32·4
14 Missions	3·8	11·0	10·9	1·5	27·2
15 Banking, Insurance and the Professions	4·1	3·5	10·1	9·0	26·7
16 Distribution	51·3	28·3	30·9	6·0	116·5
17 Domestic Services	1·1	0·8	1·8	0·5	4·2
18 Miscellaneous	1·6	1·1	6·7	5·3	14·7
GDP at Constant 1957 Factor Cost	551·6	196·8	264·7	59·2	1072·3

R. H. T. Smith on inter-regional trade in Nigeria,[1] very little is known about inter-regional commodity movements. The calculation of the regional allocation of these activities, based on proportionate consumption expenditure on imports and home-produced goods, is therefore nothing more than a guesstimate subject to a wide margin of error.

[1] A. M. Hay and R. H. T. Smith, 'Preliminary Estimates of Nigeria's Interregional Trade and Associated Money Flows', *The Nigerian Journal of Economic and Social Studies*, vol. 8, No. 1, March 1966, pp. 9–35.

Bibliography

GENERAL WORKS

ADARKAR, B. P. *The Principles and Problems of Federal Finance* (London: King & Son, 1933)

AIYAR, S. P. *Federalism and Social Change: A Commentary on Quasi-Federalism* (Bombay: Asia Publishing House, 1961)

BELASSA, B. *Theory of Economic Integration* (Homewood, Illinois: Irwin, 1961)

BHARGAVA, R. N. 'Theory of Federal Finance', *Economic Journal*, 1953; pp. 84–97. See also 'Comments' in September, 1953 and June, 1954

BIRCH, A. H. *Federalism, Finance and Social Legislation in Canada, Australia, and the United States* (Oxford: Clarendon Press, 1955)

BIRCH, A. H. 'Intergovernmental Financial Relations in New Federations', Chapter V in *Federalism and Economic Growth in Underdeveloped Countries*, U. K. Hicks *et al.* (London: George Allen and Unwin Ltd., 1961)

BOWIE, R. R. and FRIEDRICH, C. J. (Ed.) *Studies in Federalism* (Boston: Little, Brown and Company, 1954)

BUCHANAN, J. M. 'The Pure Theory of Government Finance: A Suggested Approach', *Journal of Political Economy*, vol. LVII (December, 1949), pp. 496–505

BUCHANAN, J. M. 'Federalism and Fiscal Equity', *American Economic Review*, vol. XL (September, 1950), pp. 583–599

BUCHANAN, J. M. 'Federal Grants and Resource Allocation', *Journal of Political Economy*, vol. LX, 1952, pp. 208–17

BUCHANAN, J. M. 'Reply', op. cit., pp. 536–8

BUCHANAN, J. M. *The Public Finances* (Homewood, Illinois: Irwin, 1960)

CARNEY, D. E. *Government and Economy in British West Africa* (New York: Bookman Associates, 1961)

CHELLIAH, RAJA J. *Fiscal Policy in Underdeveloped Countries* (London: George Allen and Unwin Ltd., 1960)

CURRIE, DAVID P. (Ed.) *Federalism and the New Nations of Africa* (Chicago: The University of Chicago Press, 1964)

DUE, JOHN F. *Government Finance* (Homewood, Illinois: Irwin, 1954)

DUE, JOHN F. *Taxation and Economic Development in Tropical Africa* (Cambridge: The M.I.T. Press, 1963)

DUE, JOHN F. and ROBSON, P. 'Tax Harmonization in the East African Common Market', C. S. Shoup (Ed.), *Fiscal Harmonization in Common Markets* (New York: Columbia University Press, 1966)

FRIEDRICH, CARL J. 'Public Finance in Six Contemporary Federations: A Comparative Constitutional Analysis', *Public Policy*, vol. IV, 1953, pp. 180–227

HAILEY, LORD *An African Survey*, revised edition (London: Oxford University Press, 1957)

HAZELWOOD, ARTHUR 'Trade Balances and Statutory Marketing in Primary Export Economies', *Economic Journal*, March, 1957

HICKS, LADY U. K. *Development from Below: Local Government and Finance in Developing Countries of the Commonwealth* (Oxford: Clarendon Press, 1961)

HICKS, LADY U. K. *Development Finance* (London: Oxford University Press, 1965)

HICKS, LADY U. K. *et al. Federalism and Economic Growth in Under-developed Areas* (London: Allen and Unwin, 1961)

HINRICHS, H. H. and BIRD, R. 'Government Revenue Shares in Developed and Less Developed Countries', *Canadian Tax Journal*, vol. XI, No. 5 (September–October, 1963), pp. 431–7

JOHNSON, HARRY G. 'Fiscal Policy and the Balance of Payments', chapter 9 in Alan T. Peacock and Gerald Hauser (Ed.), *Government Finance and Economic Development* (Paris: Organization for Economic Co-operation and Development, 1965)

KALDOR, NICHOLAS 'Taxation for Economic Developments', *The Journal of Modern African Studies*, March, 1963, pp. 7–23

LASKI, H. J. 'The Obsolescence of Federalism', *The New Republic*, vol. 98, 1939, pp. 367–9

MACMAHON, A. W. *Federalism, Mature and Emergent* (Garden City, N.Y.: Doubleday, 1955)

MAXWELL, J. A. *Federal Grants and the Business Cycle* (New York: NBER, 1952)

MUSGRAVE, R. A. 'Approaches to a Fiscal Theory of Political Federalism', NBER, op. cit., pp. 97–122, and Comments, pp. 122–33

MUSGRAVE, R. A. (Ed.) *Essays in Fiscal Federalism* (Washington, D.C.: The Brookings Institution, 1965)

MUSGRAVE, R. A. and SHOUP, C. S. *Readings in the Economics of Taxation* (London: George Allen and Unwin Ltd., 1964)

NATIONAL BUREAU OF ECONOMIC RESEARCH *Public Finances: Needs Sources and Utilization*, Ed. James Buchanan (Princeton: Princeton University Press, 1961)

NATIONAL BUREAU OF ECONOMIC RESEARCH *The Role of Direct and Indirect Taxes in the Federal Revenue System* (Princeton: Princeton University Press, 1964)

PEACOCK, ALAN T. 'Monetary and Fiscal Policy in Relation to African Development', in E. A. G. Robinson (Ed.), *Economic Development for Africa South of the Sahara* (London: Macmillan and Co. Ltd., 1964), pp. 654–76

PEACOCK, ALAN T. and HAUSER, GERALD *Government Finance and Economic Development* (Paris: Organization for Economic Co-operation and Development, 1965)

PREST, A. R. *Public Finance in Theory and Practice* (London: Weidenfeld and Nicolson, 1963)

PREST, A. R. *Public Finance in Under-developed Countries* (London: Weidenfeld and Nicolson, 1962)

SAWYER, GEOFFREY (Ed.) *Federalism; An Australian Jubilee Study* (Melbourne: Cheshire, for Australian National University, 1952)

SAWYER, GEOFFREY 'Taxation in a Federation', in David P. Currie, (Ed.), *Federalism and the New Nations of Africa* (Chicago: The University of Chicago Press, 1964)

SCOTT, A. 'The Economic Goals of Federal Finance', *Public Finance*, vol. XIX, No. 3/1964, pp. 241–88

SCOTT, A. D. 'The Evaluation of Federal Grants', *Economics*, vol. XIX, 1952, pp. 377–94

SCOTT, A. D. 'A Note on Grants in Federal Countries', *Economics*, vol. XVII, 1950, pp. 416–22

SHARMA, B. M. *Federalism in Theory and Practice*, 2 vols. (Chandausi, India: Bhargava & Sons, 1951)

SHIRRAS, G. F. *Federal Finance in Peace and War. With Special*

Reference to the United States of America and the British Common-wealth (London: Macmillan, 1944)

SHOUP, C. S. (Ed.) *Fiscal Harmonization in Common Markets*, Volume I: *Theory*; and Volume II: *Practice* (New York: Columbia University Press, 1967)

SHOUP, C. S. *et al. The Fiscal System of Venezuela* (Baltimore: The Johns Hopkins Press, 1959)

SMITH, S. A. DE *The New Commonwealth and Its Constitutions* (London: Stevens and Sons, 1964)

UNITED NATIONS *Taxes and Fiscal Policy in Under-developed Countries* (New York, 1954)

WALD, HASKELL P. *Taxation of Agricultural Land in Under-developed Countries* (Cambridge: Harvard University Press, 1959)

WALKER, D. 'A Recent Change in East African Company Taxation', *Public Finance*, vol. 2, 1960, pp. 166–88.

WALKER, D. 'Marketing Boards', in E. A. G. Robinson (Ed.), *Problems in Economic Development* (London: Macmillan & Co. Ltd., 1965)

WALKER, D. 'Fiscal Measures to Promote Foreign Investment' in E. F. Jackson (Ed.), *Economic Development in Africa* (Oxford: Basil Blackwell, 1965)

WALKER, D. 'Taxation and Taxable Capacity in Underdeveloped Countries', in E. F. Jackson (Ed.), *Economic Development in Africa* (Oxford: Basil Blackwell, 1965)

WALKER, D. and EHRLICH, C. 'Stabilization and Development Policy in Uganda', *Kykles*, vol. 12, 1959, pp. 341–53

WATTS, R. L. *New Federations, Experiments in the Commonwealth* (Oxford: Clarendon Press, 1966)

WHEARE, K. C. *Federal Government*, 3rd edition (London: Oxford University Press, 1953)

WILLIAMS, B. R. 'Public Expenditure and Revenue: An International Comparison', *The Manchester School of Economic and Social Studies*, vol. XXIX, 1961, pp. 43–54

WORKS ON NIGERIA

(a) Books and articles

ABOYADE, OJETUNJI *Foundations of an African Economy: A Study of Investment and Growth in Nigeria* (New York: Frederick A. Praeger, 1966)

ADEDEJI, ADEBAYO 'The Future of Personal Income Taxation in
Nigeria', *The Nigerian Journal of Economic and Social Studies*,
vol. 7, No. 2, July, 1965, pp. 159–74

ADEDEJI, ADEBAYO *A Survey of Highway Development in the Western
Region of Nigeria* (Ibadan: Ministry of Economic Planning, 1960)

ALUKO, S. A. 'Financing Economic Development in Nigeria', *The
Nigerian Journal of Economic and Social Studies*, vol. 3, No. 1,
November, 1961, pp. 39–62

ALUKO, S. A. *The Problems of Self-Government for Nigeria: A Critical
Analysis* (Ilfracombe, Devon: A. H. Stockwell, 1955)

ALUKO, S. A. 'How Many Nigerians? : An Analysis of Nigeria's Census
Problems, 1901–63', *Journal of Modern African Studies*, vol. 3,
No. 3 (1965)

ALUKO, S. A. and IJERE, M. O. 'The Economics of Mineral Oil',
The Nigerian Journal of Economic and Social Studies, vol. 7, No. 2,
(July 1965), pp. 209–220

ARIKPO, O. *Who Are the Nigerians?*, the Lugard Lectures of 1957
(Lagos: Federal Ministry of Information, n.d.)

ARIKPO, O. 'On Being a Minister', *West Africa*, 24 and 31 July, and
7, 14, and 21 August 1954, pp. 677–678, 701–29, and 731, 757–8,
and 781

ARIKPO, O. 'The Future of Nigerian Federalism', *West Africa*,
28 May, 4, 11, 18, and 25 June, and 2 July 1955, pp. 487, 511–12,
533–4, 564, 589, and 613

ARIKPO, O. *The Development of Modern Nigeria* (Harmondsworth:
Penguin Books Ltd., 1967)

AWA, E. O. *Federal Government in Nigeria* (Berkeley and Los Angeles:
University of California Press, 1964)

AWOLOWO, O. *Awo: The Autobiography of Obafemi Awolowo*
(Cambridge: Cambridge University Press, 1960)

AWOLOWO, O. *Path to Nigerian Freedom* (London: Faber, 1947)

AWOLOWO, O. *Thoughts on the Nigerian Constitution* (Ibadan: Oxford
University Press, 1966)

AYIDA, A. A. 'Contractor Finance and Supplier Credit in Economic
Growth', *The Nigerian Journal of Economic and Social Studies*,
vol. 7, No. 2 (July, 1965), pp. 175–88

BAUER, P. T. 'The Economic Development of Nigeria', *Journal of
Political Economy*, LXIII, October, 1955, pp. 399–408

BAUER, P. T. *West African Trade: A Study of Competition, Oligopoly
and Monopoly in a Changing Economy* (London: Cambridge

University Press, 1954; re-issued with a new preface by Routledge and Kegan Paul Ltd., 1963)

BOURDILLON, SIR BERNARD *Apportionment of Revenue and Duties as between the Central Government and Native Administrations*, minute by the Governor (Lagos: Government Printer, 1939)

BRETT, L. (Ed.) *Constitutional Problems of Federalism in Nigeria* (London: Sweet & Maxwell, 1961)

BUCHANAN, K. M. 'The Northern Region of Nigeria: The Background of its Political Duality', *Geographical Review*, vol. 43, 1953, pp. 451–73

BUCHANAN, K. M. and PUGH, J. C. *Land and People in Nigeria: The Human Geography of Nigeria and Its Environmental Background* (London: University of London Press, 1955)

COLEMAN, J. S. *Nigeria: Background to Nationalism* (Berkeley: University of California Press, 1960)

COTTER, WILLIAM R. 'Taxation and Federalism in Nigeria', *British Tax Review*, March–April, 1964, pp. 97–116

COX-GEORGE, N. A. 'Fiscal Experiments in Eastern Nigeria', *Public Finance*, vol. 12, 1957, pp. 173–80

DAVIES, H. O. *Nigeria: The Prospects for Democracy* (London: Weidenfeld & Nicolson, 1961)

DEAN, E. R. 'Factors Impeding the Implementation of Nigeria's Six-Year Plan', *The Nigerian Journal of Economic and Social Studies*, vol. 8, No. 1 (March, 1966), pp. 113–28

DUDLEY, B. J. 'The Concept of Federalism', *The Nigerian Journal of Economic and Social Studies*, vol. 5, No. 1 (March, 1963), pp. 95–104

DUDLEY, B. J. *Federalism in Nigeria*, an unpublished dissertation for the Degree of Master of Arts, University of Leicester, July 1959

EZENWELE, A. 'The Evolution of Modern Nigerian Finance', *Indian Journal of Economics*, vol. 40, July, 1959, pp. 37–44

EZERA, K. *Constitutional Developments in Nigeria* (Cambridge: Cambridge University Press, 1960)

FEDERAL GOVERNMENT *National Development Plan, 1962–68* (Lagos: Federal Ministry of Economic Development, 1962)

FEDERAL GOVERNMENT *National Development Plan: Progress Report 1964* (Lagos: Federal Ministry of Economic Development, 1964)

FEDERAL MILITARY GOVERNMENT *Guideposts for Second National Development Plan* (Lagos: Federal Ministry of Economic Development, 1966)

FEDERAL MILITARY GOVERNMENT *Nigeria* (Lagos: Federal Ministry of Information, 1967)

FEDERAL MILITARY GOVERNMENT *Meeting of the Nigerian Military Leaders held at Peduase Lodge, Aburi, Ghana*, 4 and 5 January 1967 (Lagos: Federal Ministry of Information, 1967)

HAWKINS, E. K. 'Marketing Boards and Economic Development in Nigeria and Ghana', *Review of Economic Studies*, No. 69, 1958

HAY, A. M. and SMITH, R. H. T. 'Preliminary Estimates of Nigeria's Interregional Trade and Associated Money Flows', *The Nigerian Journal of Economic and Social Studies*, vol. 8, No. 1 (March 1966), pp. 9–36

HAZLEWOOD, A. *The Finances of Nigerian Federation* (London: Oxford University Press, 1956)

HAZLEWOOD, A. 'The Regions' Revenues', *West Africa*, 11, 18 and 25 May 1957, pp. 439, 467, and 489

HELLEINER, G. K. 'The Fiscal Role of the Marketing Boards in Nigerian Economic Development, 1947–61', *Economic Journal*, September, 1964, pp. 582–610

HELLEINER, G. K. 'Marketing Boards and Domestic Stabilization in Nigeria', *The Review of Economics and Statistics*, vol. XLVIII, No. 1 (February, 1966), pp. 69–78

HELLEINER, G. K. *Peasant Agriculture, Government and Economic Growth in Nigeria* (Homewood, Illinois: Irwin, Inc., 1966)

HICKS, U. K. 'The New Tax System of Eastern Nigeria', *Journal of African Administration*, vol. VIII, No. 4 (October, 1956), pp. 202–5

MACKINTOSH, J. P. 'Federalism in Nigeria', *Political Studies*, vol. 10, 1962, pp. 223–247

MOREL, E. D. *Nigeria. Its People and Its Problems* (London: Smith, Elder & Co., 1911)

O'CONNELL, J. 'The Political Class and Economic Growth', *The Nigerian Journal of Economic and Social Studies*, vol. 8, No. 1 (March 1966), pp. 129–40

OGUNSHEYE, A. 'Marketing Boards and the Stabilization of Producer Prices and Incomes in Nigeria', *The Nigerian Journal of Economic and Social Studies*, vol. 7, No. 2 (July, 1965), pp. 131–44

OKIGBO, P. N. C. 'Obstacles to Planning Fiscal Policies', in Ronald Robinson (Ed.), *Overcoming Obstacles to Development* (Cambridge: Overseas Studies Committee)

OKIGBO, P. N. C. *Nigerian Public Finance* (London: Longmans, Green and Co. Ltd., 1965)

OKIGBO, P. N. C. *Nigerian National Accounts, 1950–57* (Enugu: Government Printer, 1962)

OKOTIE-EBOH, CHIEF F. S. *The Six Budget Speeches made by the Honourable Minister of Finance during the period 1958–1963* (Lagos: Federal Ministry of Finance, 1964)

OREWA, G. OKA. *Taxation in Western Nigeria* (London: Oxford University Press, 1962)

OREWA, G. OKA. 'The Role of Local Direct Taxation in a Developing Economy', *Conference Proceedings*, The Nigerian Institute of Social and Economic Research, 1963, pp. 65–72

OREWA, G. OKA *Local Government Finance in Nigeria* (Ibadan: Oxford University Press, 1966)

PACKARD, P. C. 'A Note on Gross Domestic Investment and Fiscal Policy', *The Nigerian Journal of Economic and Social Studies*, vol. 8, No. 2 (July, 1966), pp. 219–34

PREST, A. R. and STEWART, I. G. *The National Income of Nigeria, 1950–51* (Colonial Research Studies, No. 11), (London: HMSO, 1953)

ROBINSON, M. S. 'Nigerian Oil: Prospects and Perspectives', *The Nigerian Journal of Economic and Social Studies*, vol. 6, No. 2 (July, 1964), pp. 219–30

SOKUNBI, D. O. B. 'The Impact of the Oil Industry on the Economy of Nigeria', *The Nigerian Journal of Economic and Social Studies*, vol. 4, No. 1 (March, 1962), pp. 77–83

STOPLER, WOLFGANG F. *Planning Without Facts: Lessons in Resource Allocation from Nigeria's Development* (Cambridge: Harvard University Press, 1966)

STOLPER, WOLFGANG F. 'How Bad is the Plan?', *The Nigerian Journal of Economic and Social Studies*, vol. 6, No. 3 (November, 1964), pp. 261–76

TAYLOR, MILTON C. 'The Relationship Between Income Tax Administration and Income Tax Policy in Nigeria', *The Nigerian Journal of Economic and Social Studies*, vol. 9, No. 2 (July, 1967), forthcoming

TERIBA, R. O. *Western Nigeria: Public Sector and Economic Development 1948–1962* (Unpublished Ph.D. thesis for Manchester University), 1965

TERIBA, R. O. 'Nigerian Revenue Allocation Experience 1952–1965;

A Study in Inter-Governmental Fiscal and Financial Relations',
The Nigerian Journal of Economic and Social Studies, vol. 8, No. 3
(November, 1966), pp. 361–82

TUGBIYELE, E. A. 'The Nigerian Federal Union', *The Nigerian Journal
of Economic and Social Studies*, vol. 5, No. 3 (November, 1963),
pp. 364–73

(b) *Official reports*

RICHARDS, SIR ARTHUR *Proposals for the Revision of the Constitution of
Nigeria*, Cmd. 6599, (1945)

Review of the Constitution—Regional Recommendations (Lagos:
Government Printer, 1949)

Report of the Drafting Commission of the Constitution (Lagos:
Government Printer, 1950)

*Proceedings of the General Conference on Review of the Constitution,
January, 1950* (Lagos: Government Printer, 1950)

*Review of the Constitution of Nigeria: Despatch from the Secretary of
State for the Colonies. Dated 15th July, 1950*, Sessional Paper
No. 20 (Lagos: Government Printer, 1950)

*Report of the Conference on the Nigerian Constitution Held in London
in July and August, 1953*, Cmnd. 9059 (1954)

*Report by the Nigerian Constitutional Conference Held in London in
May and June, 1957*, Cmnd. 207 (1957)

*Report by the Ad Hoc Meeting of the Nigerian Constitutional
Conference Held in Lagos in February, 1958* (Lagos: Government
Printer, 1958)

*Report of the Resumed Nigerian Constitutional Conference Held
in London in September and October, 1958*, Cmnd. 569 (1958)

Nigeria Constitutional Discussions. May, 1960. Held in London,
Cmnd. 1063, 1960

Nigeria (Constitution) Order in Council, 1960, Statutory Instruments,
1960, No. 1652

*Nigeria Debates Independence: The Debate on Self-Government in the
Federal House of Representatives on the 26th March, 1957, as
Recorded in the Official Report* (Lagos: Federal Information Service,
1957)

*Report of the Commission Appointed to Enquire into the Fears of
Minorities and the Means of Allaying Them*, Cmnd. 505 (1958)

Nigeria Asks for Independence. Vol. 1: A Reprint of the Debate in the

Federal House of Representatives on January 14, 15 and 16, 1960.
Vol. 2: A Reprint of the Debate in the Senate on January 25th,
1960 (Lagos: Federal Ministry of Information, 1960)

Administrative and Financial Procedure under the New Constitution:
Financial Relations between the Government of Nigeria and the
Native Administrations (Lagos: Government Printer, 1947)

Report of the Commission on Revenue Allocation (Lagos: Government
Printer, 1950)

Report of the Fiscal Commissioner on the Financial Effects of the
Proposed Constitutional Arrangements, Cmd. 9026 (1953)

Report of the Fiscal Commission, Cmnd. 481 (1958)

Population Census of Northern Region of Nigeria, 1952; Population
Census of the Western Region of Nigeria, 1952; and Population
Census of Eastern Region of Nigeria, 1953 (Lagos: Census
Superintendent, 1954–6)

Federal Nigeria: Annual Report, 1957 (London: HMSO, 1961)

Index